ZION, CITY OF OUR GOD

Zion, City of Our God

edited by

Richard S. Hess and Gordon J. Wenham

WILLIAM B. EERDMANS PUBLISHING COMPANY
GRAND RAPIDS, MICHIGAN / CAMBRIDGE, U.K.

© 1999 Wm. B. Eerdmans Publishing Co.

255 Jefferson Ave. S.E., Grand Rapids, Michigan 49503 /

P.O. Box 163, Cambridge CB3 9PU U.K.

Printed in the United States of America

04 03 02 01 00 99   7 6 5 4 3 2 1

Library of Congress Cataloging-in-Publication Data

Zion, city of our God / edited by R. S. Hess and G. Wenham.

p.   cm.

Includes bibliographical references.

ISBN 0-8028-4426-X (pbk.: alk. paper)

1. Jerusalem in the Bible.

2. Bible. O.T. — History of Biblical events.

I. Hess, Richard S.   II. Wenham, Gordon J.

BS1199.J38Z56   1999

220.8′9569442 — dc21   99-14369

CIP

Contents

CONTENTS

Contributors

Richard S. Hess, Ph.D., is Professor of Old Testament at Denver Seminary, Denver, CO, U.S.A.

Gordon J. Wenham, Ph.D., is Professor of Old Testament at Cheltenham & Gloucester College, Cheltenham, England.

John M. Monson is Assistant Professor of Archaeology at Wheaton College, Wheaton, IL, U.S.A.

Martin J. Selman is Principal of Spurgeon's College, London, England.

Gary N. Knoppers, Ph.D., is Head of the Department of Classics and Ancient Mediterranean Studies at Pennsylvania State College, PA, U.S.A.

Thomas Renz, Ph.D., is Lecturer in Old Testament and at Oak Hill College, London, England.

Philip E. Satterthwaite, Ph.D., is Lecturer in Old Testament and Hebrew, Biblical Graduate School of Singapore.

Knut M. Heim, Ph.D., is Student Minister, Wesley House, Cambridge, England.

Rebecca Doyle, Ph.D., is Lecturer at Holy Light Theological Seminary, Kaohsiung, Taiwan.

Zion, City of Our God

For three thousand years Jerusalem has had a special place in the hearts and lives of those who worship the God of Israel. This series of selected studies presents the basis of this role in the Old Testament. The product of collaboration by an international team of scholars, *Zion, City of Our God* grew out of a special meeting of the Tyndale Fellowship Old Testament Study Group held in Cambridge in 1996. Papers from this conference, along with additional essays, touch upon some of the most significant themes that describe Jerusalem in the First Temple period of the Old Testament.

John Monson examines Jerusalem's temple of Solomon in its original ancient Near Eastern context of Syrian temple architecture. His discoveries lead to a fresh understanding of the significance of this temple as described in the book of 1 Kings. Non-Yahwistic worship in Jerusalem also played a significant role in the city's history.

Richard Hess looks at one of the most significant events in the Bible's record of pre-exilic Jerusalem: Sennacherib's attack upon Jerusalem. This attack is recorded in three sources in the Old Testament. It plays a key role in the book of the prophet Isaiah. The information is supplemented by Assyrian and other written sources as well as recent excavations at Lachish. Hess addresses some of the critical issues that surround the biblical texts, using both literary and historical methods. Many scholars perceive this event as crucial to the emergence of the Zion tradition.

The studies of Gary Knoppers and Martin Selman consider one of the most significant areas of the Old Testament that is too often overlooked, the books of Chronicles. Knoppers examines 2 Chronicles 20 to discover key themes regarding Jerusalem's temple as a starting point for battle with the enemies of Israel and of God. Selman investigates the overall theological significance of Jerusalem in the book of Chronicles. In doing so, his chapter serves as a summary statement for the key role of Jerusalem in the entire Old Testament. Here is a city central to the redemptive plan of God which, despite the rebellion of its people and their experience of divine judgment in the city's destruction, will yet be rebuilt and again become the joy of all the earth.

Thomas Renz examines the Zion tradition as it underwent its greatest challenge, the fall of Jerusalem. This is dramatically traced through the writing of the prophet Ezekiel.

Jerusalem's role in the poetry of the Hebrew Bible is aptly illustrated by two studies: Knut Heim's investigation of the city in the book of Lamentations and Philip Satterthwaite's study of Jerusalem in the Psalms of Ascent. Heim's work focuses on the theology of Lamentations as a pastoral guide for dealing with grief and suffering. While the city is here a symbol of grief and suffering, in the Psalms of Ascent Satterthwaite demonstrates its role as the goal of a pilgrim's journey of joy and praise with the realization of God's ancient promises.

Rebecca Doyle considers what Ugaritic, Old Testament, and other texts tell us about the cult of Molech and the worship of this god, both in Jerusalem and throughout the West Semitic world.

More than any other site in the Bible, Jerusalem signifies God's judgment and hope. It is the focus of much of the Old Testament, and acquaintance with this background is essential for understanding the importance of the city in Jesus' time, in our own age, and in the prophecies of the world to come.

RICHARD S. HESS
and
GORDON J. WENHAM

The Temple of Solomon:
Heart of Jerusalem

JOHN M. MONSON

*Taking advantage of the sources for the study of the temple
found in both the Bible and the contemporary ancient Near
East, the theological and political significance of this great
building is considered. Situated within Jerusalem, its structure
forms the key to understanding the centrality of the city in the
worship and praise of God's people.*

I. Introduction

The temple of Solomon was the focal point of the religious, political, and
cultural life of Israel through much of its history. The symbolism and fate of
this structure were inseparable from that of Jerusalem, the "city of the great
king" (Ps. 48:2). It is not surprising, therefore, that the temple, like Jerusalem, is mentioned throughout the Bible as a reminder of God's sovereignty,
the setting of his worship, and a barometer of Israel's spiritual health. In the
temple the people take refuge and seek deliverance (Pss. 5:7; 65). Here it is
that the nation converges to worship the Lord (Ps. 43:4; 2 Kings 23). And
through the frequent fluctuations of Israel's faith, the temple serves as the
witness to judgment and renewal alike (Ps. 79:1; Jer. 7:1-7).

The significance and nature of the temple are best reflected in the

1

light of Jerusalem during the United Monarchy, the intensifying Zion tradition, and the archaeological parallels unearthed in the northern Levant. A brief discussion of each is offered in the following pages. Emphasis is placed upon the architecture of Solomon's temple as it can be understood through recent archaeological discoveries in Syria.

II. Jerusalem during the United Monarchy

A. Texts

Without the religious and political importance accorded to it by David Jerusalem would have remained, from an international perspective, like the central hill country: "aloof, waterless, on the road to nowhere."[1] Although it had been a well-known city during the Middle and Late Bronze ages, under David it became the seat of empire.[2] In a single move the tribes of Israel and Judah were brought together, not at Hebron or Shechem, but in this hitherto unconquered Jebusite city. For a short-lived period in the tenth century B.C. the region of Benjamin was to unite, rather than divide, the northern and southern tribes of Israel.[3]

The transfer of the ark to Jerusalem was one way in which the new monarch attempted to restrain tribal rivalries and consolidate religious constituencies (2 Sam. 6; 2 Sam. 24:21).[4] In addition to building his pal-

1. G. A. Smith, *The Historical Geography of the Holy Land* (Jerusalem: Repr. Ariel Publishing House, 1966). The city and its environs did, however, always hold considerable local importance.

2. The Middle Bronze Age city had massive fortifications and was mentioned in the Execration Texts. See J. Pritchard, *Ancient Near Eastern Texts* (Princeton, NJ: Princeton University Press, 1969), p. 329. In the Late Bronze Age the king of Urusalim made several complaints to the Pharaoh of Egypt as seen in letters 286-89 of the el-Amarna archive. See W. L. Moran, *The El-Amarna Letters* (Baltimore: Johns Hopkins, 1992).

3. The city lies on the southern edge of Benjamin's tribal territory. A plateau at the center of this territory interconnects with roads from all directions. Jerusalem's well-being depended upon the fate of this plateau because the city lacked convenient access roads to the coastal plain and Jordan Valley. Immediately after the United Monarchy dissolved, great battles between Israel and Judah erupted in this region (1 Kings 12ff.).

4. H. Tadmor, "Traditional Institutions and the Monarchy: Social and Political Tensions in the Time of David and Solomon," in T. Ishida, ed., *Studies in the Period of David and Solomon and Other Studies* (Tokyo: Yamakawa-Shuppansha, 1982), pp. 239-57, esp. p. 196.

ace and repairing the city (1 Chron. 11:8), David positioned Yahweh's tabernacle dwelling as the centerpiece of his new state. This is reflected in the new priestly apparatus (2 Sam. 8:15-18), preparations for temple construction (1 Chron. 22:1-5), and a prolific psalmody in which the Lord's house figured prominently. Although he would not build the temple, David's actions would permanently marry the fortunes of the Jerusalem-based monarchy to the religious centrality of the temple mount.

Solomon's building projects further magnified the importance of the capital city and its national shrine. According to the Bible the temple was his greatest legacy. The entire nation was called to witness its dedication and behold the city which apparently directed the affairs of the Levant (1 Kings 8:2). The adjacent complex between the temple mount and the City of David included at least two palaces with throne rooms, pillared halls, and luxurious contents (1 Kings 7:1-12). Jerusalem was refortified along with strategic cities of storage, defence, and chariotry throughout the country (1 Kings 9:15-28).

According to the biblical account, Jerusalem of the United Monarchy reached unparalleled splendor. It became a place where "silver was as common as stone" and "cedar as plentiful as the sycamore of the Shephelah" (1 Kings 10:27). At its highest summit stood the temple, the epitome of God's blessing and Israel's success.[5]

B. Archaeology

Archaeological remains from the United Monarchy are mixed, and while they do not completely conform to the biblical account neither do they contradict it. The period of Solomon is well represented as a time of large-scale construction throughout the land.[6] Six chambered gates and occupa-

---

5. The temple was unusual in at least two ways. First, its measurements, if the Bible is followed, would make it one of the largest ever to be built in the Levant (see below). Second, it is perhaps the best described temple in any ancient Near Eastern text. A. Hurowitz, *I Have Built for You an Exalted House: Temple-Building in the Bible in Light of Mesopotamian and Northwest Semitic Writings,* Journal for the Study of the Old Testament Supplements (Sheffield: Sheffield Academic Press, 1995), p. 115.

6. Even many minimalists agree with this conclusion. For a general description of monumental architecture from this period see W. Dever, "Monumental Architecture in Ancient Israel in the Period of the United Monarchy," in Ishida, *Studies,* pp. 269-306.

tion levels at Hazor, Megiddo, and Gezer would seem to coincide with the account in 1 Kings 9:15 which mentions these cities by name. At Megiddo, in particular, two palaces with elaborate masonry testify to a grand scale of architecture with cultural origins in the northern Levant.[7] The long-standing attribution of these finds to tenth-century Israelites has recently come under assault, but no new hypothesis offers a better solution.[8]

With such evidence from outlying regions one would expect to find significant remains also in Jerusalem. But a century of excavation has yielded very few artifacts dating to the United Monarchy. The city at this time appears to have had three sectors: the lower city in the south, the citadel and administrative area in the center, and the temple/palace precinct in the north.[9] The temple mount in the northern part of the city has yielded nothing from the tenth century. Herod's engineers appear to have cleared away most traces of the Iron Age temple complex. In the lower city to the south only sparse traces of tenth-century occupation have been unearthed (Stratum 14).[10]

Some material from the central part of the city may be relevant, however. This elevated area between the lower city and the temple mount was the likely location of David's citadel. It was defined on its east side by a series of terraces. The most prominent terrace is known as the "stepped

7. There is considerable debate as to the age of these palaces, but the views of Yadin have prevailed. See A. Mazar, *Archaeology of the Land of the Bible* (New York: Doubleday, 1990), p. 382. The buildings are reminiscent of the *bît ḥilani* palaces of northern Syria, a fact which corroborates the biblical record of Phoenician craftsmanship in Israel at this time. See 1 Kings 5 and D. Ussishkin, "Solomon's Palace and Building 1723 in Megiddo," *Israel Exploration Journal* 16 (1966): 174-86.

8. The tenth-century material is, indeed, hard to separate from ninth-century finds, as pointed out by G. Wightman, "The Myth of Solomon," *Bulletin of the American Schools of Oriental Research* 277 (1990): 5-22, and I. Finkelstein, "The Archaeology of the United Monarchy: An Alternative View," *Levant* 28 (1996): 177-88. But a complete reworking of the stratigraphy creates as many difficulties as it solves.

9. Y. Shiloh, *Excavations at the City of David, I. Qedem 19* (Jerusalem: Hebrew University, 1984), p. 27. In later years the word *'ôpel* may have referred to the midsection of the city. This term is known from the Mesha Stele and the Bible where it indicates a protruding urban area, e.g., 2 Chron. 27:3; Isa. 32:14. See E. Mazar, "The Royal Quarter of Biblical Jerusalem," in H. Geva, ed., *Ancient Jerusalem Revealed* (Jerusalem: Israel Exploration Society, 1994), pp. 64-72.

10. These can be found in Y. Shiloh, *City of David*. They include a very small area of fills and pottery (Areas B and D1, p. 7), as well as clay installations with two complete chalices and the base of a cultic stand (Area E1, p. 12 and pl. 21: 2).

stone structure." This buttress was originally built by the Jebusites in the Late Bronze Age, judging from the pottery which lies below.[11] According to Kenyon and Shiloh this massive support is the *millô'* which was reinforced by David, Solomon, and later kings. But subsequent excavation and linguistic analysis cast considerable doubt on this interpretation.[12] To the north of the stepped structure Kenyon discovered a stretch of casemate wall and numerous blocks of reused ashlar masonry.[13] She associated these with Solomon's building projects, but here again neither feature can be dated with certainty. The reused masonry, though reminiscent of Israelite palaces at Megiddo and elsewhere, is just as likely to originate from ninth- or eighth-century construction. A final feature located near the presumed citadel is the earliest water system which some date to the United Monarchy or earlier. Warren's Shaft, as it is called, provided access to the Gihon spring from inside the city defenses. Because it is a natural geologic formation, however, it is not possible to date it with certainty.[14]

Beyond these limited finds no hints of tenth-century occupation have been discovered. No tombs, no clear buildings, no certain lines of fortification, and certainly no temple have come to light. Most noticeable is the virtual lack of tenth-century pottery among the debris and fills of later periods. Even a small settlement would produce substantial ceramic evidence, but so far such evidence is lacking. Various explanations have

11. Shiloh's Area G, p. 17.

12. Initially, the equation seems quite convincing in light of numerous biblical passages which associate the *millô'* ("fill?") with building and strengthening at the edge of the city (2 Sam. 5:9) and near the wall (1 Kings 9:15; 11:27; 2 Chron. 32:5). But only a fragmentary structure and fill layer *atop* the stepped structure can be dated with certainty to the tenth century. The pottery in the stone terrace itself is entirely from the thirteenth to the twelfth centuries B.C. Cf. J. Cahill and D. Tarler, "Excavations Directed by Yigal Shiloh at the City of David, 1978-1985," in Geva, *Ancient Jerusalem,* p. 34. Drawing from comparative linguistic and architectural material, R. Steiner has shown that the *millô'* could well have been a means of ascent from the inside of the city to the level of the walls: "New Light on the Biblical *Millo* from Hatran Inscriptions," *Bulletin of the American Schools of Oriental Research* 276 (1989): 15-23.

13. The wall is noted in *Digging Up Jerusalem* (London: Ernest Benn, 1974), pp. 114-15. The ashlar blocks and proto-aeolic capital are described in "Excavations in Jerusalem, 1962," *Palestine Exploration Quarterly* 95 (1963): 16, pl. VII.

14. Few would agree with Y. Shiloh's tenth century B.C. dating. Cf. "Jerusalem," *Encyclopaedia of Archaeological Excavations in the Holy Land,* vol. 2 (Jerusalem: Israel Exploration Society, 1993), p. 712. But there is no convincing reason to date it later, and a water system is mentioned in David's conquest of the city (2 Sam. 5).

been offered but none is entirely convincing. Jerusalem, for example, has been destroyed and rebuilt multiple times, and much of the City of David was disturbed and quarried for the construction of the late Roman city. But this still does not explain the dearth of tenth-century pottery.[15]

Archaeologically speaking, the period in which Jerusalem received its social, political, and theological grandeur is still very much an enigma. The nature of the city in the tenth century B.C. is in fact one of the greatest mysteries in biblical archaeology. Nevertheless, a viable and reasonably accurate reconstruction is still possible. In spite of the meager finds, the biblical description of the city and its great temple conforms remarkably well both to Solomonic architecture from other sites in Israel and to architectural parallels from the northern Levant.

III. The Zion Tradition

As with the architecture of Jerusalem, emerging religious traditions brought together a variety of motifs which coalesced within the crucible of David's young empire. The physical setting of Jerusalem and the properties of the temple both influenced and reflected the Zion theology on many levels. Although the precise development of the tradition is not entirely clear, its constituent parts are easily recognizable. They converge physically and theologically in the temple.

With the transferral of the ark to Jerusalem, Yahweh officially chose Mount Zion as his dwelling (Ps. 132:13-14). The place became a conduit of spiritual and political power. David's successful campaigns demonstrated anew that the God of Israel was also Lord of the entire world.[16] A host of expressions and metaphors could now be directed towards Zion because it had become a permanent locus of religious activity for the tribes and for the whole empire.[17] Vivid imagery included the divine dwelling atop a high

---

15. We are reminded of K. Kitchen's statement, "Absence of evidence is not, and should not be confused with, evidence of absence": "New Directions in Biblical Archaeology: Historical and Biblical Aspects," *Biblical Archaeology Today 1990* (Jerusalem: Israel Exploration Society, 1993), pp. 34-52, esp. p. 48.

16. E.g., Ps. 46; see J. J. M. Roberts, "Zion in the Theology of the Davidic-Solomonic Empire," in T. Ishida, *Studies,* pp. 93-108, esp. p. 98.

17. Some have argued that a previous Jebusite tradition may actually have influenced Israelite religious expression, but this cannot be known for certain. Cf. the story of Melchizedek (Gen. 14) and the threshing floor of Aruna (2 Sam. 24:15-25). There

mountain, a life-giving water source, and the conquest of chaos (figuratively and politically) — all images that were readily available in Jerusalem's topography and David's military triumphs (Pss. 29; 89; 104). The structure, style, and motifs of this emergent Zion tradition are reminiscent of other religious expressions from the ancient Near East.[18] They need not, however, be considered direct borrowing from Ugaritic and Canaanite texts, as many would assume. Rather, Israel's tradition with its temple and texts was expressing itself in the language and art of its day.[19] It retained, moreover, a number of significant distinctives.[20] In addition to the newly developed themes, individual traditions of Mount Sinai eventually were also transferred to Mount Zion, as J. Levenson has shown.[21]

These images received their highest expression in the divine abode built by Solomon. Visual reminders of creation and Eden could be found throughout this meeting point between heaven, earth, and the world below.[22] Carvings on the entry pillars, doors, and walls depicted palmettes, sacred floral designs, and cherubs. These were all motifs from the Garden, whose story had always factored into the theology of Israel. The plan of the temple reflected spheres of increasing holiness, each with its protocol for worship. Behind them all was housed the ark of the covenant and the cherub

---

was certainly a sophisticated literary tradition in the city already in the Late Bronze Age, as R. Hess has shown in "Hebrew Psalms and the Amarna Correspondence from Jerusalem: Some Comparisons and Implications," *Zeitschrift für die alttestamentliche Wissenschaft* 101 (1989): 249-65.

18. Borrowing is usually assumed, as in R. Clifford, *The Cosmic Mountain in Canaan and the Old Testament* (Cambridge, MA: Harvard, 1972). Motifs found in the Ugarit texts also appear in numerous Psalms (e.g., 2; 46; 48; 84; 122; 132) and are well represented in Isaiah. J. Lundquist has outlined the common elements found in the temples and cults of the ancient Near East: "The Common Temple Ideology of the Ancient Near East," in T. Madsen, ed., *The Temple in Antiquity* (Provo, UT: Brigham Young University, 1984), pp. 53-76.

19. This applies equally to both style and content. S. Avishur offers considerable evidence that Israelite hymns were more abstract and lyric than comparable Canaanite poetry. See *Studies in Hebrew and Ugaritic Psalms* (Jerusalem: Magnes, 1994), pp. 33-38.

20. E.g., see P. Craigie, "The Comparison of Hebrew Poetry: Psalm 104 in the Light of Egyptian and Ugaritic Poetry," *Semitics* 4 (1974): 10-21.

21. This notion is seen in Genesis 2 as well as Ezekiel 47. See the description in Levenson's book *Sinai and Zion: An Entry into the Jewish Bible* (New York: Harper & Row, 1985).

22. These are treated in J. Levenson, *Creation and the Persistence of Evil: The Drama of Divine Omnipotence* (San Francisco: Harper & Row, 1988), pp. 90ff.

throne of God from which judgment was proclaimed (Ps. 76:8-9). The significance of the place and the potency of its imagery were not lost on the pilgrims who made the ascent. In the context of the temple the liturgies demanded uprightness (Ps. 24), guaranteed security (Ps. 46), and evoked praise (Ps. 48).

Kingship, conquest, and security were not restricted to the spiritual realm. The palace which adjoined the temple served as a reminder that the king, God's agent through special covenant, was on his throne as well. If the biblical account is to be taken seriously then David and Solomon reflected the times in which they lived. The military conquests, religious imagery, and the attempt to move towards cultic centrality, all conform to the paradigm of pre-modern empires and their institutions.[23] The international climate of the tenth century suits the biblical account very well indeed.

In sum, the triad of God, monarch, and people intersected in the temple of Zion. Nowhere are the physical and emotional impact of this theology better expressed than in Psalms 68, 84, and 122. Through the vicissitudes of Israelite history this paradigm changed, however, and the Zion traditions acquired a life of their own. They intensified when Jerusalem was spared in the time of Hezekiah. They were further streamlined with the reforms of Josiah. And after the exile of 586 B.C. they were invoked to stir renewal and point to glory in an age to come. From the beginning the temple and its setting lay at the heart of the Zion theology. It would remain the tradition's primary vehicle of expression even after it was destroyed (Rev. 21:9–22:5).

IV. Solomon's Temple: The Quest for Parallels

The temple of Solomon is the best-described structure in the Hebrew Bible, but it is also the most enigmatic. The descriptions of the temple in the Bible provide a general picture which allows for a variety of reconstructions. Until the advent of modern archaeology depictions of the shrine usually reflected the era of each given interpreter.[24] Today a

23. C. Meyers, "The Israelite Empire: In Defense of King Solomon," *Michigan Quarterly Review* 22/3 (1983): 412-28.

24. Past reconstructions ranged from medieval castles to Egyptian mortuary temples. These can be seen in the opening pages of Th. Busink, *Der Tempel von Jerusalem von Salomo bis Herodes; eine archäologische-historische Studie unter Berücksichtigung des westsemitischen Tempelbaus. I Der Tempel Salomos* (Leiden: Brill, 1970).

much more reliable reconstruction is possible, thanks to parallels from northern Syria.[25] Nevertheless, the text also includes numerous terms for which no clear archaeological *realia* have been found. A precise understanding of these features continues to elude archaeologists and biblicists alike. Among them are the *ṣĕlaʿot* (side chambers?), *lûl* (ladder?), and *ḥallonê šĕqupîm ʾaṭumîm* (recessed windows?) which are discussed below.

The most striking architectural parallel to Solomon's temple is the recently published but little discussed temple of ʿAin Dara in northern Syria. In the following pages the biblical description of the temple is reviewed briefly. Next, select comparative material is evaluated. Finally, the attributes of the ʿAin Dara temple are used to clarify several enigmatic features of Solomon's temple.

A. Biblical Sources

The well-known descriptions in 1 Kings 6, 2 Chronicles 2–3, and Ezekiel 41–43 are quite clear about the temple's basic layout. It was built according to the long-room plan and had three interior divisions, each twenty cubits wide.[26] The portico *(ʾûlam)* was ten cubits long, the hall *(hêkal)* forty cubits long, and the Holy of Holies *(dĕbîr)* a cube with sides of twenty cubits each.[27] The height of the Holy of Holies was twenty cubits, ten cubits less than the thirty cubits of the first two rooms. According to 1 Kings 6:5-6 and Ezekiel 43:3 the central shrine was enclosed on three sides by multistoried side chambers. The entire structure stood atop a platform at the summit just north of the City of David (Ezek. 41:8, 13-14).

On several other matters the text is less clear and there is consider-

---

25. The most detailed analyses are found in two works: J. Ouellette, "The Temple of Solomon" (Ph.D. dissertation, Hebrew Union College, Cincinnati, 1966); V. Fritz, *Tempel und Zeit: Studien zum Tempelbau in Israel und Zeltheiligtum die Priesterschrift, Wissenschaftliche Monographien zum Alten und Neuen Testament* 47 (Neukirchen-Vluyn: Neukirchener Verlag, 1977).

26. This is the most common temple plan in the Levant. See G. R. H. Wright, *Ancient Building in South Syria and Palestine*, vol. 1 (Leiden: Brill, 1985), pp. 255ff.

27. If the royal cubit of 52.5 cm. is read here, the width of the main temple was approximately 12 m. and its length roughly 40 m. For a summary of proportions see V. Fritz, "Temple Architecture: What Can Archaeology Tell Us about Solomon's Temple?" *Biblical Archaeology Review* 13 (1987): 38-49.

able debate. What, for example, were the protrusions on the side chambers? And what was the nature of the Holy of Holies? It may have been an elevated room, which would account for its lower height. Or perhaps it housed a small shrine with a lower ceiling, or even the tabernacle itself.[28] This design would require secondary, less substantial walls between the two innermost chambers of the temple rather than a large stone wall as at Tell Taynat. Such an arrangement is hinted at in the text and known from other temples in the Levant.[29]

Many secondary features of the temple are also difficult to understand. We read of "blocked" windows, a pentagon-shaped door, cedar panels, floral patterns, palmettes, cedar panelling, and lavish gold from floor to ceiling. The nature of these features must be sought in comparative material from the archaeological record.[30]

B. The Quest for Archaeological Parallels

In his 1939 essay, A. Alt argued convincingly that the architecture of the Jerusalem temple belonged to the traditions of the northern Levant.[31] This was confirmed by G. E. Wright and later by D. Ussishkin who detailed the striking similarities between the building projects of Solomon and the palace-temple complexes found at Tell Taynat, Hamath, and elsewhere in northern Syria.[32] At Tell Taynat in particular, the small temple adjoining

28. R. Friedman argues this point based on Chronicles 9 and later Jewish sources: "The Tabernacle in the Temple," *Biblical Archaeologist* 43 (1980): 241-48.

29. A. Mazar, "Temples of the Middle and Late Bronze Ages and from the Iron Age," in E. Netzer and R. Reich, eds., *The Architecture of Ancient Israel* (Jerusalem: Israel Exploration Society, 1992), pp. 161-92, esp. p. 184.

30. K. Kitchen, for example, found Egyptian recessed chambers of different widths which provide us with a better understanding of the recessed side chambers described in Solomon's temple: "Two Notes on the Subsidiary Rooms of Solomon's Temple," *Eretz Israel* 20 (1989): 107*-12*; cf. 1 Kings 6:5-6, 8, 10. In a similar study A. Millard, following Noth, explained the technical terms for doorways by contrasting them with descriptions of lintels and doorways from elsewhere in the Levant, "The Doorways of Solomon's Temple," *Eretz-Israel* 20 (1989): 135*-39*.

31. "Verbrietung und Herkunft des syrischen Tempeltypus," *Pälastina-Jahrbuch* 35 (1939): 83-99.

32. G. E. Wright, "The Significance of the Temple in the Ancient Near East: III The Temple in Syria-Palestine," *Biblical Archaeologist* 7 (1944): 65-77; L. Waterman, "The Damaged Blueprints of the Temple of Solomon," *Journal of Near Eastern Studies* 2 (1943): 284-94.

the palace seemed to have much in common with the temple of Solomon.[33] Later, J. Ouellette was one of the few scholars who attempted to combine the technical terms and comparative architecture into one study. Although he gathered a substantial amount of linguistic and archaeological data, no comprehensive synthesis resulted from his work, and it is no longer up-to-date.[34] Decades of research on Solomon's temple culminated in 1970 with Th. Busink's comprehensive book which brought most discussion to a close for some time.[35]

Since then, more long room temples have been unearthed in the northern Levant, though most of them date to the second millennium B.C. The temples at Ebla, Tell Munbaqa, and Emar all have tripartite division (some with internal walls), raised platforms, pillared entrances, and in some cases comparable construction techniques. They reveal a common Syrian tradition of temple building which no doubt influenced the temples of Phoenicia and Israel.[36]

Israelite "temples" found outside of Jerusalem contribute very little to the study of Solomon's temple, in spite of their notoriety. The shrine at Lachish is post-exilic and there is, in fact, no discernible temple at Beer-sheba to accompany the horned altar. The interpretation of the Arad shrine is also fraught with problems. My use here of the word "shrine" instead of "temple" is deliberate. Once the subsequent construction layers of the fortress are accounted for, very little remains of the cultic structure itself. The relation of this edifice to the Jerusalem temple has been greatly overestimated. First, its dating and layout are different from what Aharoni supposed. Second, except for its orientation and altar the structure has nothing in common with the temple of Solomon.[37] There

33. D. Ussishkin, "Building IV in Hamath and the Temples of Solomon and Taynat," *Israel Exploration Journal* 16 (1966): 104-10; D. Ussishkin, "Solomon's Palace and Building 1723; D. Ussishkin, "King Solomon's Palaces," *Biblical Archaeologist* 36 (1973): 78-105. For a full bibliography see Busink, *Tempel Salomos*.

34. Ouellette, *Temple of Solomon*.

35. Busink, *Tempel Salomos*.

36. See J. Margueron, "Les origines syriennes du temple de Jerusalem," *Le Monde de la Bible*, XX (1981): 31-33; J. Margueron, "Les fouilles francaises de Meskéné-Emar (Syrie)," *Comptes rendus de l'Academie des inscriptions et belles-lettres* (1975): 201-13; A. Mazar in Netzer, *Architecture,* p. 163.

37. Y. Aharoni's eagerness to connect the two structures is perhaps understandable in view of the fact that no other Israelite temples have been discovered. But the association has received uncritical acceptance ever since, even though it is not altogether convincing. See Y. Aharoni, "The Solomonic Temple, Tabernacle and the Arad

may have been alternate cult sites in the land at certain times in Israelite history, but none discovered to date have any direct bearing on the temple of Solomon.

C. The ʿAin Dara Temple: A New Parallel from Syria

The ʿAin Dara temple represents a significant new resource for the study of Solomon's temple. This neo-Hittite temple, located sixty-seven kilometers northwest of Aleppo in Syria, dates to the early first millennium B.C. It was published in 1990 but has received little attention from biblical archaeologists.[38] This is quite surprising because its design and ornamentation are closer to Solomon's temple than the highly publicized temple from Tell Taynat which was discovered more than fifty years ago.

The temple stands on the acropolis of the tell and is built upon an elevated terrace which is approached by way of a basalt flagstone courtyard. Large ornate reliefs of lions, cherubs, palmettes, and guilloche patterns flank the staircase and the porch through which the temple is entered.[39] As in the Tell Taynat temple, the two massive pillars on the porch are slightly inset and appear to have supported the roof. These features are reminiscent of the entryway to the well-known bît ḥilani palace type.[40] Meter-long carved footprints between the colossal door sockets perhaps represent the feet of the deity entering into the first room. The vorcella (or antechamber) of the temple is also flanked with orthostats which have been carved with representations of divine figures (Ishtar?) and flowery ribbons.

The "cella," or central room, of the temple is square and very large, measuring approximately 16 × 16 m. It is reached by ascending three ad-

Sanctuary," in Harry A. Hoffner Jr., ed., *Orient and Occident Essays Presented to C. H. Gordon on the Occasion of His 65th Birthday, Alter Orient und Altes Testament* 22 (1973): 161-92; W. Dever, "Israelite Religion and Archaeology," in P. Miller et al., eds., *Ancient Israelite Religion* (Philadelphia: Fortress, 1987), pp. 209-47. For the opposing view, see D. Ussishkin, "The Arad Temple Redated," *Israel Exploration Journal* 38 (1988): 80-91.

38. Ali Abu-Asaf, *Der Tempel von ʿAin Dara,* Damaszener Forschungen, Bd. 3 (Mainz am Rhein: Philipp von Zabern, 1990).

39. Abu-Asaf, p. 14.

40. J. Ouellette: "Le vestibule du Temple de Salomon était-il un *bît ḥilani?*" *Revue Biblique* 76 (1969): 365-78.

View through central axis of ʿAin Dara temple, front to back
Photo by Tony Appa

ditional stairs and passing through a doorway. Although this room was largely destroyed by later construction, several features are worthy of note. The large elevated area, or "podium," opposite the entrance takes up the rear third of the room. Originally, it was reached by a ramp. The rear wall of the room had a niche and a pedestal with depictions of a deity and divine creatures that is now on display in the Aleppo Museum.[41] Several holes in the southwestern wall appear to have been brackets for supporting a wooden wall.[42] A wall such as this may have blocked off the back part of the area to form a secondary room or "Holy of Holies." These types of internal divisions have been discovered in several second-millennium temples such as Emar and Munbaqa.[43]

41. Abu-Asaf, p. 17.
42. Abu-Asaf, p. 17 and temple plan, Ill. 12.
43. Margueron, "Meskéné-Emar."

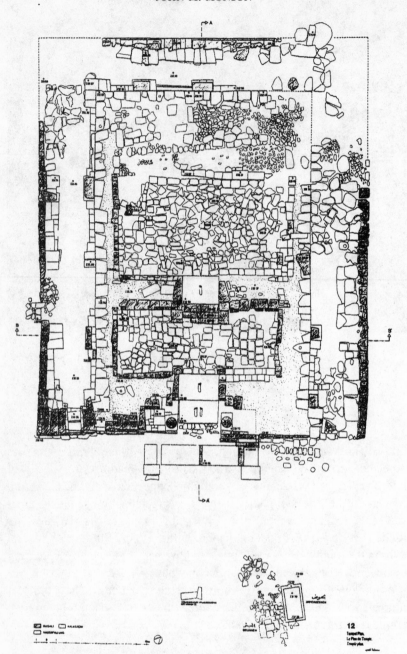

Site sketch of ʿAin Dara temple

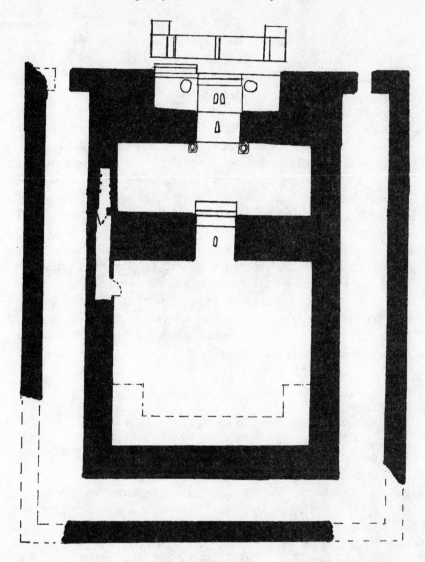

'Ain Dara temple plan

One of the most significant features for our study is the covered walkway which surrounded the temple on three sides. Two levels of well-carved panels and orthostats hint at the superstructure of a second story. Originally the hallway was entered by two doors, one on each side of the main entrance to the temple. Today only the western door remains, but it is still flanked by several impressive winged lions. Grooves and sockets inside the door indicate that it could be locked from the inside of the building.[44] A secondary opening was later added inside the east wall of the inner sanctuary between the first room (vorcella) and main hall (cella). Abu-Asaf's report leaves little doubt that the carved sockets arranged in the corridor behind the northeast wall of the vorcella are the remains of a staircase that led to the second floor of the side chamber.[45]

To summarize, the architecture and ornamentation of the ʿAin Dara temple bears many close similarities not only to second-millennium temples such as Emar, Munbaqa, and Ebla (Temple D) but also to the temple of Solomon and the eighth-century temple from Tell Taynat. Abu-Asaf may therefore be correct in saying that this temple closely resembles the "precursor to the so-called Phoenician temple type" which has yet to be discovered but is thought to have been the inspiration for Solomon's temple.[46]

D. Solomon's Temple in the Light of the ʿAin Dara Temple

What can be said about the temple of Solomon in light of these discoveries? The author of the ʿAin Dara publication did not develop the striking parallels that this structure gives to the biblical description of Solomon's temple. I would argue that the ʿAin Dara temple does in fact have many implications for our understanding of Solomon's temple — more than even the Tell Taynat temple, acclaimed since the 1930s as the closest parallel. To begin with, the ʿAin Dara temple, with its length of 38 m. (as opposed to Tell Taynat, 25 m.), is among the largest Syrian temples discovered to date, and the closest in size to Solomon's temple. Only a few of the additional similarities can be addressed here.

44. Abu-Asaf, p. 16.
45. Abu-Asaf, pp. 18, 16, Fig. 11.
46. Abu-Asaf, p. 42.

1. Platform/Terrace

The 'Ain Dara temple is located on the acropolis of the tell. It was constructed atop a terrace whose outer surfaces were lined with reliefs. Since the temple of Solomon, too, was built on a hilltop, it may have required a similar platform. Such a feature is alluded to in Ezekiel 41:8, 13-14. The *yaṣia'* of 1 Kings 6:5-6, moreover, seems to have been a foundational platform of some sort, whether for the whole temple or just for the side chambers.[47]

2. Pillars, Porch, and Hall *('ûlam)*

The main elements of the 'Ain Dara temple are the porch, the middle room, and the inner room. The small entrance porch and wide hall, like the entrances to many second-millennium temples, were integrated with an open courtyard and were not as closed in as the inner chambers. The *'ûlam* of Solomon's temple, likewise, seems to have served as a type of transitional passageway linking a courtyard to the temple proper. The middle room (hall or vorcella) at 'Ain Dara measures 6×15.5 m. On account of its short length it actually is a broad room like the rooms of the Hamath temple published by Ussishkin. Because it is relatively small, this room cannot be associated with the biblical *hêkal,* which was the main activity area of Solomon's temple. Rather, it should be compared to the biblical *'ûlam.* In this case the name of the porch remains unknown.[48] The middle room at 'Ain Dara is lined with beautiful reliefs of lions, guilloche, and window-like panels, which again remind us of Solomon's temple: "He carved all the walls of the house round about with carved figures of cherubim and palm trees and flowers, in the inner and outer rooms" (1 Kings 6:29).

The pillars at the entrance to the 'Ain Dara temple, like those in the Tell Taynat temple, seem to have had an architectural function in addition to their cultic significance. While this is not certain, it may add to the cumulative evidence that *Jachin* and *Boaz,* the pillars in the temple of Solomon, supported part of the roof.[49] There are many divergent interpreta-

---

47. J. Ouellette: "The *yaṣia'* and the *ṣĕla'ot:* Two Mysterious Structures in Solomon's Temple," *Journal of Near Eastern Studies* 31 (1972): 187-91.

48. I thank Prof. Amihai Mazar for pointing this out to me. He corrected Yadin's erroneous interpretation of a similar temple in Area H at Hazor (Netzer, *Architecture,* p. 172).

49. Such a notion is consistent with the findings of J. Ouellette's comparative study of the temple of Solomon and the porticoes of *bît ḥilani* palaces (Ouellette, *"bît ḥilani?"*); Ussishkin, "Solomon's Palace and Building 1723."

tions of these pillars, which are described in 1 Kings 7:21. Besides a possible association with the palmette (the tree of life or tree of good and evil?), the pillars may have displayed sacred texts.[50]

3. Main Hall *(hêkal)*

According to the biblical description in 1 Kings 7:31ff., the *hêkal,* or main hall, of Solomon's temple was the center of cultic activity and measured approximately 12 × 24 m. It housed the lamp stands, a small incense altar, and a table for the "bread of presence" (1 Kings 7:31ff.). The corresponding room at ʿAin Dara is square and measures approximately 16 × 16 m. Although it is not as well-preserved as other parts of the building, the lower panels of basalt relief can still be seen lining the walls. In addition, the remains of an elevated podium, a niche, and sockets for a secondary wall are clearly visible.

4. Inner Shrine *(dĕbîr)*

The shrine area at ʿAin Dara, like the *dĕbîr* of Solomon's temple, was a small section at the innermost part of the temple. However, some of its features are still hard to interpret. The *dĕbîr* of Solomon's temple, as described in 1 Kings 6:20, was a cube-shaped room which contained the ark and the cherubim. It is unclear from the text whether it was a shrine built within the *hêkal* (main hall) itself, as J. Ouellette and R. Friedman have argued, or a separate architectural unit built of stone, as in the Taynat, Munbaqa, and Ebla temples.[51] In the shrine at ʿAin Dara, carved sockets and grooves on the wall were likely used in the construction of an interior wooden partition. The niche and elevated area to the rear of the partitioned room would then be considered the "Holy of Holies." Unfortunately, the ruins of Syrian temples, even when we consider them alongside the biblical text, do not provide conclusive evidence on this matter. Judging from the biblical description, it seems more likely that the *dĕbîr*

50. The pillars and the general symbolism of Solomon's temple are discussed in E. Bloch-Smith, "'Who Is the King of Glory?' Solomon's Temple and Its Symbolism," in M. Coogan et. al., eds., *Scriptures and Other Artifacts: Essays in Bible and Archaeology in Honor of Philip J. King* (Louisville: John Knox, 1995), pp. 18-31.

51. J. Ouellette: "The Solomonic Dᵉbîr According to the Hebrew Text of 1 Kings 6," *Journal of Biblical Literature* 89 (1970): 338-43; Friedman, "Tabernacle." For descriptions of these temples see Margueron, "Les Origines."

of Solomon's temple was a secondary room within the main hall as at ʿAin Dara. But one cannot rule out the possibility that the room was separated from the hall by a substantial stone wall as at Tell Taynat.

A second question concerns the height of the inner shrine in relation to the temple. According to 1 Kings 6:2 the height of Solomon's temple was 30 cubits, but in 1 Kings 6:20 we read that the inner sanctuary was only 20 cubits high. At Tell Taynat the shrine room is reached by ascending a small flight of stairs. In the ʿAin Dara temple a poorly preserved ramp ascends from the main room to the platform area. In both cases the floor was elevated above the floors of the main hall. Such a construction would accord well with the smaller height of the *děbîr* in Solomon's temple.

5. Reliefs

In 1 Kings 6:29 we read that Solomon "carved all the walls of the house round about with carved figures of cherubim and palm trees and open flowers, in the inner and outer rooms." The imposing winged creatures, lions, and stylized floral designs on the outer and inner walls of the ʿAin Dara temple match this description quite well even though they are largely influenced by neo-Hittite style.[52] These similarities of decoration and relief are worthy of their own independent study.[53]

6. Side Chambers

Generations of commentators have tried to determine the precise nature of the *şěla ʿot,* usually translated "side chambers," of Solomon's temple (1 Kings 6:5). The multistoried hallways which flank the ʿAin Dara temple on three sides are the first clear example of this enigmatic feature to be found outside third-millennium Egypt.[54] These newly discovered side chambers, which had paved floors and beautiful wall reliefs, were entered

52. Abu-Asaf, Pls. 18-22, Ills. 16-17.

53. E.g., see J. Strange, "The Idea of Afterlife in Ancient Israel: Some Remarks on the Iconography in Solomon's Temple," *Palestine Exploration Quarterly* 117 (1985): 35-40; E. Bloch-Smith, "Symbolism." The usefulness of such study is readily seen in I. Winter's articles, such as " 'Idols of the King': Royal Images as Recipients of Ritual Action in Ancient Mesopotamia," *Journal of Ritual Studies* 6 (1992): 13-42.

54. They should not be seen as casemates (contra G. R. H. Wright, *Ancient Building,* p. 258). For Egyptian parallels see Kitchen, "Subsidiary Rooms," above.

through doors on the main (south) facade of the temple. This accords well with the biblical *ṣĕlaʿot*: "The entrance for the lowest *ṣelaʿ* (story) was on the right side of the house; and one went up by *lûlîm* to the middle story" (1 Kings 6:8). A likely example of the *lûlîm*, variously translated as "stairs," "ladders," "winding staircases," etc., has also been found at ʿAin Dara. As noted above, Abu-Asaf has reconstructed two flights of a staircase based upon wall sockets and debris found inside the northeast section of the wall adjoining the antechamber. We now have comparative archaeological examples for a part of Solomon's temple which until now could only be reconstructed in theory.[55]

Besides illuminating for us the text of 1 Kings 6 and Ezekiel 41:4-7, the side chambers at ʿAin Dara raise several questions. The beautiful workmanship on the walls of these hallways leads us to believe that the rooms were not merely storage areas but likely had some ceremonial or cultic function as well. In addition, the side chambers have independent foundations and appear to have been constructed later than the central shrine.[56] This leaves open the possibility that the same building sequence occurred in the Jerusalem temple. Perhaps the side chambers in the Jerusalem temple were constructed later in Solomon's reign or during the reign of a later king. This scenario is promoted by a number of literary critics who for textual reasons consider 1 Kings 6 to be a compilation of source documents from different dates.[57] Finally, the newly published side chambers have conventional walls which do not exactly compare to the recessed walls and wider upper stories of the temple of Solomon (1 Kings 6:6). This aspect of Solomon's temple remains a mystery.

7. Windows and Doors

There have been many attempts to understand the *hallonê šĕqupîm ʾăṭumîm* of Solomon's temple (windows with recessed frames? 1 Kings 6:4). The ʿAin Dara publication sheds important — even decisive — new light on the subject. Most commentators translate this term as "latticed windows" based on etymologies. L. E. Stager's translation, which is informed by a proper understanding of the archaeology, seems closer to the

---

55. Compare the features (Abu-Asaf, pp. 16-18, Fig. 11) with Ouellette's analysis thirty years ago ("The *yaṣîaʿ*," p. 190).

56. See the temple plan of Abu-Asaf, Ill. 18 and pp. 17-19.

57. D. Gooding, "An Impossible Shrine," *Vetus Testamentum Supplements* 15 (1965): 405-20.

original meaning. According to him the term refers to wood or stone frames which were "filled up with rubble masonry," hence the word *'aṭam*, "to shut up, close."[58]

It is now possible to take this suggestion one step further. The wall panels in the first room (vorcella) at ʿAin Dara include at least two window frames which have been carefully cut into the stone and are remarkably well-preserved. These "decorative windows" are not lacking in any detail.[59] Each has a recessed, indented frame on each side, including the top, where it is slightly arched. Horizontal "figure eight-shaped ribbons" fill the upper half of each window.[60] These may indeed represent the window lattice described in 1 Kings 6:4-5 and elsewhere in the Hebrew Bible.[61] Some of the windows have been carved with side posts which apparently represent the opening capability of functional windows.[62] In light of the overall similarity between the two temples and the apparent meaning of the biblical phrase, we may infer that the "blocked, latticed windows" of Solomon's temple were beautiful decorative stone reliefs such as the ones at ʿAin Dara. The interior of the Solomonic temple must have been a dark place indeed, with some light entering through the doorways when they were opened. Perhaps higher windows or the rafters of the roof construction provided additional light and ventilation.

The doors of Solomon's temple are described in 1 Kings 6:1-33 as fitting into "pentagonal" (?) and "four-sided" (?) lintels and doorposts. The exact design is still unclear although A. Millard has warned against the dangers of hasty emendation.[63] At ʿAin Dara door sockets were found only inside the entrance to the vorcella.[64]

58. L. E. Stager, "The Archaeology of the Family in Ancient Israel," *Bulletin of the American Schools of Oriental Research* 260 (1985): 13.

59. Abu-Asaf, p. 15, Pl. 42, Figs. D2-D4.

60. Abu-Asaf, p. 15, Pl. 42, Figs. D2-D4.

61. For additional references and related terms see A. Even-Shoshan, ed., *A New Concordance of the Bible* (Jerusalem: Qiryat Sepher, 1981), pp. 371-72.

62. Abu-Asaf, p. 15.

63. For the doors of the ʿAin Dara temple see Abu-Asaf, pp. 15-16 and the plan of the temple, Ill. 18. See Millard, "Doorways," above.

64. Abu-Asaf, pp. 15-16; Millard, "Doorways."

V. Conclusion

The biblical description of Jerusalem and its temple accord well with what is known of the cultural record and political framework of the Levant in the tenth century B.C. Like other monarchs of the Near East David and Solomon attached their dynasty to a national shrine. It is not surprising to find a high degree of similarity in architectural, literary, and artistic expression between Israel and its neighbours during this cosmopolitan era. With the aid of Phoenician workers the temple was constructed in a city which had a long history of cultural ties with Syria. Whatever traditions had existed on the site before, Israel developed its own theology of Zion. The tradition eventually became a code word for Jerusalem and the temple. Hereafter the temple of Solomon would be the heart of Jerusalem, the focal point of the nation.

In the long quest to understand Solomon's temple the ʿAin Dara temple represents another significant landmark. In our attempt to reach a more informed reading of the biblical descriptions we have presented only a few of the many similarities between the two temples. We must always keep in mind, however, that each temple had its own character and individual features. Each temple was unique to some degree. While similar in style and construction, these structures were, after all, built by different kingdoms, each with its own concerns and distinct religion. It is unlikely, in fact, that an exact prototype of Solomon's temple will ever be found.

Yet the symbolism of the temple far outlived the fleeting empire in which it was built. The crisis of 586 B.C. did not diminish the standing of the temple in the collective Israelite psyche, even though the nation would never again see such a golden age. In the exile and beyond, the temple inspired the reunited Jews and animated many visions of the future. One thousand years later the (rebuilt) temple was destroyed amidst nationalist aspirations. Again the image of the temple lived on. Today the same temple mount still draws international attention as it stirs the faith, aspirations, and passions of people worldwide.

> "Our fathers worshiped on this mountain; and you say that in Jerusalem is the place where men ought to worship." . . . Jesus said to her, "The hour is coming, and now is, when the true worshipers will worship the Father in spirit and in truth" (John 4:20-24).

Hezekiah and Sennacherib in 2 Kings 18–20

RICHARD S. HESS

This study examines a major event in the history of Old Testament Jerusalem, one that is recorded in three places in the Hebrew Bible. The effects of the invasion of Sennacherib in 701 and his threat to the existence of Jerusalem and the dynasty of David remained with the citizens of Jerusalem. This study surveys some of the recent attempts to make sense of the biblical account and proposes a literary approach to 2 Kings 18–20 (as well as the other occurrences of the life of Hezekiah in Isaiah and 2 Chronicles), using techniques found elsewhere in the Hebrew Bible.

The Assyrian attack on Jerusalem in 701 B.C. arose out of the resistance that the new king of Jerusalem, Hezekiah, offered the ruler of Assyria, Sennacherib. When Sennacherib began his reign (705), he was confronted with rebellions throughout his empire, perhaps orchestrated by the Babylon resistance fighter, Merodach-baladan, from his base in southern Babylonia. It was not until 701 that Sennacherib was able to turn his attention to the West and the Syrian city-states who had rebelled. The campaign of Sennacherib, in which he destroyed the Judean cities of Lachish and Libnah, and besieged Hezekiah in Jerusalem, is recorded in the Assyrian chronicles as well as the Bible.

The end of the eighth century in Judah and the invasion of Sennacherib are well attested by literary, iconographic, and archaeological sources.[1] The biblical sources include Isaiah 36–39 and 2 Kings 18–20 which resemble one another in many details, as well as 2 Chronicles 32. Extrabiblical literary sources include Sennacherib's Annals (Taylor Prism) of his third Royal Campaign, the Bull Inscription, and the Nebi Yunis Slab.[2] There is also an account contained in the works of the Greek historian Herodotus (Book II, 141) that may be related to this event. It describes how Herodotus was told about a statue in Egypt that commemorated an event during which the Assyrian army was stopped in its advance by mice who ate the Assyrians' bowstrings. Although the account would appear to fit surprisingly well with the events of 701 B.C., not all scholars agree. Cogan and Tadmor[3] deny that it has any relevance to the period of Sennacherib, preferring to see it as a late ascription of Esarhaddon's (Sennacherib's successor) achievements confused with the Jerusalem story by Jewish immigrants in Egypt and used to explain the origins of an Egyptian statue and its inscription.

In Jerusalem additional archaeological and textual evidence attest to this period. For example, there are the Siloam tunnel and Siloam inscription. The tunnel was built at the time of Sennacherib's threat of invasion and designed to bring water into the city so it could withstand a siege in 701.[4] The inscription recounts the process of construction and is the longest connected inscription in Hebrew from before the Exile.[5] Other material remains include those found on the Western Hill in Jerusalem from this period. These could have been part of the mishneh or second city built to enclose the expanding population and provide for its defence.

1. For the written sources, cf. J. von Beckerath, "Ägypten und der Feldzug Sanheribs im Jahre 701 v. Chr.," *Ugarit Forschungen* 24 (1992): 3-8.

2. As A. R. Millard has observed, the initial reports were written within a year of the event. Later copies and briefer summations support the earlier accounts.

3. M. Cogan and H. Tadmor, *II Kings: A New Translation with Introduction and Commentary,* Anchor Bible 11 (Garden City: Doubleday, 1988).

4. D. Gill, "How They Met: Geology Solves Long-Standing Mystery of Hezekiah's Tunnelers," *Biblical Archaeology Review* 20/4 (July/August 1994): 20-33, 64.

5. See S. B. Parker, "Siloam Inscription Memorializes Engineering Achievement," *Biblical Archaeology Review* 20/4 (July/August 1994): 36-38, although this has now been challenged.

Outside Jerusalem, at Lachish excavations of the Southwest corner of the tell uncovered the Assyrian siege ramp and evidence of special strengthening of the walls at this corner.[6] Level III on the site preserves the Assyrian destruction of 701 B.C. In terms of the iconography of the period, there is a wall relief of the siege of Lachish from the palace of Sennacherib in Nineveh. Today it comprises an entire room in the Assyrian exhibit of the British Museum.[7] In the territory conventionally assigned to Judah, Tel Halif, Beer-Sheba, Beth Shemesh, Tell Beit Mirsim, as well as Arad and other sites exhibit destruction layers at the end of the eighth century.[8]

Aharoni, who excavated at Arad, identified an altar for burnt offerings in the Israelite cultic site there. He argued[9] that it went out of use at the time of Hezekiah's reform (stratum VIII). Na'aman[10] argues that the evidence for Hezekiah's reform in 2 Kings 18:4, 22 is not clear. He notes that the termination of the altar at Arad has been dated a century or more later by Ussishkin.[11] Further, Tel Beersheba's altar does not have a clear date for its destruction. There is thus no archaeological evidence for this

6. Along with evidence of the conflict itself, i.e., "holed" stones for hurling at the defenses, arrowheads, pieces of Assyrian armor, etc., cf. D. Ussishkin, "The Assyrian Attack on Lachish: The Archaeological Evidence from the Southwest Corner of the Site," *Tel Aviv* 17 (1990): 53-86.

7. A study of cities on Assyrian reliefs has led R. Jacoby, "The Representation and Identification of Cities on Assyrian Reliefs," *Israel Exploration Journal* 41 (1991): 130, to conclude that the portrayal of Lachish by Sennacherib contains some conventional materials as well as factual details. Using the Assyrian technique of the "simultaneous succession" of events, the battle itself is presented. This style corresponds in some ways to the literary repetition of events as discussed below. The details of the city and its fortifications are presented in a conventional stereotypical fashion (the shields on the wall indicate a western city). The identity of the city is determined by its name in the attached inscription as well as the portrayal of hills (wavy lines), vines, and fig trees native to the Lachish area.

8. G. W. Ahlström, *The History of Ancient Palestine from the Palaeolithic Period to Alexander's Conquest,* JSOT Supplement 146 (Sheffield: JSOT Press, 1993), p. 699.

9. Y. Aharoni, "Arad: Its Inscriptions and Temple," *Biblical Archaeologist* 31 (1968): 26-27.

10. N. Na'aman, "The Debated Historicity of Hezekiah's Reform in the Light of Historical and Archaeological Research," *Zeitschrift für die alttestamentliche Wissenschaft* 107 (1995): 184-89.

11. D. Ussishkin, "The Date of the Judean Shrine at Arad," *Israel Exploration Journal* 38 (1988): 142-57.

cult centralization and closing of the high places. The Lachish reliefs exhibit two bronze incense burners taken as booty from Lachish. This indicates cultic activity there despite the statements of the Bible. Thus the Deuteronomistic History transformed an archival note about the destruction of the Nehustan into a major cultic reform.

However, Halpern[12] finds possible signs of a change in cult at Arad before Josiah in the covering over of the large fieldstone altar and in the plastering over of the two pillars in the "holy of holies." Borowski disputes the later dating of the altar's termination.[13] He concludes that the Beersheba stratum in which the destroyed altar was found is identical to the period in which Lachish was destroyed by Sennacherib. However, the incense burning shrine at Tel Halif continued in operation, perhaps because it was not used for sacrifice. Could this also explain the incense burners on the Lachish reliefs? It would appear agreement has not been reached on the interpretation of the archaeological evidence from Arad and its meaning for a cultic reform in Judah at the end of the eighth century B.C.

The focus of this study will be upon the literary studies of this event as found in the biblical texts, especially 2 Kings but also Isaiah and 2 Chronicles. For convenience, scholars divide the account in 2 Kings 18–20 into two parts: A and B. The A account is 18:13b-16 and B is 18:17–19:37.[14] A is concise with no theology or moral judgment. B is narrative with mention of Isaiah's role. Titles of Hezekiah also differ. In A Hezekiah is "the king of Judah" whereas in B he is "the king." In A Hezekiah pays Sennacherib the tribute that he demands. The Assyrian chronicle mentions a siege of Jerusalem and also includes the tribute exacted upon Hezekiah.

---

12. B. Halpern, "Jerusalem and the Lineages in the Seventh Century BCE: Kinship and the Rise of Individual Moral Liability," in B. Halpern and D. W. Hobson, eds., *Law and Ideology in Monarchic Israel,* JSOT Supplement 124 (Sheffield: JSOT Press, 1991), p. 66.

13. O. Borowski, "Hezekiah's Reform and the Revolt against Assyria," *Biblical Archaeologist* 58 (1995): 148-55.

14. F. J. Gonçalves, *L'expédition de Sennachérib en Palestine dans la littérature hébraïque ancienne* (Paris: Gabalda, 1986), pp. 342-50, followed by H. Williamson, *The Book Called Isaiah* (Oxford: Clarendon, 1994), pp. 198-99, argues that this account derived from Kings and the Deuteronomistic History, not from Isaiah. This is because the date formula in the first verse has parallels in the Deuteronomistic History when a new event in a particular ruler's reign is introduced. Specific dates can introduce invasions but do not introduce prophetic stories. 2 Kings 18:14-16 requires v. 13 if it is to be understandable.

In the B account of 2 Kings, Hezekiah receives official envoys who address him in the language of Judah (Hebrew) and he receives a letter from Sennacherib which challenges his God as impotent in the face of the Assyrians. Hezekiah prays to God with this letter and the response is God's defense of Jerusalem "for my own sake and for the sake of my servant David" (v. 34). There is a slaughter of 185,000 Assyrians by the angel of the Lord (v. 35) causing a withdrawal. The subsequent murder of Sennacherib by his sons is also recorded (681 B.C. with Assyrian attestations). Isaiah 36–37 also recounts the B text. 2 Chronicles 32 is an elaboration of the B account where Sennacherib is conducting a siege at Lachish when he sends the envoys.[15]

All the biblical accounts are followed by a story concerning Hezekiah's illness and miraculous recovery, the news of which comes through the prophet Isaiah who visits him. Hezekiah is given fifteen additional years. A sign promising this is given in which Hezekiah's sun dial moves backward ten degrees. Isaiah brings Hezekiah God's word of promised healing and life and protection. He also heals Hezekiah with a fig cake and then calls upon God for the sign of the sun dial.[16]

This is followed by an account in which Merodach-baladan, guerrilla leader of Babylon's resistance against Assyria, sends a party to Hezekiah at Jerusalem to discuss resistance plans against Assyria. Hezekiah shows the Babylonians all his defenses and treasures. Isaiah predicts an exile of Hezekiah's dynasty in Babylon.[17] Note that nowhere is the exhibition to the Babylonians explicitly condemned. Only 2 Chronicles suggests a moral aspect to what was done, "God left him to himself in order to try him and to know all that was in his heart."

---

15. S. Japhet, *I & II Chronicles. A Commentary,* Old Testament Library (Louisville: Westminster/John Knox, 1993), p. 976, regards this chapter as based on Kings but involving "extensive reworking through omissions, additions, rephrasing and epitomization." Some of Hezekiah's preparations in vv. 3-6 she ascribes to "an additional independent source" (p. 978). There is an attempt to idealize Hezekiah and to parallel his account with that of Josiah as much as any other king of Judah (p. 998). I. Kalimi, "Literary-Chronogical Proximity in Chronicles," *Vetus Testamentum* 43 (1993): 318-38, has suggested that the Chronicler has juxtaposed events in the text for theological purposes. Thus Hezekiah's ritual reform and Sennacherib's failure are associated even though they may not have occurred at the same time. God's response to Hezekiah's prayer appears to be immediate and Sennacherib's unsuccessful campaign against Judah leads directly to his assassination in Nineveh.

16. See Isa. 38; 2 Kings 20:1-11; 2 Chron. 32:24-26.

17. See Isa. 39; 2 Kings 20:12-20; and the single verse in 2 Chron. 32:31.

The most significant problem in this account is the question of the A and B accounts in 2 Kings. Why are there two accounts? Alongside this problem is that of the accounts of Hezekiah's illness and of the Babylonian envoys. What is the reason for their placement and order in the text? Finally, we may question why this material is repeated in Isaiah at the end of the section ascribed to Isaiah of Jerusalem. There are three groups of approaches to these problems, historical, critical, and literary.

I. Historical Approaches

This approach was developed in the U.S. by Albright and followed by Bright. It argues that A and B represent two separate accounts of two campaigns by Sennacherib against Judah. As such the first one took place in 701 B.C. Sennacherib reigned until 681 and Hezekiah for another fifteen years after 701. Thus there would be fifteen years in which a second war could have occurred. As the latter part of Sennacherib's reign is not well documented in the Assyrian sources, an unrecorded campaign against Jerusalem that resulted in an ignominious defeat could easily have been ignored in the Assyrian accounts.

An additional later campaign would explain the reason for the account of the Babylonian envoys appearing after the account of the Assyrian attack. If there was only one Assyrian war, then this account would make better sense before the war, as the Babylonian alliance would logically have preceded and caused the Assyrian attack. However, if there were two Assyrian wars, then the earlier one in 701 could have been followed by the search for allies by Hezekiah to support continued resistance in the face of diminished resources. This would have led to the alliance with Merodach-baladan that could have precipitated the second later war with Sennacherib. This second war, preserved in the B account, would have been the last event in 2 Kings' record of Hezekiah's life.[18] However, as the writer may have grouped together similar themes, such as the wars of the king, it was placed alongside the A account of the first war. Indeed, the writer/editor may have confused the two wars and understood a single conflict.

18. N. Na'aman, "Hezekiah and the Kings of Assyria," *Tel Aviv* 21 (1994): 235-54, concludes that the promise of an additional fifteen years for Hezekiah came in his recovery from illness shortly before the war of 701 B.C.

This interpretation has been used to explain the appearance of Tirhakah at the head of the Egyptian army (2 Kings 19:9; Isaiah 37:9). According to some Egyptian chronologies, Tirhakah would have been an infant in 701 and thus unable to lead the Egyptians. Therefore, a second campaign some years later, would have given Tirhakah sufficient time to grow old enough to lead a campaign. However, this is no longer necessarily a difficulty because recent discussions have suggested that Tirhakah was a prince in 701 and old enough to lead an army.[19] His coronation in 690 would have been as a sole ruler of Egypt.[20]

Cogan and Tadmor[21] criticize this view as one that ignores the historical circumstances behind the revolt of 701, with the change of rulership in Assyria and the rise of Merodach-baladan in Babylonia. These phenomena were not repeated after 701. Cogan and Tadmor compare the variety of written sources from 701 with the conflicting reports that emerge from a modern battle with various biases and positions reflected in them.

Motyer[22] also suggests two assaults by Sennacherib, but they follow one immediately after the other. He suggests that the battle of Eltekeh shattered Egypt's hopes and left Sennacherib free to deal with Judah. Following a strong assault, Hezekiah asked for terms. The Assyrians imposed a heavy fine that Hezekiah paid. However, Sennacherib proved treacherous and returned to attack Jerusalem again. At this point Hezekiah expressed faith in God. He and the city were rescued. Although this view agrees with the biblical texts, the absence of any explicit mention of treachery by Sennacherib is difficult to explain.

19. See K. A. Kitchen, *The Third Intermediate Period in Egypt (1100-650 B.C.)*, 3rd ed. (Warminster: Ares & Phillips, 1989), pp. 557-58; review of W. H. Barnes, *Studies in the Chronology of the Divided Monarchy of Israel* (Atlanta: Scholars Press, 1991), in *Evangelical Quarterly* 65 (1993): 251-52.

20. See F. J. Yurco, "The Shabaka-Shebitku Coregency and the Supposed Second Campaign of Sennacherib against Judah: A Critical Assessment," *Journal of Biblical Literature* 110 (1991): 35-45; K. A. Kitchen, "Late-Egyptian Chronology and the Hebrew Monarchy: Critical Studies in Old Testament Mythology, I," *Journal of the Ancient Near Eastern Society of Columbia University* 5 (1973): 225-33; idem, *The Third Intermediate Period in Egypt (1100-650 B.C.)* (Warminster: Ares & Phillip, 1973), pp. 161-72.

21. Cogan and Tadmor, *II Kings: A New Translation with Introduction and Commentary*.

22. A. Motyer, *The Prophecy of Isaiah* (Leicester: Inter-Varsity Press, 1993), p. 20.

This might be expected considering the biblical authors' low view of the Assyrian king.

Laato analyzes the Assyrian and Babylonian sources, as well as Herodotus' account and concludes: "many features of this text (2 Kings/ Isaiah) correspond well to the historical circumstances of the time of Isaiah."[23] Laato regards the slaughter of 185,000 as an exaggeration reflecting a bubonic plague or some other disease. After defeating the other rebellious cities, including Ekron, Sennacherib went to Lachish and captured it. Hezekiah offered tribute (2 Kings 18:14-16) which Sennacherib received along with Padi the king of Ekron whom Hezekiah held prisoner. But Sennacherib was not satisfied and required Hezekiah to open the gates of Jerusalem. He sent the Rabshekah with a large force. Many of Hezekiah's troops fled (Isa. 22:3), having heard of the Assyrian vengeance against Ekron. A plague broke out causing the Assyrians to withdraw. This plague may also have affected Jerusalem (Isa. 22:2). Hezekiah sent a large tribute to Sennacherib in Assyria to assure him of his loyalty and prevent the return of the Assyrian army. Like the approach of Motyer, this explanation suffers from the difficulty that the biblical texts, otherwise quick to accuse Sennacherib of faults, ignore such treachery against Hezekiah.

Shea has renewed the argument for a second Assyrian campaign.[24] He interprets and applies Sennacherib's "letter to God," as reconstructed by Na'aman, to this event.[25] It is not certain, however, that this reconstructed text (assuming that the reconstruction itself is correct) must be applied to an additional campaign by Sennacherib against Judah, one otherwise unattested in the Assyrian records.

II. Critical Approaches

This approach, with its attempt to address the role of Isaiah and of the place of this account in the subsequent history of Judah, is championed by

23. A. Laato, "Assyrian Propaganda and the Falsification of History in the Royal Inscriptions of Sennacherib," *Vetus Testamentum* 45 (1995): 223-26.

24. W. H. Shea, "Sennacherib's Second Palestinian Campaign," *Journal of Biblical Literature* 104 (1985): 401-18.

25. N. Na'aman, "Sennacherib's 'Letter to God' on His Campaign to Judah," *Bulletin of the American Schools of Oriental Research* 214 (1974): 25-39.

many biblical scholars.[26] Sources are identified along with a series of editorial stages, ranging from two[27] to seven.[28]

A. For Clements, Isaiah was opposed to Hezekiah's union with others in rebellion against Assyria. The prophecies in which Isaiah predicts the success of the rebellion are not original to Isaiah and date to a later time. Following Childs, he regards the two accounts of 2 Kings 18:13-16 and 2 Kings 18:17–19:37 as in agreement with Sennacherib's Annals in their basic message that Sennacherib threatened Jerusalem without an actual siege, that he was paid off by Hezekiah, and that he returned home. 2 Kings 19:35, with its account of God's destruction of the army, is one of the later embellishments. This positive account of Jerusalem's salvation with its affirmation of the Davidic monarchy and of Zion theology's view of Jerusalem's inviolability, dates from Josiah's reign.

Scholars who follow this approach divide the B account into two sections, B_1 (18:17–19:9a and 36) and B_2 (19:9b-35).[29] B_1 includes the

26. E.g., B. S. Childs, *Isaiah and the Assyrian Crisis, Studies in Biblical Theology* 2/3 (London: SPCK, 1967); R. E. Clements, *Isaiah and the Deliverance of Jerusalem,* JSOT Supplement 13 (Sheffield: JSOT, 1980); Cogan and Tadmor, *II Kings: A New Translation with Introduction and Commentary;* I. W. Provan, *Hezekiah and the Book of Kings,* Beihelfte zur Zeitschrift für die alttestamentliche Wissenschaft [hereafter BZAW] 172 (Berlin: de Gruyter, 1988); M. A. O'Brien, *The Deuteronomistic History Hypothesis: A Reassessment,* Orbis Biblicus et Orientalis 92 (Friebourg: Universitätsverlag; Göttingen: Vandenhoeck & Ruprecht, 1989); C. Hardmeier, *Prophetie im Streit vor dem Untergang Judas: Erzählkommunikative Studien zur Entstehungssituation der Jesaja- und Jeremiaerzählungen in II Reg 18-29 und Jer 37-40,* BZAW 187 (Berlin: de Gruyter, 1990); A. Laato, *Josiah and David Redivivus: The Historical Josiah and the Messianic Expectations of Exilic and Postexilic Times,* Coniectanea Biblica Old Testament Series 33 (Stockholm: Almqvist & Wiksell, 1992); idem, "Assyrian Propaganda and the Falsification of History in the Royal Inscriptions of Sennacherib," *Vetus Testamentum* 45 (1995): 198-226.

27. G. W. V. Chamaza, "Literarkritische Beobachtung zu 2 Kön 18,1-12," *Biblische Zeitschrift* 33 (1989): 222-33.

28. E. Ruprecht, "Die ursprüngliche Komposition der Hiskia-Jeaja-Erzählungen und ihre Umstrukturierung durch den Verfasser des deuteronomistischen Geschichtswerkes," *Zeitschrift für Theologie und Kirche* 87 (1990): 33-66.

29. See Childs, *Isaiah and the Assyrian Crisis,* pp. 73-103; Gonçalves, *L'expédition de Sennachérib en Palestine dans la littérature hébraïque ancienne,* pp. 373-489; Provan, *Hezekiah and the Books of Kings,* pp. 122-28, identifies B_1 as 18:17-37; 19:1-8, 35-37; and B_2 as 19:9-34. He places all of 19:9 with B_2, arguing that the Egyptian advance described there forms the reason for sending the letter.

visit of Sennacherib's envoys. B_2 replaces this with a letter from Sennacherib. Cogan and Tadmor attribute B_1 to a contemporary record of the events. B_2, with its focus on the role of Isaiah, they date to a few generations later and ascribe it to Isaiah's disciples. Provan[30] concludes that, because A contains materials that foreshadow B_1 (but not B_2), then B_1 is contemporary with A and pre-exilic while B_2 is exilic. Clements[31] argues that B preserves no historical value other than what it obtained from A.

For Clements, Hezekiah's illness (2 Kings 20:1-11) is a further example of Zion theology. It is related in its ascribed date (v. 6) to Sennacherib's threat. Both events support the Davidic dynasty. Hezekiah's faithfulness and lack of need for repentance suggest that this was composed after Josiah's death as a nuance to the Zion theology; i.e., that David's successors were guaranteed their reigns only if they were faithful and blameless, serving God "with a whole heart." As Cogan and Tadmor observe, there is a transposition of the fig cake healing, which 2 Kings 20:7-8 places before the sun dial promise, to its logical position after this incident in Isaiah 38:21-22. Cogan and Tadmor regard the fig cake incident as separate from the rest of the narrative, in the wonder worker tradition of Elijah/Elishah.[32]

For Clements, Merodach-baladan's emissaries, Hezekiah's entertainment of them, and the consequent judgement (2 Kings 20:12-19) refer to Jehoiachin's surrender to Babylon in 598 with Jehoiachin's deportation and the temple being stripped of valuables (2 Kings 24:12-16). Note that Merodach-baladan's visit is out of sequence (it would have taken place before Sennacherib's attack against Judah), the reasons for the judgment are weak (mere entertainment of the embassy), and the promised punishment does not include the destruction of the temple which took place in 587. All these factors explain this account as a rationale for the events of 598, written after they took place and after the two previous incidents from the life of Hezekiah were written, but written before the events of 587. This conclusion was reached independently by Cogan and Tadmor.

---

30. Provan, *Hezekiah and the Book of Kings,* p. 129.

31. Clements, *Isaiah and the Deliverance of Jerusalem.*

32. In 1QIs[a], the key verse at issue is omitted and later written in the margin by another scribe (Isa. 38:21). However, both vv. begin with the same word so that it would have been easy for a scribe's eye to skip one v. and continue with v. 22, a phenomenon known as haplography.

This third story of Hezekiah further provides a conditional aspect for the Zion theology and the promises to the Davidic dynasty.

For Clements, Zion tradition flourishes only during the reform period of Josiah and emerges as Deuteronomistic authors (Clements' Assyrian redactors) of Josiah's age look back upon Hezekiah's confrontation with Sennacherib and interpret it in light of their own theological notions of the guarantee of the Davidic dynasty.[33] Isaiah and Micah did not share this belief, but by the time of Jeremiah and Ezekiel it had become a dogma that they needed to address. The incorporation of these three narratives into the Deuteronomistic history lies before 587, during Zedekiah's reign. Childs and Cogan and Tadmor, however, regard the Zion tradition as original with Isaiah and not the product of a later development. Begg has also found the substance of the account of the Babylonian embassy to be based on annalistic sources older than the Deuteronomist.[34]

B. The last eight years have seen a great variety in scholarly evaluations of the biblical texts and their value for any historical reconstruction. A few may be summarized here. O'Brien[35] uses thematic patterns for his evaluation of B_1 and B_2. He argues that the Deuteronomist used certain criteria for comparing Hezekiah and Josiah with the ideal of David: fidelity to Yahweh, fidelity to centralized worship, and fidelity to the prophet/king form of leadership through consultation at a critical moment in the king's reign. Because B_2 does not include the element of a prophetic consultation, B_1 was brought in to frame it and to include this item.[36] The Deuteronomistic history did not contain A which was added later to contrast with other accounts of plundering the temple in the historical books.[37] A and 2 Kings 20:12-19 are later additions that frame the whole series of accounts of Hezekiah's reign. The latter's portrayal of the Babylonians as aggressors against Judah would fit the exilic period rather than the time of Josiah or earlier.

33. See I. Provan, *Hezekiah and the Books of Kings,* p. 130.

34. C. T. Begg, "2 Kings 20:12-19 as an Element of the Deuteronomistic History," *Catholic Biblical Quarterly* 48 (1986): 27-38.

35. O'Brien, *The Deuteronomistic History Hypothesis: A Reassessment,* pp. 220-26.

36. For O'Brien the prophetic consultation itself is composed of the event, the prophetic consultation, the prophecy and its fulfillment.

37. 1 Kings 14:25; 2 Kings 12:18-19; 16:5-9.

C. Dion[38] reverses the analysis of B_1 and B_2. B_1 is the original source for the composition of B_2. A and B_1 reflect the same original context. B_1 was written after the events and reflects only a limited knowledge of them. Its purpose was religious.

D. Others also deny any historical value to one or both of the accounts of Hezekiah in the Bible. Gonçalves reaches the conclusion[39] that the text lacks historical basis and should be understood as a narrative statement of a theological conviction that Isaiah and his "successors" found salvation only in Yahweh. In this understanding, the Assyrian army's slaughter becomes a symbol of the Passover.

E. Høgenhaven argues that 2 Kings 18–20 and Isaiah 36–39 are fabrications of the Deuteronomist with no authentic traditions regarding Isaiah.[40] He regards Isaiah as supporting originally a pro-Assyrian policy.[41] Isaiah opposed the policy of Hezekiah with the latter's anti-Assyrian position. This is based on Isaiah 30:1-7 and 31:1-3 with its attack of any hope for support from Egypt. Isaiah 8:11-18 should be applied to Hezekiah's time with Isaiah's warning to his followers not to accept the anti-Assyrian plot or conspiracy at the court.

L. Camp[42] and C. Hardmeier[43] would see the B texts as without historical value. With Gonçalves[44] and most scholars, Hardmeier agrees that A has a historical basis. In general, the accounts of Kings are propaganda docu-

---

38. P. E. Dion, "Sennacherib's Expedition to Palestine," *Eglise et Théologie* 20 (1989): 5-25.
39. F. J. Gonçalves, "Senquerib en Palestina y la Tradición Biblica: De la terrible derrota de Jud a la maravillosa liberación de Jerusalém," *Efemerides Mexicana* 8 (1990): 57-69.
40. J. Høgenhaven, "The Prophet Isaiah and Judaean Foreign Policy under Ahaz and Hezekiah," *Journal of Near Eastern Studies* 49 (1990): 351-54.
41. Isaiah 7 should be seen as originally having Isaiah praising Ahaz for his policy. This original stratum is preserved in the names of the children which describe the success of this policy for Judah.
42. L. Camp, *Hiskija und Hiskijabild: Analyse und Interpretation von 2 Kön 18–20,* Münsteraner Theologische Abhandlungen 9 (Altenberge: Telos, 1990).
43. Hardmeier, *Prophetie im Streit vor dem Untergang Judas.*
44. Gonçalves, *L'expédition de Sennachérib en Palestine dans la littérature hébraïque ancienne;* "Senaquerib na Palestina et a tradiç o bíblica. Da grande derrota de Jud à maravilhosa salvação de Jerusalém," *Didaskalia* 5 (1990): 30-44.

ments written after the events of 588 by the anti-Babylonian party in order to argue against Jeremiah and Ezekiel. A's purpose is to show that tribute payment only leads to further assault (B). But this does not explain why such documents have survived when the message of Jeremiah was the one that the Bible accepted, nor does it appreciate the similarities of these chapters to the language and ideas of Jeremiah.[45]

G. De Jong examines 2 Kings 18:13–19:37 in a doctoral thesis prepared at the Free University of Amsterdam.[46] He finds five separate layers of literary and editorial work, based on linguistic criteria. The most significant are the exilic and late exilic, with affinities to Jeremiah and Deutero-Isaiah respectively. The Kings account predates the Isaiah text.

H. Seitz sees in 2 Kings 18:14-16 a portrayal of the untrustworthy character of Sennacherib as a blasphemer who proceeds to attack Hezekiah even after receiving tribute from him.[47] The purpose of the text is to teach how dealings with foreign kings are fruitless. Seitz views 18:14-16 as non-historical on the basis of discrepancies with Sennacherib's annals.[48] He concludes that this was a literary creation of the Deuteronomist who wanted to exalt Josiah at Hezekiah's expense, portraying him as the ideal Davidic ruler (cf. Laato). Thus 18:14-16 is an intentional comparison with Ahaz of 16:5-9, showing that Hezekiah was like Ahaz in not following God.

I. Smelik thinks that most of the biblical accounts in Kings, Chronicles, and Isaiah are a literary retrojection back into the past of a theological discussion of the meaning of events in the Exile.[49] The Rabshakeh's speech,

45. S. De Jong, "Het verhaal van Hizkia en Sanherib. 2 Koningen 18.17-19, 37/ Jesaja 36–37 als narratieve reflectie op de Ballingschap," *Amsterdamse Cahiers voor Exegese en Bijbelse Theologie* 10 (1989): 57-71.

46. S. De Jong, *Het verhaal van Hizkia en Sanherib. Een synchronische en diachronische analyse van II Kon. 18,13–19,37 (par. Jes 36–37)* (Amsterdam: Centrale Huisdrukkerij V. U., 1992).

47. C. R. Seitz, "Account A and the Annals of Sennacherib: A Reassessment," *Journal for the Study of the Old Testament* 58 (1993): 47-57.

48. C. R. Seitz, *Zion's Final Destiny: The Development of the Book of Isaiah: A Reassessment of Isaiah 36–39* (Minneapolis: Fortress, 1991).

49. K. A. D. Smelik, *Converting the Past. Studies in Ancient Israelite and Moabite Historiography,* Oudtestamentische Studiën 28 (Leiden: Brill, 1992), pp. 93-128.

for example, represents the easy distortion of biblical prophecy. Only Source A in 2 Kings can be used for reconstructing the history. This is based on the argument that the text is a literary unity with signs of its composition as late as after the Exile. Therefore, the whole cannot be earlier than the Exile.

J. By comparing the Qumran, Septuagint, and Masoretic texts of Kings and Isaiah, Konkel argues that Kings is older than Isaiah and that both originally come from a pre-exilic source whose literary form can still be discerned.[50] His argument is based on the antiquity of the *kaige* recension found in the Septuagint (Vaticanus) of Kings.

Behind some of these views lie assumptions that one can separate the historical from the theological and that the theological is not historical. Yet, the theologically significant B source is not unusual when compared with contemporary Ancient Near Eastern annalistic accounts. The narrative presentations of wars are regularly punctuated with descriptions of divine intervention by deities of the victorious party. Divisions into historical and theological sources are artificial and do not adequately explain the text in its Ancient Near Eastern context.[51]

III. Literary Approaches

Wiseman observes that the B account is parallel to the A account.[52] It is an elaboration of the first account, emphasizing Hezekiah's faith and the role of the prophetic promise. It is the concern of this third approach to elaborate this view by considering it in the light of literary techniques identified in the Old Testament.

50. A. H. Konkel, "The Sources of the Story of Hezekiah in the Book of Isaiah," *Vetus Testamentum* 43 (1993): 462-82.
51. M. Weinfeld, "Divine Intervention in War in Ancient Israel and in the Ancient Near East," in H. Tadmor and M. Weinfeld, eds., *History, Historiography and Interpretation: Studies in Biblical and Cuneiform Literatures* (Jerusalem: Magnes, and Leiden: Brill, 1984), 121-47; and A. R. Millard, "Sennacherib's Attack on Hezekiah," *Tyndale Bulletin* 36 (1985): 61-77, provide examples from other Ancient Near Eastern sources of descriptions of warfare and divine miracles similar to that found in these accounts.
52. D. J. Wiseman, *1 and 2 Kings,* Tyndale Old Testament Commentaries (Leicester: InterVarsity Press, 1993), pp. 275-76.

A literary approach studies the conventions of biblical narratives and attempts to apply these to understanding why the material is arranged in its present position. In so doing it does not deny validity to the historical and critical approaches, but it does suggest a rationale for the present arrangement of the material within its literary context, a rationale that is key to the interpretation of the material as we have it.[53] The approaches considered here develop from those applied to other biblical narratives.

The A and B accounts in 2 Kings 18–20 need not be understood as the mere juxtaposition of two different narratives. Instead, the techniques of resumption and expansion are applied to demonstrate that, as in other biblical cases, there are two parallel accounts set side by side. The use of these techniques in the Bible creates stories where the first account is usually shorter and presents a summary of the narrative. The second account is longer and provides further details of what happens.

This occurs in Genesis 1 and 2. The first description of creation considers the cosmos and all creation. The second one provides specifics of the people created and their home and work.[54] Sprinkle has identified it in the Book of the Covenant, where the arrangement of the laws uses this principle to introduce a category and then to develop it further.[55] In the narratives of Joshua it may also appear.[56] For example, the visit of the spies to Rahab is summarized in 2:1 and then expanded in vv. 2-14. Their escape from Jericho is also summarized (2:15) and then expanded (vv. 16-21). This same technique may also enable the reader to better understand what appear to be multiple accounts of crossing the Jordan River in Joshua 3–4.

Its analysis as a phenomenon in biblical narrative and prophetic tales

53. See, e.g., R. Alter, *The Art of Biblical Narrative* (London: George Allen & Unwin, 1981) (especially his chapter, "The Techniques of Repetition"), and M. Sternberg, *The Poetics of Biblical Narrative: Ideological Literature and the Drama of Reading,* Indiana Studies in Biblical Literature (Bloomington: Indiana University Press, 1985).

54. R. S. Hess, "Genesis 1–2 in Its Literary Context," *Tyndale Bulletin* 41 (1990): 143-53.

55. J. M. Sprinkle, *The Book of the Covenant: A Literary Approach,* JSOT Supplement 174 (Sheffield: JSOT, 1994).

56. W. Moran, "The Repose of Rahab's Israelite Guests," pp. 275-83 in *Studi sull'Oriente e la Bibbia. Offerti al p. Giovanni Rinaldi nel 60j compleanno da allievi, colleghi, amici,* Genova Studio e vita (1967); R. S. Hess, *Joshua,* Tyndale Old Testament Commentary Series (Leicester: InterVarsity Press, 1996).

has been studied by Brichto[57] who identifies it as the synoptic/resumptive technique:

> Essentially it is the treatment of one event two times. The first narration of the event (and an event may be simple or compounded of a number of actions) is usually *briefer* (hence *synoptic*) than the second, is an independent, freestanding literary unit. . . . The second treatment seems to go back to the opening point of the first episode and, resuming the theme of that treatment, provide a more detailed account (hence *resumptive-expansive*) of how the bottom line of the first episode (hence *conclusive*) was arrived at.

The two episodes may be simultaneous. "In the *synoptic/resumptive technique,* the pattern of repetition is there; the function of the pattern must be separately determined in and for each occurrence." Although the late Rabbi Brichto produced a volume studying examples of this technique in the Deuteronomistic History (and an additional volume on the patriarchal narratives has been published posthumously), he did not apply this approach to the A and B accounts of 2 Kings 18–20.[58] Such an application is relevant for understanding the structure of these texts.

A is the summary account that describes the most important events of the narrative that begin and conclude the action. B is an elaboration of these events with a full discussion of the detail in between. Thus the tribute paid by Hezekiah in A may be something that happened after the deliverance recorded in B. This would seem more logical in any case. Sennacherib, forced to retire due to a sudden crisis in his army, would still threaten Hezekiah with subsequent campaigns. In order to guarantee that this would not occur, Hezekiah submitted to the king and paid him tribute. Note that in the Assyrian account of the siege of Jerusalem, Sennacherib mentions that Hezekiah "later" paid tribute. The first deliverance (in the B text) is one that occurs specifically as a result of Sennacherib's threat and blasphemy against God. Sennacherib's remaining power might have been sufficient to threaten Hezekiah although he may no longer have blas-

57. H. C. Brichto, *Toward a Grammar of Biblical Poetics: Tales of the Prophets* (Oxford: Oxford University Press, 1992), pp. 13-19.
58. Its appearance in narratives elsewhere in the biblical text argues against the view that this is merely an *ad hoc* approach to the texts under study. The implications for source analysis lie beyond the limitations of this essay. While the two methods are not logically contradictory or incompatible, they do not go together comfortably in the analysis of component parts of the same texts.

phemed God.[59] This is in Sennacherib's own conclusion to his campaign against Jerusalem:[60]

> Thus I reduced his country, but I still increased the tribute and the *katrû*-presents (due) to me (as his) overlord which I imposed (later) upon him beyond the former tribute, to be delivered annually. Hezekiah himself, whom the terror-inspiring splendor of my lordship had overwhelmed and whose irregular and elite troops which he had brought into Jerusalem, his royal residence, in order to strengthen (it), had deserted him, did send me, later, to Nineveh, my lordly city, together with 30 talents of gold, 800 talents of silver, precious stones, antimony. . . . In order to deliver the tribute and to do obeisance as a slave he sent his (personal) messenger.

A related literary concept may be applied to B_1 and B_2. The two parts of B can be explained as two refrains. This concept of narrative parallelism has its poetic correspondent on a smaller scale in poetic parallelism, especially synonymous parallelism whose purpose may be to reinforce the statement in psalms and proverbs.[61] Thus the confrontation between the representatives of Sennacherib and Hezekiah complements the letter from Sennacherib to Hezekiah. They serve to reinforce one another and emphasize the serious threat to Jerusalem and the slander against the God of Israel.

The conflict of two healings in the account of Hezekiah's illness can also be so understood. The account in Isaiah is sequential according to what happened. The account in 2 Kings, however, follows the repetitive

59. See A. Laato, "Assyrian Propaganda and the Falsification of History in the Royal Inscriptions of Sennacherib," pp. 198-226, who, although not identifying the literary methods used here, comes to some similar conclusions regarding the events of the narrative.

60. A. L. Oppenheim (translator), "Babylonian and Assyrian Historical Texts," pp. 265-317 in J. B. Pritchard, ed., *Ancient Near Eastern Texts Relating to the Old Testament,* 3rd ed. (Princeton: Princeton University Press, 1969), p. 288.

61. So the discussions of J. L. Kugel, *The Idea of Biblical Poetry* (New Haven: Yale University Press, 1981), pp. 88-113; J. Gammie, "Alter vs. Kugel: Taking the Heat in the Struggle over Biblical Poetry," *Bible Review* 5/1 (February 1989): 26-33. For the larger context of poetic parallelism within West Semitic literature, see the discussions of W. G. E. Watson, *Classical Hebrew Poetry: A Guide to Its Techniques,* JSOT Supplement 26 (Sheffield: JSOT Press, 1986); *Traditional Techniques in Classical Hebrew Verse,* JSOT Supplement 170 (Sheffield: Sheffield Academic Press, 1994).

style of biblical narrative. 2 Kings 20:7 is a parallel to vv. 8-11. It is a summary statement of what 8-11 go on to elaborate with a different emphasis. Thus the healing of v. 7 could occur after the events of vv. 8-11 without the narrator feeling it necessary to place v. 7 after 8-11. The New International Version's incorporation of a pluperfect at the beginning of v. 8 is another way of doing something similar. It is grammatically permissible and seems to be what the author intended, since it is more likely that the author would compose a logical account than one which contradicts the expected order of the narrative.[62]

The three events of Hezekiah's life discussed here can be understood as serving a triple sequence of actions, common to biblical narrative. They are not necessarily historically in sequence. It is likely that the Babylonian embassy preceded the revolt and the illness of Hezekiah may have occurred before or in the same year as the Assyrian war.[63] The triple sequence of accounts provides an increased tension in the narratives of the threat to Jerusalem and to the Davidic dynasty (for 2 Kings) and they provide a conclusion to Isaiah's prophecies of the eighth century and an introduction of the book's address to Babylon which begins in chapter 40.[64] The use of this technique in narratives is attested in the Hebrew Bible:[65]

62. D. J. Wiseman, *1 and 2 Kings,* p. 287, observes how Hezekiah's psalm of thanksgiving precedes his healing. He suggests this may be intended to demonstrate the king's faith.

63. A. F. Rainey, "Manasseh, King of Judah, in the Whirlpool of the Seventh Century B.C.E.," pp. 147-64 in A. F. Rainey, ed., *kinattutu ša darâti. Raphael Kutscher Memorial Volume,* Tel Aviv Occasional Publications No. 1 (Tel Aviv: Tel Aviv University, Institute of Archaeology, 1993), p. 149.

64. E. J. Young, *The Book of Isaiah,* 3 vols. (Grand Rapids: Eerdmans, 1965-1972). Distinctive purposes have also been identified for variant elements within these two accounts. Thus H. Williamson, *The Book Called Isaiah,* pp. 206-7, argues that the psalm of Hezekiah in Isaiah 38:19-20 is distinctive from that in Kings. Whereas in Kings the focus is on Hezekiah, in Isaiah his restoration symbolizes a restoration of the exiled community by the restoration of worship at the temple. On the literary purpose of the account of the Babylonian envoys being placed last, cf. Knoppers, "'There Was None Like Him': Incomparability in the Books of Kings," *Catholic Biblical Quarterly* 54 (1992): 424: ". . . placing this affair at the end of Hezekiah's reign serves a double purpose. It preserves, even as it ultimately qualifies, the result of Hezekiah's trust during the Assyrian crisis. . . . It succeeds in emphasizing Hezekiah's resolve during the Assyrian crisis, even as it acknowledges that this resolve did not vouchsafe dynasty or city indefinitely."

65. R. Alter, *The Art of Biblical Narrative,* pp. 95-96.

4. *Sequence of actions.* This pattern appears most commonly and most clearly in the folktale form of three consecutive repetitions, or three plus one, with some intensification or increment from one occurrence to the next, usually concluding either in a climax or reversal. (For example, the three captains and their companies threatened with fiery destruction in 2 Kings 1; the three catastrophes that destroy Job's possessions, followed by a fourth in which his children are killed; Balaam's failure to direct the ass three times.)

These events are parallel with those that occur a century later in the time of Josiah and the last kings of Judah. These parallels are conscious efforts of the author of 2 Kings who sees the same God at work throughout Israel's history.

Jerusalem in Chronicles

MARTIN J. SELMAN

*Through tracing God's purposes for Jerusalem as God's cho-
sen city and the place of God's temple, the Chronicler affirms
Jerusalem's continuing significance after the exile. The Chronicler regarded the repopulation of Jerusalem and the proper
use of the temple as the key to Israel's future restoration,
though the principle is also affirmed that failure to acknowledge God's laws leads to destruction for the temple and the
city and to exile. The disastrous effects of the exile can be
countered by responding to the invitation contained in Cyrus'
edict and faithfully worshipping God in the Jerusalem temple.*

I. Jerusalem and the Will of God

In many works of literature the real meaning is made plain only at the end,
and the Books of Chronicles are no exception to this practice. Though
"made plain" is perhaps an exaggeration in the case of Chronicles, the final paragraph of 2 Chronicles 36 undoubtedly provides an important clue
to the meaning of the entire work:

> The land enjoyed its sabbath rests; all the time of its desolation it rested,
> until the seventy years were completed in fulfilment of the word of the
> LORD spoken by Jeremiah.

In the first year of Cyrus king of Persia, in order to fulfil the word of the LORD spoken by Jeremiah, the LORD moved the heart of Cyrus king of Persia to make a proclamation throughout his realm and to put it in writing.

"This is what Cyrus king of Persia says: 'The LORD, the God of heaven, has given me all the kingdoms of the earth and he has appointed me to build a house for him at Jerusalem in Judah. Anyone of his people among you — may the LORD his God be with him, and let him go up'" (2 Chron. 36:21-23).

The truncated nature of the final sentence, which is almost certainly based on the longer version in Ezra 1:2-5,[1] highlights the Chronicler's view that the land of Israel and the city of Jerusalem have a continuing place in the purposes of God. To be more precise, according to this passage, God has two main intentions in restoring his people after the exile: (i) to bring the "desolation" of the land to an end in fulfillment of Jeremiah's prophecy of it resting for seventy years; and (ii) to rebuild the temple in Jerusalem. The Chronicler does not therefore view the future of Jerusalem as an end in itself. He regards it as a highly significant element in God's long-term will concerning both the land of Israel and the temple.

II. Invitations to Jerusalem

Before these ideas are developed, however, a comment must be made about the Chronicler's distinctive mode of expression in this passage. The final abbreviated sentence (which now also concludes the Hebrew Bible!) is in the form of an invitation, addressed apparently to the exiles but also by implication to the Chronicler's readers. The Chronicler's mention of the combined authority of Yahweh and the Persian emperor Cyrus suggests that he expects those who receive the invitation to travel to Jerusalem for the special task of rebuilding the temple.

A similar element of invitation and response is present in other key passages in Chronicles, suggesting that the end of the work confirms an

1. H. G. M. Williamson, *Israel in the Books of Chronicles* (Cambridge: Cambridge University Press, 1977), pp. 9-10. It is not necessary to adopt Williamson's related view that 2 Chron. 36:22-23 is not the work of the Chronicler (cf. M. J. Selman, *2 Chronicles,* Tyndale Old Testament Commentaries [Leicester: InterVarsity Press, 1994], p. 551).

already existing emphasis rather than that it was added as an appendix. Two passages may be quoted in support of this view. The first is God's reply to Solomon's prayer at the dedication of the temple, when God promises among other things to heal the land of Israel if only the people will turn towards him in prayer (2 Chron. 7:14). On any understanding of Chronicles, the divine oracle in 2 Chronicles 7:12-22 is a key passage, and there seems little doubt that it shows that the purpose of the Jerusalem temple is to bring restoration to the nation.[2] Unfortunately, the Chronicler does not make explicit his understanding of the concept of the healing of the nation. The same terminology only occurs in one other context, where it is concerned with forgiveness for cultic impurity (2 Chron. 30:19-20), but while cultic issues are certainly important for the Chronicler, the concept of healing here is clearly of wider significance. What is important for our purposes, however, is to note that as in 2 Chronicles 36:23, the Chronicler invites the people to participate in the restoration of their land by means of the Jerusalem temple. The main difference between the two passages is that whereas in 2 Chronicles 7, Israelites are invited to pray in or towards a temple that is newly constructed and dedicated, in 2 Chronicles 36 they must build it all over again.

The second passage to be considered occurs at the end of the genealogies in 1 Chronicles 9:2-34. It has not received the attention it deserves, mainly because as part of the genealogies it has often been viewed as an addition to the Chronicler's work. But its value and its origins have been greatly clarified in recent years, especially by Oeming who has argued for the unity of 1 Chronicles 1-9 and its kerygmatic connection with the narrative that follows.[3] In Oeming's view, 1 Chronicles 9:2-34 completes the last two stages of a concentric structure moving inwards from the world (ch. 1) towards the tribes of Israel (chs. 2–8), Jerusalem (9:2-34), and finally the temple (9:10-33). Two issues are important here in relation to the role of Jerusalem. Firstly, the list of those who settled in the towns of Judah (vv. 2-21) concentrates almost entirely on the city of Jerusalem (vv. 3-21). Secondly, since evidence exists to suggest that this list represents the process of repopulating Jerusalem approximately half a generation later than in Nehemiah 11, the Chronicler is probably describing how the peo-

2. H. G. M. Williamson, *1 and 2 Chronicles,* New Century Bible Commentary (Grand Rapids/London: Eerdmans/Marshall, Morgan & Scott, 1982), pp. 225-26; M. J. Selman, *2 Chronicles,* pp. 331-42.
3. M. Oeming, *Das wahre Israel,* Beiträge zur Wissenschaft vom Alten und Neuen Testament 128 (Stuttgart: Kohlhammer, 1990).

ple of Judah were responding to Cyrus' invitation around the end of the fifth century B.C. A further point about the structure of this passage is also worthy of note. It is clear from the mention of the much larger number of cultic officials (vv. 10-33) than of laymen (vv. 3-9), as well as the fact that only the cultic officials are named and their responsibilities listed, that the focus of the repopulation of the city was on those who served in the temple and on their role in Israel's worship. Where Cyrus had merely invited people to return to Jerusalem to rebuild the temple, here the priests, Levites, and gatekeepers are described as actually taking up their responsibilities in the house of God. For the Chronicler, rebuilding the temple meant not just the task of construction but the practical details of worship such as preparing the sacrifices and guarding the temple gates.

III. Jerusalem and the Davidic Covenant

Underlying this interest of the Chronicler in the repopulation of Jerusalem and the restoration of temple worship are the promises of the Davidic covenant. This has already been implied by the Chronicler's version of Cyrus' edict, since Cyrus' words, "he has appointed me to build him a house in Jerusalem," are remarkably similar to the promise about David's successor, "He is the one who will build a house for me."[4] Though the Chronicler presumably found the language about building a house already present in Ezra's account, he would surely have found in it an unmistakable echo of Nathan's promise. This is all the more likely given that Chronicles also emphasizes that God kept his promise to David by enabling Solomon to build the first temple. Solomon declared, "I have built the temple for the name of Yahweh, the God of Israel" (2 Chron. 5:10) in response to God's word about David's successor: "He is the one who will build a house for my name" (2 Sam. 7:13).[5] Responding to Cyrus' invitation, therefore, was not simply a matter of recognizing God's providence behind the words of a Persian emperor, but of becoming involved in the ongoing fulfillment of the Davidic covenant.

4. Cf. 1 Chron. 17:12; 2 Chron. 36:23. See also 1 Chron. 22:10; 28:6; 2 Chron. 6:9-10.

5. Though this phrase becomes "He is the one who will build a house for me" in 1 Chron. 17:12, the failure to use "the name" here does not appear significant, since it is frequently used elsewhere in Chronicles in relation to the temple (1 Chron. 22:7, 10, 19; 28:3; 2 Chron. 2:1, 4; etc.).

A. *Jerusalem the Chosen City*

The Chronicler recognizes that the continued relevance of the Davidic covenant in the post-exilic period had several implications for the city of Jerusalem. Firstly, as Solomon himself had acknowledged, Jerusalem was a city chosen by God:

> Since the day when I brought out my people from the land of Egypt, I did not choose any city among any of the tribes of Israel to build a house there for my name. Neither did I choose any man to be a prince over my people Israel. But now I have chosen Jerusalem for my name to be there and I have chosen David to be over my people Israel (2 Chron. 6:5-6).

This is of greater significance than first appears, since it could be argued that by taking over the basic wording from his *Vorlage* in 1 Kings 8:16, the Chronicler has simply reiterated the view of his pre-exilic predecessors. However, the Chronicler has not just quoted his source, he has expanded it and given it a more emphatic sense. Where Kings puts the choice of Jerusalem negatively ("I did not choose any city among any of the tribes of Israel to build a house there for my name"), the Chronicler adds a positive complementary phrase: "But now I have chosen Jerusalem for my name to be there." The reason for the addition is that for the Chronicler, the election of Jerusalem has a more specific meaning than in the Deuteronomic History, which is related to the broader theme of election in Chronicles. Though the Chronicler has preserved from Kings all the references to God's choice of Jerusalem in passages which have parallels in his own work,[6] he has amplified the theme of election by adding several references to God's choice of Solomon as the chosen temple builder[7] and to God's choice of the temple itself.[8] Japhet interpreted the Chronicler's emphasis as a return to Deuteronomy's idea of God choosing the temple in contrast to the view of the Deuteronomic historians who thought that God's chosen "place" was "the city" or "Jerusalem."[9] But this distinction cannot be sustained, since it is

6. 1 Kings 8:16, 44, 48; 14:21; 2 Kings 21:7; cf. 2 Chron. 6:5, 6, 34, 38; 12:13; 33:7. Only 1 Kings 11:13, 32 do not appear in Chronicles, since 1 Kings 11 has no equivalent in Chronicles.
7. 1 Chron. 28:6, 10; 29:1; cf. R. L. Braun, "Solomon, the Chosen Temple Builder," *Journal of Biblical Literature* 95 (1976): 581-90.
8. 2 Chron. 7:12, 16.
9. S. Japhet, *The Ideology of the Book of Chronicles* (Frankfurt: P. Lang, 1989), p. 90.

clear that the Chronicler emphasizes both the choice of the temple and the choice of the city. For the Chronicler, God's choice of Jerusalem also involves the choice of both the temple site and the temple builder.

B. Jerusalem the City of David

Secondly, the Chronicler frequently associates Jerusalem with the person of David, especially in the phrase "the City of David." Now it is true that this phrase is used for the most part in a general way, in relation to burial notices and to the building activities of certain kings.[10] But it also has a special association with the ark, as the place to which David first took the ark and from which it was then transferred to the temple.[11] The later association between Jerusalem and the temple is anticipated by this association between the City of David and the ark. In the same context, the Chronicler also emphasizes the identification of Zion with the City of David. Despite a much briefer account of David's capture of Jerusalem from the Jebusites than the *Vorlage* in 2 Samuel 5, the Chronicler twice retains the mention of Zion in the same passage.[12] The Chronicler is therefore keen to emphasize the fact that even in the post-exilic period, Jerusalem was the city which David himself had established and to which the ark belonged. It was a place with a quite specific history which still resonated in the different circumstances of post-exilic times.

C. Jerusalem the Temple City

Thirdly and most importantly, however, Jerusalem is the city where the temple is located, and as far as the Chronicler is concerned, this is undoubtedly its primary significance. This is particularly evident from a number of specific activities which the Chronicler associates with the temple and which in most cases are given much more prominence than in his *Vorlage*.[13] God's choice of Jerusalem as the place for his name has al-

10. It is used in burial notices in 2 Chron. 9:31; 12:16; 14:1; 16:14; 21:1, 20; 24:16, 25; 27:9, and in relation to building works in 2 Chron. 32:5, 30; 33:14.
11. 1 Chron. 13:13; 15:1, 29; 2 Chron. 5:2.
12. 1 Chron. 11:5, 7; cf. 2 Sam. 5:7, 9.
13. Cf. 1 Chron. 21:22–22:1 and 2 Sam. 24:21-25; 1 Chron. 13:1–16:3 and 2 Sam. 5:11–6:20. 1 Chron. 16:4-6, 37-38 has no parallel in 2 Samuel.

ready been noted as an important feature (2 Chron. 6:6), but even more significant are the various preparations which took place in advance of the temple's construction. These include the purchase of the temple site from an inhabitant of the city when it was known as Jebus (1 Chron. 21:22–22:1), the bringing of the ark to a specially prepared site in the City of David (1 Chron. 13:1–16:3), and David's establishing a regular pattern of worship there while the tabernacle and the altar of burnt offering remained at Gibeon (1 Chron. 16:4-6, 37-38). The last of these events has no parallel at all in the Chronicler's sources. In terms of its restoration as well as its origin, therefore, the temple was central to the Chronicler's understanding of the role of Israel's capital city.

What, however, was the Chronicler's view of the temple? Since this is not the place for a detailed investigation of this important question, only a brief summary of the main issues can be attempted here. The first point to note is that of course the temple had no significance for its own sake. As with other Old Testament writers, the Chronicler regarded it as something that enabled God to fulfill God's intentions for his people. Conversely, it was not something that Israel could either take for granted or use for their own religious or political agenda. The temple belonged to God, and from time to time he asserted his rights over it. The incidents involving the cloud and the glory at the temple's opening ceremony and the cautionary tale of Uzzah and the ark are merely the clearest illustrations of this principle.[14] This attitude was in sharp contrast with that of many Israelites. It was precisely because they had not treated the temple as Yahweh's exclusive and distinctive preserve but had regarded it just like any other ancient Near Eastern sanctuary, as a building for religious objects and activities for the cultus of divine beings, that it had been destroyed in the first place. The Chronicler illustrates this in both theory (2 Chron. 7:19-22) and in practice (2 Chron. 36:15-19).

1. The Nature of the Temple

The Chronicler refers at length to God's intentions for the temple and to the ways it was to be used. As far as its nature is concerned, the temple was:

Firstly, the place on earth where God wanted his name to be. This idea is clearly taken over from Deuteronomy and the Deuteronomic His-

14. 1 Chron. 13:9-14; 2 Chron. 5:13–6:2; 7:1-3.

tory, though as Japhet notes, the Chronicler makes a point of showing that this is identical in meaning to the place where God himself was to be found.[15] The importance of this emphasis is underlined by the fact that "every context pertaining to the Temple's construction mentions the *name* of God."[16]

Secondly, the temple as the place of God's name is closely associated with the temple as an expression of God's presence among his people. The clearest example of this is surely the extended account of the filling of the newly dedicated temple with the cloud of God's glory (2 Chron. 5:13-14; 7:1-3), though the most evocative expression must be God's promise about his eyes, ears, and heart: "now my eyes will be open and my ears attentive to the prayers offered in this place. I have chosen and consecrated this temple so that my name may be there for ever. My eyes and my heart will always be there" (2 Chron. 7:15-16). This passage illustrates the way in which the Chronicler combines the twin understandings of God being present on earth and in heaven. His eyes and ears are looking towards the temple from his heavenly dwelling, while his eyes and heart are in his earthly dwelling. If anything, the mention of God's heart being in the temple suggests that God was just as much at home in the temple as he was in heaven.

Thirdly, the temple represents God's resting-place, with the ark as his footstool (1 Chron. 28:2; 2 Chron. 6:41). This may represent either the concept of rest as the completion of God's work as at creation (cf. Gen. 2:1-3), or the rest which expresses God's and Israel's mutual acceptance of each other as covenant partners. It is notable that all three of these designations convey the idea of the temple as very closely associated with the person of God.

However, a fourth and rather different feature of the temple should also be noted, namely, that the temple is a place where the promises and prophecies of Scripture become reality. The temple was built because God kept his promise to David and Solomon, but the Chronicler's account of the building of the temple also reflects the fulfillment of many other scriptural passages. David's purchase of the temple site, for example, is based on the account of Abraham's purchase of a family burial ground (1 Chron.

15. Cf. S. Japhet, *The Ideology*, p. 69. Note the following phrases in 1 Chron. 22: "he charged [Solomon] to build a house for Yahweh the God of Israel" (v. 6); "I had it in my heart to build a house for the name of Yahweh my God" (v. 7).

16. S. Japhet, *The Ideology*, p. 67.

21:22-25; cf. Gen. 23:9), and the actual construction of the temple contains a number of reminders of the building of the tabernacle, both in its pattern (2 Chron. 3–4; cf. Exod. 36:1–39:32) and in the appearance of the cloud of God's glory at the opening ceremony (2 Chron. 5:13-14; 7:1-3; cf. Exod. 40:34-35; Lev. 9:23-24). Even the very site of the temple which only the Chronicler identifies as Mt. Moriah is surely intended to evoke memories of the sacrifice of Isaac on a mountain in the land of the same name (2 Chron. 3:1; cf. Gen. 22:2).

2. The Use of the Temple

The Jerusalem temple, however, was not simply a place associated with great theological themes, but somewhere where God was actually worshipped. The Chronicler's concept of the temple is of a living reality, where the manner in which the people worshipped God was crucial to the success of Israel's relationship with him. The Chronicler summarizes this emphasis on worship with a phrase which does not occur in his *Vorlage*, namely, that God had "chosen this place for myself as a house for sacrifices" (2 Chron. 7:12; cf. 1 Kings 9:3). The Chronicler goes on to express the significance of Israel's worship by highlighting four different aspects of sacrifice:

Firstly, as Kelly has correctly observed, "the Chronicler's principal cultic interest lies in the regular cycle of daily, weekly and seasonal offerings."[17] As soon as the temple was completed, the Chronicler records Solomon instituting the regular pattern of worship (2 Chron. 8:12-15), in fulfillment of the purpose for which the temple had originally been designed (2 Chron. 2:4). Offerings were to be made on behalf of the people in Jerusalem on a daily basis, indicating that worship was to be central to Israel's pattern of life as a nation under God.

Secondly, it is impossible to avoid the emphasis the Chronicler places on the Passover.[18] Indeed, his inclusion of Hezekiah's Passover has proved something of an embarrassment, since not only does it not even warrant a mention in Kings, its actual existence seems positively to be excluded by the statement in 2 Kings 23:22 about Josiah's Passover that "not since the days of the judges who led Israel, nor throughout the days of the

17. B. Kelly, *Retribution and Eschatology in Chronicles,* JSOT Supplement 211 (Sheffield: Sheffield Academic Press, 1996), p. 169.
18. 2 Chron. 30:1-27; 35:1-19.

kings of Israel and the kings of Judah, had any such Passover been observed." But in fact, the Chronicler includes Hezekiah's Passover, not in order to create something which did not exist in reality, but for the even more extraordinary reason that it was acceptable to God despite the people breaking all the ceremonial rules. Even though it was celebrated in the wrong month, the priests were unprepared, and the majority of the people were ritually impure, yet still God accepted that Passover through Hezekiah's prayer: "And Yahweh heard Hezekiah and healed the people" (2 Chron. 30:20). Taken together with the celebrations at the opening ceremony which continued straight into the Feast of Tabernacles, the Chronicler clearly intends to portray the Jerusalem temple as a place where God's people can celebrate in God's presence, even though they may not be formally qualified to do so.

Thirdly, and most strikingly, the Chronicler presents Israel's worship in music and song as a necessary accompaniment to the various animal and vegetable sacrifices. His preoccupation with the Levites gives particular prominence to this musical ministry, which is clearly intended to be understood as an integral part of the entire sacrificial ritual. Not only did this provide Israel's worship with specific verbal content alongside the mute sacrifices on the altar, in particular it enabled the people as a whole to participate in worship. For example, "the whole assembly bowed in worship," as Hezekiah gave the order for the burnt offering to begin accompanied by singing (2 Chron. 29:28; cf. 1 Chron. 16:36; 2 Chron. 7:3).

Finally, as if to underline the Chronicler's wholehearted view of worship, he refers in a unique passage to the self-offering of the people. David's invitation to participate in the temple building project is expressed in explicit sacrificial terms: "Who is willing to consecrate themselves today to Yahweh?" (1 Chron. 29:5).

This brief summary of the role of the Jerusalem temple as a place where the people as a whole could experience the real presence of the living God certainly reflects the Chronicler's emphasis, though it has to be said that for the most part this remained an ideal rather than a reality. For in addition to these very positive portrayals, there is also a dark side to the Chronicler's view of Jerusalem and its temple. There were times when both the city and the temple were under direct threat, from both internal and external influences.

IV. Jerusalem under Threat

The rather neglected final section of God's reply to Solomon's dedicatory prayer deals directly with the possibility that God may become so displeased with his people that the temple might be destroyed and the Israelites removed from their land (2 Chron. 7:19-22). The possibility of the loss of the temple is made more prominent than in the parallel text in 1 Kings 9:6-9, where the original reference to the land as a proverb and an object of ridicule has now been transferred to the temple. In contrast with his *Vorlage,* therefore, this passage concentrates almost entirely on Israel's attitude to the temple, apart from two brief references to the land.[19] The circumstances under which such a disaster might take place are summarized as disobedience to God's decrees and commands, particularly through idolatry, and despite the Chronicler's greater emphasis on Israel's restoration than in Kings, he is keen to continue the strong element of warning from his sources.

The importance of this for the Chronicler emerges from the several occasions when this hypothetical threat to Jerusalem and its temple became a reality. These threats fall into three types. The first reflects the precise circumstances of 2 Chronicles 7:19-22, when the people were subjected to the indignity of exile as a result of the idolatrous practices of Ahaz and Manasseh. Though this pattern is already well established in the books of Kings, the Chronicler highlights the seriousness of the matter by describing the consequences of Ahaz' unfaithfulness quite differently from the earlier account. Whereas 2 Kings 16:5-18 puts its emphasis on Ahaz' being forced to submit to Assyria and his desecration of the Jerusalem temple by introducing a pagan altar, the Chronicler reports that God handed him over to Syria and Israel as well as to Assyria because of his unacceptable religious practices.[20] As a result, Judah became as "an object of dread, horror and scorn," and "our fathers have fallen by the sword and our sons and daughters and wives are in captivity."[21] In the Chronicler's view, the pattern of disobedience and exile was established already in the eighth century B.C., and Israel's attitude to the Jerusalem temple was a key element in their fortunes.

19. Cf. S. Japhet, *I and II Chronicles,* Old Testament Library (London: SCM, 1993), p. 617, though Japhet has failed to mention a second reference to the land which has been retained at the end of v. 21.
20. 2 Chron. 28:5-23.
21. 2 Chron. 29:8-9; cf. 2 Chron. 7:19-22.

The second kind of threat is more surprising, since it came from David whom the Chronicler is often accused of presenting in whitewashed terms. In fact, 1 Chronicles 21 describes the consequences of David's census more seriously than 2 Samuel 24 by describing "the angel of Yahweh standing between heaven and earth, with a drawn sword in his hand extended over Jerusalem" (1 Chron. 21:16). It was only when David took full responsibility for his actions and presented offerings on an altar built on the piece of land he had purchased that Yahweh ended the threat by instructing the angel to put away his sword (1 Chron. 21:27). The reality of the threat to Jerusalem brought about by David was just as serious as that which arose from the actions of kings such as Ahaz and Manasseh.

The third kind of threat came from external sources, which God sometimes used to punish his people for their disobedience. This was the case, for example, with Shishak's invasion of Judah, and the Chronicler makes explicit what is already implied in 1 Kings 14:22-28 that this was because "he and all Israel with him abandoned the law of Yahweh" and "they had been unfaithful to Yahweh" (2 Chron. 12:1-2). But on at least four other occasions, invasions took place which cannot be explained in terms of divine retribution. These include Jeroboam I's attack against Abijah (2 Chron. 13:2-20), Zerah the Cushite's advance against Asa with a vast army (2 Chron. 14:9-15), Jehoshaphat's defense against a coalition of Moabite and Ammonite forces (2 Chron. 20:1-30), and Sennacherib's attempt to overrun the kingdom of Judah in Hezekiah's day (2 Chron. 32:1-23). In the view of the Chronicler, these threats could be repulsed by an attitude of faith, usually involving some combination of prayer offered in or towards the temple, sacrifice on the temple altar, and praise led by the Levites.[22] In particular, the Levites' musical ministry is often given a redemptive aspect, based on a pattern established by the psalm in 1 Chronicles 16:8-36.[23] The main adaptation of this psalm of praise in comparison with its earlier forms in the Psalter occurs in the final two verses, which have a much greater emphasis on Yahweh's power to deliver and emphasize the people's commitment to their prayer for God's help (1 Chron. 16:35-36; cf. Ps. 106:47-48).[24] In this psalm and elsewhere, the Levites'

22. 2 Chron. 13:10-18; 14:11-15; 20:5-23; 32:6-8, 20-23.
23. J. Kleinig, *The Lord's Song: The Basis, Function and Significance of Choral Music in Chronicles,* JSOT Supplement 156 (Sheffield: JSOT Press, 1993); B. Kelly, *Retribution.*
24. See M. J. Selman, *1 Chronicles,* Tyndale Old Testament Commentaries (Leicester: InterVarsity Press, 1994), pp. 170-72.

ministry of praise played a key role in reversing potential and actual threats to the well-being of God's people.

V. Jerusalem as a Meeting Place for God and His People

This leads naturally and finally to a consideration of Jerusalem as the chief focus of the interface between God and his people. The Chronicler's interest in the people of Israel and Judah is well known, and has been examined in some detail by Japhet under the term "democratization."[25] However, her remarks can be amplified in a number of respects, especially as she tends to concentrate on the relationship between king and people rather than on the role of the people *per se*. The Chronicler in fact gives special prominence to the people or inhabitants of Jerusalem. First of all, the people of Jerusalem may exercise authority in their own right, for example by appointing a new king as in the case of Ahaziah (2 Chron. 22:1) or honoring a dead one such as Hezekiah (2 Chron. 32:33). In neither instance does a comparable phrase appear in the Chronicler's *Vorlage*. Secondly, the Chronicler refers to a much larger number of popular assemblies in Jerusalem than do his sources. The various assemblies addressed by David in preparing for Solomon's reign and for the temple, for example, are without parallel in Samuel (1 Chron. 22, 28–29), but these are not the only instances. Mention should also be made of David's assembly of all Israel which decided to bring the ark to Jerusalem (1 Chron. 13:1-6), Solomon's assembly of the leaders and people to bring the ark into the temple (2 Chron. 5:2-3), Jehoshaphat's assembly for fasting and prayer in response to military invasion (2 Chron. 20:4-5), Hezekiah's assembly which decided to celebrate the Passover out of due time (2 Chron. 30:2-5), and Josiah's assembly of the elders when he read the contents of the recently discovered law scroll (2 Chron. 34:29). Though it is true that most of these gatherings were called by the various monarchs, the assemblies of the people made several vital decisions on national issues and ensured they were carried out. Thirdly, some of these popular assemblies had as their particular purpose the making of covenants with God and with one another. Three such occasions are included, under Asa (2 Chron. 15:10-15), Jehoiada the priest for the purpose of overthrowing Athaliah (2 Chron. 23:1-3), and Josiah (2 Chron. 34:32). Each of these ceremonies

25. S. Japhet, *The Ideology,* pp. 417-27.

probably took place at the temple, though explicit evidence is lacking in Asa's case. The important point here, however, is that Jerusalem is the place where God's people regularly renewed their commitment to God and expressed that conviction in various practical ways.

VI. Jerusalem as the City of Opportunity

The city of Jerusalem and its temple are clearly central to the Chronicler's understanding of God's purposes for his people in post-exilic times. He constantly adapts his sources to give greater prominence to both the city and the temple, presenting them as a place of opportunity where the people as a whole could again meet with their God and be involved in his work of restoration of the land. Though the Chronicler saw a continuing role for God's promises concerning the Davidic line, the "healing of the land" was dependent on the people rather than the old royal family. One might even surmise that he looked for a further occasion when the people might renew their covenant with God, or more probably give fuller expression to the covenant already renewed under Nehemiah.[26] If Oeming's view of the structure and purpose of 1 Chronicles 1–9 is to be accepted, the return to the land should have culminated in God's people living again in the city that he had chosen and meeting with him as a worshipping community in the temple. Despite all that had happened in the past, the Chronicler recognized that a heaven-sent opportunity still existed for the Israelites to commit themselves to God's purposes for his chosen city and so contribute directly to the restoration of his people.

26. Nehemiah 9:38–10:39.

56

Jerusalem at War in Chronicles

GARY N. KNOPPERS

This essay challenges von Rad's influential view that holy war in Chronicles was entirely cultic in character by giving special attention to two neglected features of Jehoshaphat's war against the eastern coalition (2 Chronicles 20): the critical function of the temple in war and the specific instructions issued to Jehoshaphat in this military crisis. The Chronicler can be seen as bringing out the historical, theological, and military significance of the Jerusalem temple. Themes of exodus and conquest figure prominently in the battle narratives of Exodus, Numbers, Deuteronomy, and Joshua, but in Chronicles the divine warrior battles against Israel's enemies, fighting for the temple and people he established and promised to defend. Like the battle against the Egyptians in the Exodus, the battle against the eastern coalition becomes one in which YHWH is pitted exclusively against Israel's foes. Jehoshaphat's recourse to the temple, the divinely sanctioned place for prayer, is therefore appropriate and does not warrant the general conclusion that the Chronicler embraced a quietistic or a nonparticipatory stance toward war.

I. Introduction

In his treatment of holy war in the Hebrew scriptures, Gerhard von Rad argued that holy war was "one of the sacral institutions of ancient Israel."[1] Like earlier scholars who had used the term "holy war," von Rad stressed the importance of religious rituals in preparation for war and in the conduct of war itself.[2] Von Rad constructed a typology of ancient Israelite warfare by culling texts, mostly in Deuteronomy, Joshua, and Judges, and isolating what he deemed to be the typical elements of war during the Israelite confederation.[3] In von Rad's judgment, holy war went into decline during the monarchy, the Babylonian exile marking its final demise. But von Rad recognized that texts depicting sacral war did not cease to be written after the Babylonian deportation. There are a variety of poems and narratives from the exilic and post-exilic periods that deal with holy war. Chronicles, for instance, contains an abundance of military information and records many accounts of sacral warfare. In von Rad's view, "a free intellectual toying with isolated ideas" occurs in the post-exilic period with respect to holy war.[4] According to von Rad, post-exilic works such as Chronicles and certain psalms evince a "strong spiritualization" of sacral war.[5] Employing as an example 2 Chronicles 20:1-30, King Jehoshaphat's battle against a coalition of nations to the east and south of Judah, von Rad asserted that holy war in Chronicles had been completely severed from its institutional moorings in history. In the Jehoshaphat campaign one finds a variety of formal elements, which are not found in von Rad's typology of holy war: Levitical officials playing a prominent role, non-belligerence on the part of king and people, a national assembly, a long royal prayer, a national procession from Jerusalem, communal singing, and a dramatic divine interven-

---

1. *Der heilige Krieg im alten Israel* (Zürich: Zwingli, 1951), recently translated into English as *Holy War in Ancient Israel* (Grand Rapids: Eerdmans, 1991). Quotations follow the English edition.

2. The locution does not appear in the Old Testament itself. For earlier scholarly usage of the term, see F. Schwally, *Der heilige Krieg im alten Israel* (Leipzig: Deiterich, 1901), and M. Weber, *Ancient Judaism* (Glencoe: Free Press, 1952), pp. 118-46. B. C. Ollenburger provides a helpful overview, "Introduction: Gerhard von Rad's Theory of Holy War," in von Rad, *Holy War,* pp. 1-33.

3. Von Rad, *Holy War,* pp. 41-51.

4. Von Rad, *Holy War,* p. 129.

5. Von Rad, *Holy War,* p. 128.

tion against Israel's enemies. For von Rad the presence of these motifs was sufficient to demonstrate that war had become entirely cultic in character.[6]

A number of recent scholars differ from von Rad in their reconstruction of holy war, but offer similar assessments about its function in the Chronicler's History. Jones agrees that war in Chronicles is entirely cultic in character, while De Vries speaks of a "ritualized drama" and the "complete sacramentalization of *Heilsgeschichte*" in Chronicles.[7] Ackroyd suggests that the Chronicler is promoting "a strongly quietistic doctrine."[8] Similarly, Gabriel and Niditch contend that Chronicles offers a biblical war ideology that is critical of war itself.[9] Indeed, Niditch thinks that of all the battle narratives in the Hebrew scriptures, 2 Chronicles 20 "best approaches the ideal of non-participation in fighting."[10] Welten also sees a strong cultic emphasis, but in addition argues for a movement in Chronicles toward apocalyptic.[11] Davies thinks that the story addresses the integrity of the society of "Israel," that is, its ethnic and cultic definition.[12] Some scholars are even unsure whether 2 Chronicles 20:1-30 is a holy war narrative. De Vries types the passage a "quasi-holy-war" narrative.[13] De-

6. Von Rad, *Holy War,* pp. 128-31. Unfortunately, von Rad did not spell out precisely what this meant.

7. G. H. Jones, "The Concept of Holy War," in R. E. Clements, ed., *The World of Ancient Israel* (Cambridge: Cambridge University Press, 1988), pp. 315-16; S. J. De Vries, "Temporal Terms as Structural Elements in the Holy War Tradition," *Vetus Testamentum* 25 (1975): 105.

8. P. R. Ackroyd, *Chronicles, Ezra, Nehemiah, Nehemiah,* Torch Bible Commentaries (London: SCM, 1973), p. 151.

9. I. Gabriel, *Friede über Israel. Eine Untersuchung zur Friedenstheologie im Chronik I 10–II 36,* Osterreichisch biblische Studien 10 (Klosterneuberg: ÖKB, 1990), pp. 139-43; S. Niditch, *War in the Hebrew Bible: A Study in the Ethics of Violence* (New York: Oxford University Press, 1993), pp. 136, 139. Niditch realizes, however, that there are exceptions within Chronicles to this stance, pp. 141-43.

10. Niditch, *War in the Hebrew Bible,* pp. 146-49.

11. P. Welten, *Geschichte und Geschichtsdarstellung in den Chronikbüchern* (Neukirchen: Neukirchener Verlag, 1973), pp. 201-6.

12. P. R. Davies, "Defining the Boundaries of Israel in the Second Temple Period: 2 Chronicles 20 and the 'Salvation Army,'" in E. C. Ulrich et al., eds., *Priests, Prophets, and Scribes: Essays on the Formation and Heritage of Second Temple Judaism in Honour of Joseph Blenkinsopp,* JSOT Supplement 149 (Sheffield: JSOT Press, 1992), pp. 43-54.

13. S. J. De Vries, *I and II Chronicles,* Forms of Old Testament Literature (Grand Rapids: Eerdmans, 1989), pp. 326-28.

scribing 2 Chronicles 20 as "an odd account of holy war," McCarthy prefers to term the narrative a liturgy.[14]

In this essay I would like to take issue with von Rad's influential construction: the "strong spiritualization" of battles in Chronicles. Claims that the Chronicler's wars are only of cultic significance or that his presentation witnesses the final stage in the spiritual sublimation of holy war should be contested. The evidence is more complex. Von Rad's holy war schema is not only idealized, as many scholars have observed,[15] but too narrow and rigid when applied to biblical books outside Deuteronomy, Joshua, Judges, and Samuel. As for the Chronicler's view of war, one should not isolate 2 Chronicles 20 from other battle narratives as somehow epitomizing the Chronicler's view of war. The Chronicler narrates a variety of conflicts in the history of the united and divided monarchies. Because of this diversity, no one contest can be taken as entirely representative of the whole. Moreover, as will become clear in the following discussion, Jehoshaphat's holy war is unusual even in the context of Chronicles.

I will argue that the confluence of traditional features of YHWH war with a highly liturgical focus is deliberate compositional technique on the part of the Chronicler.[16] Despite the elaboration of some elements, the ac-

14. D. J. McCarthy, "Covenant and Law in Chronicles–Nehemiah," *Catholic Biblical Quarterly* 44 (1982): 32.

15. M. Weippert, "'Heiliger Krieg' in Israel und Assyrien: Kritische Anmerkungen zu G. von Rads Konzept des 'Heiligen Krieges im alten Israel,'" *Zeitschrift für die alttestamentliche Wissenschaft* 84 (1972): 460-93; N. K. Gottwald, "Holy War," Suppplementary Volume to *Interpreter's Dictionary of the Bible* (1976): 942-44; P. C. Craigie, *The Problem of War in the Old Testament* (Grand Rapids: Eerdmans, 1978), pp. 48-50; T. R. Hobbs, *A Time for War: A Study of Warfare in the Old Testament,* Old Testament Studies 3 (Wilmington: Michael Glazier, 1989), pp. 203-7; G. H. Jones, "'Holy War' or 'Yahweh' War'?" *Vetus Testamentum* 25 (1975): 651-53; A. Van der Lingen, *Les guerres de Yahvé: L'implication de YHWH dans les guerres d'Israël selon les livres historiques de l'Ancien Testament,* Lectio Divina 139 (Paris: Éditions du Cerf, 1990), pp. 11-17. F. Stolz points out how dependent von Rad's typology was on the views of the deuteronomic and deuteronomistic writers, *Yahwes und Israels Kriege: Kriegstheorien und Kriegserfahrungen im Glauben des alten Israels,* Abhandlungen zur Theologie des Alten und Neuen Testaments 60 (Zürich: Theologischer Verlag, 1972).

16. Some scholars, e.g., Jones, "'Holy War,'" pp. 642-58, distinguish between the actual practice of war, designated "YHWH war," and the ideology supporting such campaigns, designated "holy war." Others distinguish between the wars of YHWH (ancient Israelite sacral wars) and holy wars (sacral conflicts in other lands within the

count of 2 Chronicles 20:1-30 still follows the overall pattern of a war of YHWH. The Chronicler adapts and incorporates liturgical motifs centering on the temple into a larger pattern of sacral war. Liturgy, understood as a sequence of public rites, is of course an intrinsic component in earlier battles fought in the name of YHWH. Two essential elements of the Chronicler's History have been overlooked by von Rad and the scholars who follow his reconstruction: the critical function of the Jerusalem temple in the Chronicler's understanding of war and the particular instructions issued to Jehoshaphat in this military crisis. It will be useful to begin with some brief observations about the Chronicler's perspective toward the wars of YHWH and then address the particular circumstances in which Jehoshaphat's battle is waged.

II. The Critical Function of the Jerusalem Temple in Times of War

Israelite literature uses adaptations and transformations in various texts. By the time of the post-exilic age the Chronicler is able to draw from a rich variety of martial traditions. His perspective toward the wars of YHWH needs to be situated within the context of these developments. Themes of exodus and conquest figure prominently in the battle narratives of Exodus, Numbers, Deuteronomy, and Joshua. According to "the Song of the Sea," YHWH, by delivering his people into Canaan confirms his kingship and establishes his sanctuary.[17] The divine warrior acts on behalf of Israel, defeating both cosmic and historical enemies. The locus of holy warfare in early Israel is, therefore, not discovered in a primordial battle of creation, but in the Lord's liberation of his people from Egypt and his bringing them into the land.[18]

With the rise of the monarchy the sanctuary is, of course, identified with the temple. The ideology of the Davidic covenant and the Lord's

---

ancient Near East). Since my chief concern is the Chronicler's theology, and not the actual reconstruction of past events, this essay will employ the terms "holy war," "sacral war," and "YHWH war" interchangeably.

17. Exod. 15:17-18; Ps. 29:10; 2 Sam. 22:2-51; Deut. 33:2-5, 26-29; F. M. Cross, *Canaanite Myth and Hebrew Epic* (Cambridge, MA: Harvard University Press, 1973), pp. 112-44.

18. P. D. Miller, *The Divine Warrior in Early Israel*, Harvard Semitic Monographs 5 (Cambridge, MA: Harvard University Press, 1973).

promises to Jerusalem come to the fore. The past deeds of conquest are re-
cited (e.g., Psalm 89), but so also is the Lord's establishment of Zion.[19] In
such contexts one finds celebrations of or petitions for YHWH's warfare
against the enemies of his anointed. With the prophets, further transformations occur. On the one hand, Amos (5:18-24) boldly depicts YHWH as
turning in wrath against Israel itself.[20] On the other hand, the prophet in
Isaiah 52:7-12 envisions YHWH leading a new Exodus-Conquest the goal
of which is not Canaan, but more particularly Zion. The prominence of
Zion in later war theology is also evident in Joel:

> YHWH roars from Zion,
> and raises his voice from Jerusalem,
> so that the heavens and the earth quake.
> But as for his people,
> YHWH is a refuge,
> and a stronghold for Israel's sons (Joel 4:16).

If one were to search for precedents to the Chronicler's view of
God's involvement in conflagrations, it would seem that the Chronicler
revives and reapplies traditional holy war theology as that theology has
developed during the Judahite monarchy. Like the Deuteronomist, the
Chronicler emphasizes the temple as sanctioned by God; but the Chronicler, unlike the writer of Kings, consistently pursues the military implications of this relationship.[21] In this regard, the provisions dealing with
war in Solomon's temple prayer are pertinent.[22] Solomon's seven petitions detail a variety of predicaments in which the nation may find itself,
including defeat by the enemy (2 Chron. 6:24-25), the siege of towns or

19. Pss. 2:1-12; 20:2-20; 33:1-22; 46:1-12; 68:1-36; 78:1-72.
20. In the view of von Rad, the prophets were responsible for sustaining the tradition of holy war during the monarchy, albeit in an oppositional mode, *Holy War,* pp.
94-114. Note, however, that one also finds the YHWH against Israel theme in the historical books, Van der Lingen, *Les guerres de Yahvé,* pp. 189-212.
21. On the importance of Solomon's prayer in the context of the Deuteronomistic History, see my "Prayer and Propaganda: The Dedication of Solomon's
Temple and the Deuteronomist's Program," *Catholic Biblical Quarterly* 57 (1995):
229-54, and the references cited there.
22. The Chronicler's version of Solomon's prayer in 2 Chronicles 6 is repro-
duced from his *Vorlage* of 1 Kings 8, with some differences. See S. L. McKenzie,
"1 Kings 8: A Sample Study into the Texts of Kings Used by the Chronicler and Translated by the Old Greek," *Bulletin of the International Organization for Septuagint and
Cognate Studies* 19 (1986): 15-34.

cities (6:28-30), and open pitched battles (6:34-35).[23] In each case Solomon prays that God might listen from his heavenly dwelling and be attentive to the prayers of his people. Both the Deuteronomist and the Chronicler mention a divine response to Solomon's prayer, but the Chronicler includes an additional divine message to King Solomon (7:14), assuring the Israelite monarch that his prayers will be answered. Should the people suffer calamity or find themselves in duress, they may respond in four ways: "humbling themselves" *(nkn')*, "praying" *(htpll)*, "seeking *(bqš)* divine favor," and "turning *(šwb)* from their evil ways." If Israel reacts to disaster along these lines, God promises that he will hear from the heavens, forgive their sins, and heal their land (7:14).

With justification, Williamson and Dillard have called this divine assurance a charter, which anticipates later developments in the course of Judah's history.[24] When later monarchs and their subjects respond to adversity in this manner, God intervenes and restores them. The implications of Solomon's prayer for the Chronicler's understanding of war should be apparent. The context for God's action differs in Chronicles from that found in certain earlier books, upon which von Rad relied so heavily. In Chronicles the divine warrior battles against Israel's enemies, fighting for the temple and people he established and promised to defend.[25]

That the basis for divine activity is different in the Chronicler's work can be seen by reference to those battle narratives, which are unique to his history. In King Abijah's holy war against the northern kingdom, for example, Abijah mentions both the Lord's promises to David and the worship associated with the Jerusalem temple as grounds for the failure of Jeroboam and his forces, should Jeroboam press on in battle (2 Chron. 13:4-

23. I. Eph'al argues for distinctions between these different kinds of conflicts, "On Warfare and Military Control in the Ancient Near Eastern Empires: A Research Outline," in H. Tadmor and M. Weinfeld, eds., *History, Historiography and Interpretation* (Jerusalem: Magnes, 1983), pp. 88-106.

24. H. G. M. Williamson, *1 and 2 Chronicles,* New Century Bible Commentary (Grand Rapids: Eerdmans, 1982), pp. 216-27; R. B. Dillard, *2 Chronicles,* Word Bible Commentary 15 (Waco: Word, 1987), pp. 52-53, 157.

25. In this respect the Chronicler's perspective is akin to a number of prophetic passages and psalms which petition or depict the divine warrior's action on behalf of Judah or Zion (e.g., Nah. 1:4; 2:1-14; Isa. 17:12-14; Ps. 9:1-21; 20:2-8; 46:4-7; 48:10-15; 76:2-7; 132:13-18). See further B. C. Ollenburger, *Zion, the City of the Great King,* JSOT Supplement 41 (Sheffield: JSOT Press, 1987), pp. 66ff.

12).[26] Similarly, when King Asa is confronted with an invasion by Zerah the Cushite, Asa calls out to the Lord for deliverance in accordance with the petitions of Solomon's prayer (14:7-10). God intervenes on behalf of Judah and Asa is able to inflict tremendous damage on his foe (14:11-14). In contrast, then, to the early portrayals of the divine warrior as fighting against Israel's enemies, leading Israel in exodus-conquest, and establishing his sanctuary in the land, the Chronicler depicts the divine warrior as fighting for that sanctuary already established in the temple.

III. The Pattern of Holy War in 2 Chronicles 20

The image of YHWH battling for his people with special reference to the petitions offered at the Jerusalem temple elucidates the cultic orientation of king and people toward the temple in 2 Chronicles 20:1-30. Before exploring the configuration of this conflict, it is necessary to address briefly its context. The Chronicler presents a generally favorable, although complex, portrait of Jehoshaphat.[27] This clash occurs during one of the salutary periods in Jehoshaphat's reign. After the fiasco of a failed alliance with King Ahab (18:1–19:3), Jehoshaphat recovers and embarks on a praiseworthy measure. He initiates a judicial reform from Beer-sheba to the highlands of Ephraim (19:4-11). Sometime after his judicial reformation, Jehoshaphat is confronted, however, with a crisis that threatens to overwhelm his people. The invasion by a coalition of Moabites, Ammonites, and Meunites (20:1-30) is not mentioned in the Deuteronomistic History.[28] In the context of

26. See further A. Ruffing, *Jahwekrieg als Weltmetapher: Studien zu Jahwekriegstexten des chronistischen Sondergutes,* Stuttgarter biblische Beiträge 24 (Stuttgart: Katholisches Bibelwerk, 1992), pp. 19-57; S. Japhet, *I & II Chronicles,* Old Testament Library (Louisville: Westminster John Knox, 1993), pp. 685-96; and my "'Battling against Yahweh': Israel's War against Judah in 2 Chron. 13:2-20," *Revue biblique* 100 (1993): 511-32.

27. G. N. Knoppers, "Reform and Regression: The Chronicler's Presentation of Jehoshaphat," *Biblica* 72 (1991): 500-24; K. Strubind, *Tradition als Interpretation in der Chronik: König Josaphat als Paradigma chronistischer Hermeneutik und Theologie,* Beihefte zur Zeitschrift für die alttestamentliche Wissenschaft 201 (Berlin: de Gruyter, 1991).

28. In 2 Chronicles 20:1, I read with LXX[AB], *mhm'wnym,* "from the Meunites." The reading of MT, *mh'mwnym,* "from the Ammonites," evinces a metathesis of *mem* and *'ayin.* See the list of the coalition partners in vv. 10, 22, and 23 (the Ammonites, Moabites, and inhabitants of Mt. Seir), as well as 2 Chron. 26:7, which again mentions the Meunites.

Jehoshaphat's reign, this onslaught is both unprovoked and mercenary.[29] Of the wars unique to Chronicles, this contest is among the most spectacular.[30]

When the news of the enemy expedition reaches Jehoshaphat, he is afraid and sets his face to seek *(drš)* the Lord (2 Chron. 20:3).[31] He then proclaims a national fast. Holding a fast in response to peril is known not only from prophetic writings (e.g., Jer. 36:6, 9; Zech. 8:19; Joel 2:12f.), but also from battle reports, such as Judges 20:26 and 1 Samuel 7:6. The summoning of volunteers willing to fight for their nation is a characteristic of some war narratives in Judges and Samuel, but in this case people "from all the towns of Judah" gather "to seek *(bqš)* YHWH" at the temple in Jerusalem.[32] Not only is the solidarity of the people and its leadership noteworthy, but also its focus. In resorting to Jerusalem, they honor the divine directive given at Solomon's temple dedication to seek *(bqš)* the Lord in times of need (2 Chron. 7:14).[33] This orientation toward the Jerusalem temple by Jehoshaphat, the cultic personnel, the inhabitants of Jerusalem, and all of Judah continues throughout the narrative.

Jehoshaphat's prayer (2 Chron. 20:6-12), which follows the assembly of all Judah, is uttered on behalf of all Judah in the new court of the temple. With some justification this prayer has been called a national lament.[34] But within this context of a sacral war, I would argue that it also

29. It cannot be attributed to any wrongdoing on Jehoshaphat's part (pace Niditch, *War,* p. 146), because Jehoshaphat has just introduced his judicial reforms. Indeed, the innocence of Jehoshaphat and his people is a prominent motif in the following prayer (2 Chron. 20:6-12).

30. Strübind, *Tradition als Interpretation,* pp. 176-88.

31. On the significance of the expression, see C. T. Begg, "Seeking Yahweh and the Purpose of Chronicles," *Louvain Studies* 9 (1982): 128-41.

32. Again, the locution is typical of the Chronicler's style. The pan-Judah focus mentioned in v. 3 continues throughout the narrative (vv. 4, 15, 17, 20, 27).

33. The whole scenario is reminiscent of earlier occasions in which the people are gathered together on a momentous occasion, such as the anointing of David (1 Chron. 11:1-3), the elevation of the ark to Jerusalem (1 Chron. 15–16), the bringing of the ark into the temple (2 Chron. 5), and Solomon's temple prayer (2 Chron. 6:1–7:10). An atmosphere of national unity pervades these accounts.

34. E.g., O. Eissfeldt, *The Old Testament: An Introduction* (New York: Harper & Row, 1965), pp. 112-13; Williamson, *Chronicles,* p. 295; Dillard, *Chronicles,* p. 154; M. A. Throntveit, *When Kings Speak: Royal Speech and Royal Prayer in Chronicles,* Society of Biblical Literature Dissertation Series 93 (Atlanta: Scholars Press, 1987), pp. 67-72; Ruffing, *Jahwekrieg,* pp. 161-64. De Vries prefers to call it simply a prayer, *Chronicles,* pp. 323-25.

functions basically as an inquiry of the deity, a typical element in other battle narratives.[35] Like many Mesopotamian monarchs[36] and a number of other salutary monarchs in Chronicles, Jehoshaphat petitions the deity in the context of an international crisis.[37] Jehoshaphat's oration recalls specific features of two previous royal prayers in Chronicles: David's farewell blessing (1 Chron. 29:10-19) and Solomon's temple prayer. The opening address used by Jehoshaphat resonates with that used by David.[38] Both David and Jehoshaphat ascribe complete sovereignty to YHWH. Jehoshaphat acclaims God as "ruling over all the kingdoms of the nations; in your hand lies power and strength; none can withstand you" (2 Chron. 20:6), while David acclaims "that all in heaven and on earth is yours . . . you rule over everything; in your hand lies power and strength" (1 Chron. 29:11-12).[39] Both addresses express trust in God's will and power to save. Because these ascriptions contrast divine omnipotence with human helplessness, they lay the foundation for the summations and petitions that follow.[40]

Having addressed the deity, Jehoshaphat presents a highly compressed redemptive history that draws upon earlier biblical texts. Citing both a familiar refrain from the deuteronomistic literature,[41] referring to the divine warrior's lead in conquest, and Isaiah 41:8, Jehoshaphat asks:

35. Judges 20:23, 27-28; 1 Sam. 7:8-9; 14:37; 15:12; 23:2, 4, 10-11; 28:6; 30:6-8; 2 Sam. 5:23; 1 Kings 20:14; 22:6-8; 2 Kings 3:11-12; 6:8-12; 19:15-19. See also S-.M. Kang, *Divine War in the Old Testament and in the Ancient Near East,* Beihefte zur Zeitschrift für die alttestamentliche Wissenschaft 177 (Berlin: de Gruyter, 1989), pp. 215-17.
36. Weippert, "'Heiliger Krieg,'" 471-72; Kang, *Divine War,* pp. 42-43. For a sample of royal Assyrian prayers associated with battle, see R. L. Pratt, "Royal Prayer and the Chronicler's Program" (diss., Harvard Divinity School, 1987), pp. 58-61.
37. David (1 Chron. 14:9, 14); Asa (2 Chron. 14:11); Jehoshaphat (2 Chron. 18:31); Hezekiah (2 Chron. 32:20); Manasseh (2 Chron. 33:12-13). Pratt provides a detailed discussion, "Royal Prayer," pp. 285-353.
38. Similarly, Japhet, *Chronicles,* p. 789.
39. Asa's acclamation (2 Chron. 14:10), also spoken in the context of an enemy invasion, is similar.
40. Throntveit, *When Kings Speak,* pp. 67-71; S. E. Balentine, *Prayer in the Hebrew Bible: The Drama of Divine-Human Dialogue,* Overtures to Biblical Theology (Minneapolis: Fortress, 1993), pp. 97-100.
41. Cf. Deut. 4:37-39; 7:5; 11:23. A helpful list of kindred expressions is provided in M. Weinfeld, *Deuteronomy and the Deuteronomic School* (Oxford: Clarendon, 1972), pp. 341-42.

Did you not[42] drive out the inhabitants of this land from before your people Israel and give it to the seed of your friend[43] Abraham forever? And they dwelt in it and built[44] in it a sanctuary for your name (2 Chron. 20:7-8).

Jehoshaphat's historical retrospect begins with God's past activity on behalf of Israel. That Judah resides in the land promised in perpetuity to Abraham results from divine action, not Judah's own prowess. Updating the historical review to the time of the monarchy, the king refers to the descendants of Abraham building a sanctuary for Yhwh.[45] In the Chronicler's historical overview, Yhwh leads his people in conquest resulting in their occupation of the land and the establishment of a sanctuary for their God. By appealing to the significance of the temple built for Yhwh's name, Jehoshaphat updates the basis for the deity in his role as divine warrior to act in the present. To make the point explicit, the Judahite king alludes to the petitions in Solomon's temple prayer:

If calamity, sword, judgment,[46] plague, or famine come up against us, we will stand before this house and before you, because your name is in this house, and we will cry out to you on account of our afflictions, that you might heed and deliver.[47]

42. I have translated *hl'* as introducing a rhetorical question, but it is also possible to construe *hl'* as an asseverative (Balentine, *Prayer,* pp. 99-100; NEB; NJPS). In this case, one would translate: "truly, you drove out the inhabitants of this land." D. Sivan and W. Schniedewind are uncertain, however, whether the Chronicler recognized the asseverative sense of *l',* "Letting Your 'Yes' Be 'No' in Ancient Israel: A Study of the Asseverative לֹא and הֲלֹא," *Journal of Semitic Studies* 38 (1993): 209-26.

43. Isaiah 41:8 and the MT read *'ohabka,* while the LXX[AB] has the passive participle τῷ ἠγαπημένῳ σου (= qal passive participle **'hwbk?*). MT and LXX[AB] may represent two interpretations of an original orthographically ambiguous **'hbk.*

44. Reading *wybnw* with the LXX[AB], the Syriac, and Vg. *(lectio brevior).* MT adds explicating "for you" *(lk).*

45. P. C. Beentjes discusses the Chronicler's exegetical blend of older texts in more detail, "Tradition and Transformation: Aspects of Innerbiblical Interpretation in 2 Chronicles 20," *Biblica* 74 (1993): 258-61.

46. So MT, *špwṭ* ("judgment"). LXX[L] reads "flood" akris (= *štp*). It is possible that MT has suffered metathesis, e.g., W. Rudolph, *Chronikbücher,* Handbuch zum Alten Testament 21 (Tübingen: Mohr, 1955), p. 258, but the Chronicler may be punning on the root *špṭ* (see v. 12).

47. 2 Chron. 20:9, alluding to 2 Chron. 6:28, 36-37.

Jehoshaphat's prayer is, therefore, couched with the people's present predicament very much in view. His appeal is based on the existence of the temple, because this sanctuary was accepted by YHWH as the place where efficacious prayers could be offered (2 Chron. 7:1-2, 14). Indeed, the emphasis throughout this prayer is on God having a personal stake in this particular national crisis: YHWH's "name is in this house," Israel is "your possession" and "your people," who "built a sanctuary for your name."

Since Zion is prominent in the Chronicler's theology and holy war involves the deity's defense of his sanctuary and people, one should not be surprised by transformations in the rites of sacral war. The orientation by king, priests, and people toward the Jerusalem temple in this narrative is perfectly understandable, even expected, given the Chronicler's presuppositions. There is, for example, no need to view the references to Levitical singers in this passage (vv. 19, 21-22) as later additions.[48] The appointment of Levitical singers is a constituent feature of the national cultus established during the united monarchy. Nor should the appearance of prayers and singing be dismissed as "spiritual sublimation,"[49] because the Chronicler associates such activities with normative worship at the temple.[50]

Having summarized God's past favors to Israel, Jehoshaphat defends his people's innocence against an undeserved threat. The Judahite king observes that the very nations, which Israel was neither allowed to encroach upon nor destroy when Israel originally left Egypt, are now rewarding Judah by invading their land and endangering their hold on it.[51]

---

48. Contra T. Willi, *Die Chronik als Auslegung,* Forschungen zur Religion und Literatur des Alten und Neuen Testaments 106 (Göttingen: Vandenhoeck & Ruprecht, 1972), p. 198.

49. Contra von Rad, *Holy War,* p. 129.

50. Contrary to the standard view expressed in treatments of 2 Chronicles 20, the singing associated with the march against the enemy is not unique. On the paean sung by soldiers as they joined battle in ancient Greece, see W. K. Pritchett, *The Greek State at War: Part 1* (Berkeley: University of California Press, 1974), pp. 105-8. Pritchett also discusses, however briefly, paeans sung before or after a battle. Hymns and songs of battle are also attested, ironically, in the books from which von Rad drew his typology of holy war. See, for instance, the "Song of the Sea" (Exod. 15:1-18), the "Song of Miriam" (Exod. 15:20-21), and the "Song of Deborah" (Judg. 5:1-31). Most of these ancient Israelite poems are, however, associated with the successful conclusion of a battle and are not situated within the context of the battle itself.

51. 2 Chron. 20:10-11. See Num. 20:14-21, Deut. 2:1-19, Judg. 11:15-18, and the discussions of G. von Rad, *Das Geschichtsbild des chronistischen Werkes* (Stuttgart: Kohlhammer, 1930), pp. 77-78, Ruffing, *Jahwekrieg,* pp. 249-52, and Beentjes, "Tradition," pp. 261-63.

The incursion violates Israel's right to the land God gave it. In other words, the present invasion not only constitutes a tremendous threat to Judah, but also a direct offense against the God of Israel. Jehoshaphat's defense carries a juridical force.[52] Hence, he asks God to judge *(špt)* the invaders (2 Chron. 20:12). Emphasizing his own helplessness before the onslaught of this great horde, Jehoshaphat concludes his oration by expressing trust and asking God what course of action to take.

As we have seen, Jehoshaphat's prayer bears some affinities with the form of a national lament. However, one must ask a further question about context: what role does this prayer have in the larger setting of the Chronicler's narrative? It seems that in the context of an ominous military threat Jehoshaphat is leading the people in typical sacral war fashion by consulting the deity. Hence, the prayer appropriately ends with Jehoshaphat stating, "we do not know what to do, but our eyes are set on you."

Following the conclusion to Jehoshaphat's prayer, the spirit of YHWH descends upon Jahaziel, who, as the designate priest in other sacral war descriptions, assures Judah of victory.[53] Jehaziel implores king and people not to be afraid of this great horde and instructs them on a proper course of action.[54] Although some have classified Jahaziel's response simply as a salvation oracle,[55] the components of this oracle: (1) definition of addressee(s); (2) "fear not" formula; and (3) substantia-

52. Pace Ruffing, *Jahwekrieg,* p. 253. See R. M. Good, "The Just War in Ancient Israel," *Journal of Biblical Literature* 104 (1985): 385-400.

53. The martial nature of Jahaziel's address has also been recognized by A. Schmidt, "Das prophetische Sondergut in 2 Chronicles 20,14-17," in L. Ruppert and E. Zenger, eds., *Künder des Wortes: Beiträge zur Theologie der Propheten* (Würzburg: Echter Verlag, 1982), p. 279; E. W. Conrad, *Fear Not Warrior: A Study of ''al tîrā' Pericopes in the Hebrew Scriptures,* Brown Judaic Studies 75 (Chico: Scholars Press, 1985), pp. 65-69; and R. Mason, *Preaching the Tradition: Homily and Hermeneutics after the Exile* (Cambridge: Cambridge University Press, 1990), p. 64.

54. The expression *hmwn (rb)* recurs in this and other holy war passages in Chronicles to describe huge numbers of the enemy (e.g., 2 Chron. 13:8; 14:10; 20:2, 12, 15, 24; 32:7).

55. E.g., Welten, *Geschichte,* p. 150; Ackroyd, *Chronicles,* p. 150; Dillard, *Chronicles,* p. 154. The Chronicler's dependence upon the oracle of Exodus 14:13-14 is not determinative as Ruffing (*Jahwekrieg,* pp. 173-77) thinks, because the two speeches occur in somewhat different contexts. Whereas in Exodus 14, Moses' speech follows the complaints of the people, in 2 Chronicles 20 Jahaziel's speech follows Jehoshaphat's prayer for divine help and instruction. In any case, the two categorizations — war oracle and salvation oracle — are not mutually exclusive. Jahaziel's battle instructions portend the deliverance of Judah.

tion, are also found in the war instructions of Deut. 20:2-4.[56] There the duties of the priest designated to exhort the people before battle are prescribed.[57]

> Hear O Israel, you are drawing near for battle this day against your enemies. Let not your heart soften, do not fear, do not be alarmed, and do not be frightened because of them, for the LORD your God is going with you to do battle for you with your enemies to deliver you (Deut. 20:3-4).

Because both the presence of a priestly figure and the form of his speech comport with the mandate authorized by the authors of Deuteronomy, the Chronicler's description fits within the larger pattern of a war of YHWH.[58]

As commentators have observed, the content of Jehaziel's speech is partially drawn from other holy war narratives. That Jehaziel counsels complete confidence in YHWH is not surprising in light of similar prescriptions given in other sacral war narratives.[59] What is remarkable is the adept enlistment of prominent authorities in older sources to fit the present context. Both leaders cited, Moses at the Red Sea: "stand still and see the salvation of the LORD . . ." (v. 17; Exod. 14:13-14) and David against Goliath: "the battle is not yours but the LORD's" (1 Sam. 17:47), confront not only great odds, but also a reluctant and doubting people (Exod. 14:10-12; 1 Sam. 17:11, 24).

In response to Jehoshaphat's inquiry, Jahaziel's speech provides specific directions to the people along with an accompanying rationale. The entire populace is to march down against the enemy the next day by the Ascent of Ziz. There they will encounter the enemy at the end of the wadi, by the wilderness of Jeruel (2 Chron. 20:16). In other words, the people are to leave the relative safety of Jerusalem, journey into the

56. In the view of Schmidt, the formal elements within Jahaziel's oracle are also attested at Mari, "Das prophetische Sondergut," pp. 277-79.
57. Weinfeld contends that Deut. 1:29-33; 2:24-25, 31; 3:21-22; 7:17-24; 9:1-6; 11:22-25; 31:1-6 are examples of such military orations, *Deuteronomic School,* pp. 45-49.
58. See also Judg. 20:18, 23, 28; 1 Sam. 7:9; 14:36; 23:2, 4, 9-12; 28:6; 30:7-8; 2 Sam. 5:19, 23.
59. E.g., Deut. 20:3; 2 Chron. 13:18; 14:10; 20:15, 17, 20; 32:7-8. For the appearance of the formula in older narratives, see von Rad, *Holy War,* pp. 45-46; Conrad, *Fear Not Warrior;* and Van der Lingen, *Les guerres de Yahvé,* pp. 242-46.

open terrain, and encounter the enemy at a specific location. They are to put themselves in harm's way, but they are told explicitly not to fight. Unlike the earlier sacral wars in Chronicles fought by Kings David, Abijah, and Asa in which the Israelite forces play a military role, Judah under Jehoshaphat is simply instructed, as Israel was at the Red Sea, to "stand still."[60] It would seem that the defense of Judah's innocence advanced so cogently by Jehoshaphat has won divine acceptance. This has become strictly a battle between YHWH and the forces arrayed against Judah. Like the Israelites encamped by the Red Sea awaiting divine intervention, the residents of Jerusalem and Judah will play the role of onlookers.[61] Precisely because of the particular circumstances surrounding this conflict, it is hazardous to infer a purely cultic or quietistic interpretation of sacral war from Judah's non-combativeness in this particular battle. As at the Red Sea, non-participation is nothing more and nothing less than the divinely mandated role the people are to play in a particular conflict.[62]

Exhibiting no doubts, Jehoshaphat and all the people respond to Jehaziel's oracle with worship and action. Manifesting the certainty of victory spoken of in other combat accounts, the Levites begin to praise YHWH with "an exceedingly loud voice" (2 Chron. 20:19). The inhabitants of Jerusalem and Judah obey Jehaziel's directions by proceeding the next day to the wilderness of Tekoa, where they are exhorted again, in this case by Jehoshaphat. The Judahite monarch reinforces the advice given the day before by Jahaziel: "Trust in the LORD your God and you will be established; trust in his prophets and you will succeed" (20:20). This royal speech, spoken prior to battle, is remarkable not only for its reuse of Isaiah 7:9, but also for its place in the Chronicler's overall depiction of Jehoshaphat's reign. Such admonitions to steadfast faith first from Jehaziel and later by Jehoshaphat himself stand out in bold relief to the proclivities displayed by Jehoshaphat elsewhere in his reign. Both Jehoshaphat's alliance with Ahab (2 Chron. 18:3-34//1 Kings 22:1-36) and his later alliance with Ahaziah (2 Chron. 20:35-37//1 Kings 22:50) encounter prophetic condemnation only in Chronicles (2 Chron. 19:2-3;

60. 1 Chron. 14:11, 16; 2 Chron. 13:17-19; 14:12-14. The involvement by Israelite forces in these campaigns is stressed by Japhet, *Ideology*, pp. 125-36.

61. J. G. McConville, *Chronicles*, The Daily Study Bible (Edinburgh: St. Andrew Press, 1984), p. 194.

62. Within the Chronicler's History the unilateral divine action is rivalled only by YHWH's reaction to Sennacherib's invasion (2 Chron. 32:21).

20:37). In both cases Jehoshaphat elicits divine wrath by "doing evil," and "loving those who hate YHWH" (2 Chron. 20:35; 19:3).[63]

The resonances with the prophecies of Isaiah go beyond Isaiah 7:4-9. Other Isaianic oracles which condemn Judah's alliances and dependence upon other nations are more explicit in grounding the basis for hope.[64] Rather than Judah seeking security from abroad, Isaiah promises that "YHWH Sebaoth will descend to fight upon Mt. Zion and upon its hill" (Isa. 31:4). Jehoshaphat's response to this invasion is therefore exemplary: his posture is a significant counterexample both to the posture adopted by Ahaz in Isaiah and to the accommodational approach he himself adopts elsewhere in his reign. Moreover, the kind of divine intervention Isaiah anticipates is depicted by the Chronicler as actually occurring in Jehoshaphat's reign.

The transformations of holy war in this account continue. In some war portrayals the priests blow the trumpets and the people sound the battle cry.[65] In this case, Jehoshaphat consults with the people and then appoints "singers to YHWH and those praising the One appearing in holiness as they went forth before the head of the army."[66] At the very moment they begin to sing, YHWH sets ambushers presumably of a heavenly derivation in the midst of the enemy coalition, resulting in disunity and annihilation.[67] God does not kill them directly; the members of the al-

63. On the Chronicler's distinctive treatment of pacts in light of earlier biblical portrayals, see my "'YHWH is not with Israel': Alliances as *Topos* in Chronicles," *Catholic Biblical Quarterly* (forthcoming).

64. E.g., Isa. 19:1-2; 30:27-30; 31:1-4; 37:33-35.

65. On the priests blowing horns or trumpets, see Num. 10:8-9; 31:6; Josh. 6:5; Judg. 7:19-20; 2 Chron. 13:12. For examples of the battle cry, see Josh. 6:16, 20; 1 Sam. 17:20, 52; Jer. 4:19; Hos. 5:8; Amos 1:14; 2:2; Job 39:24-25.

66. 2 Chron. 20:21. The context is difficult, but I translate *lhdrt-qdš* as "to the One appearing in holiness," rather than in "beautiful apparel" as it is often translated, because the phrase seems to refer to the deity himself and not to the appearance of his worshipers. The translation of NJPS is similar: "the One majestic in holiness as they went forth ahead of the vanguard." The expression *bhdrt-qdš* also occurs in Ps. 29:2; 96:9 (//1 Chron. 16:29). For discussions of its meaning in these contexts, see further, P. R. Ackroyd, "Some Notes on the Psalms," *Journal of Theological Studies* 17 (1966): 393-96, and Cross, *Canaanite Myth,* pp. 152-53.

67. The identity of the "ambushers" in 2 Chron. 20:22 is unclear. As in the sacral wars of old there are two levels of action: divine and human. Hence, the question is not one of divine agency, but the mechanism by which YHWH sows disunity among Judah's adversaries. Some commentators (e.g., Japhet, *Chronicles,* pp. 797-98) believe that human ambushers are in view (cf. Judg. 8:1-29; 9:32-35; 18:9-12; 20:33-38;

liance exterminate each other.[68] As with the miracle at the Red Sea, not one of the enemy survives (2 Chron. 20:23; Exod. 14:28). The death of all the coalition partners confirms the very terms of Jehaziel's oracle, though in a surprising way. The Judahites encounter the enemy horde, as Jahaziel promised, but only as a mass of corpses (2 Chron. 20:24).

Victory in holy war is always ascribed to the deity, but this element is magnified in 2 Chronicles 20. As in the triumph over the Egyptians at the Red Sea, YHWH wins the battle alone.[69] Judah need only gather three days' worth of bountiful spoils.[70] After praising YHWH in the Valley of Berakah, all Judah returns to the temple in Jerusalem with great joy (2 Chron. 20:27-28). As in a number of other holy wars "the fear of YHWH" descends upon "all the kingdoms of the lands."[71] The narrative begins with Jehoshaphat afraid because of the threat confronting him, but it closes with Jehoshaphat at peace from every side and fear gripping Judah's neighbors, when they heard that as of old "YHWH fought with the enemies of Israel."[72]

---

2 Chron. 13:13), while others (e.g., Dillard, *Chronicles,* p. 159) think that the ambushers belong to Yhwh's heavenly host (cf. Josh. 5:13-15; Judg. 5:20; 2 Kings 7:5-7; 19:35; Isa. 13:4; Ezek. 1:24; 2 Chron. 32:21). Similar ambiguity exists in the account of Asa's war: does "his camp" (*mhnhw;* 2 Chron. 14:12) refer to God's heavenly army, or to his earthly army? Welten (*Geschichte,* p. 134) advances a number of arguments for the latter interpretation, but I am not so sure. The antecedent in 2 Chron. 14:12 is YHWH.

68. Cf. Judg. 7:22 and 1 Sam. 14:20.

69. Exod. 14:4, 14, 18; 15:3-10; 2 Chron. 20:22-24. The parallels between Exodus 14 and 2 Chronicles 20 are also noted by Niditch, *War,* pp. 146-49, and Beentjes, "Tradition," pp. 265-68.

70. 2 Chron. 20:25. Cf. Gen. 14:11, 16; Num. 31:25-54; Deut. 2:35; 3:7; 20:14; Josh. 8:27; Judg. 5:30; 8:21, 24-26; 21:23; 1 Sam. 14:32; 21:10; 30:19-20, 24-25; 31:8-10; Isa. 9:2; 1 Chron. 18:7-8; 20:2; 26:26-28; 2 Chron. 14:13-14. In Exod. 14:28 (cf. Exod. 3:21-22) the Israelites receive spoils from the Egyptians before they leave Egypt.

71. Cf. Exod. 15:14-16; Deut. 2:25; 11:25; Josh. 2:9, 11, 24; 5:1; 9:24; 10:1-2; 1 Sam. 4:7-8; 14:15; 1 Chron. 14:7; 2 Chron. 14:13; 17:10. The motif is also present in royal Assyrian inscriptions, where the scope of the victory can be so overwhelming that it induces neighboring nations to offer terms of peace or to submit outright, H. W. F. Saggs, "Assyrian Warfare in the Sargonid Period," *Iraq* 25 (1963): 145-54; Weippert, "'Heiliger Krieg,'" pp. 468-83.

72. 2 Chron. 20:30; cf. Josh. 10:14, 42; Judg. 20:35; 1 Chron. 22:9; 2 Chron. 13:23; 14:4, 6; 15:15. On the importance of peace and rest in Chronicles, see Gabriel, *Friede über Israel,* pp. 180-91, and B. E. Kelly, *Retribution and Eschatology in Chronicles,* JSOT Supplement 211 (Sheffield: Sheffield Academic Press, 1996), pp. 190-99.

IV. Conclusions

Having discussed the specific nature of this conflict, it will be helpful to explore its function within the Chronicler's larger presentation. What interest does the Chronicler have in reviving the concept of YHWH's wars? Considering that the Chronicler is living in the post-exilic age when Persian authority is regnant, what is the purpose of his reformulation and reapplication of holy war ideology? Welten's view that this narrative is proto-apocalyptic calls attention to the paradigmatic nature of the Chronicler's historical writing. Nevertheless, this passage does not resemble the typical literary genres, which an apocalyptic perspective normally takes.[73] Nor is there clear evidence in the Chronicler's depiction of this past event that it purports to be predictive of God's eschatological intervention into human affairs.

The suggestion of Ackroyd and Niditch that the Chronicler is pursuing a quietistic agenda calls attention to Judah's non-participation in this conflict. Nevertheless, one wonders why a number of the Chronicler's other holy wars do mention Judah's involvement in the destruction of their enemies. One also has to ask why the Chronicler would take such an interest in military matters and write extensive accounts of sacral war, if only to stress passive contemplation and non-participation in the events of the world. Although they are not called upon to fight, the people, priests, and king all have to engage in public action and render themselves completely vulnerable to a severe menace. Nor does the stress on not accommodating or entering alliances with other nations evident in 2 Chronicles 18–20 entail a quietistic stance as the historical example of Hezekiah and his reforms indicates. Indeed, the proscription of accommodation with other nations is consistent with the independent posture Israel was to take in the context of fighting the enemy (Exod. 23:32; 34:12-16; Deut. 7:1-4).

In many respects the interpretive option advanced by von Rad presents a false dichotomy. Every holy war is by its very nature spiritual, ritualistic, and cultic. As von Rad himself stressed in his reconstruction of holy war during the Israelite confederation: "holy war is an eminently cultic undertaking — that is, prescribed and sanctioned by fixed, traditional, sacred rites and observances."[74] Yet in so far as a holy war involves groups of people, weapons, conflict, injury, and death, it is also political,

73. P. D. Hanson, *The Dawn of Apocalyptic: The Historical and Social Roots of Jewish Apocalytic Eschatology* (Philadelphia: Fortress, 1979), pp. 1-31.

74. Von Rad, *Holy War,* p. 51.

social, and martial. Admittedly, historical assessments of 2 Chronicles 20:1-30 vary widely.[75] But whether one can reconstruct either the dimensions of a historical war against a southeastern coalition or a holy war institution in the period in which Chronicles was written does not determine if the story has strictly a cultic designation. A narrative depicting a war of YHWH can have political, historical, and social significance, regardless of whether there was such a thing as an institution of holy war at the time when the author wrote.[76] Even a battle description with a highly liturgical focus, such as 2 Chronicles 20, may have an impact on the political and historical views of the author's audience. The stress on YHWH's sovereignty in Jehoshaphat's prayer, for instance, could affect how a Judean reader would view the Achaemenids — their deities and their military might. Indeed, it is the very nature of sacral war stories to relativize the importance of military power, politics, and large numbers. The insistence that the land pledged to Abraham was given in perpetuity might influence how people in Yehud viewed the possession of their land. The depiction of the Moabites, Ammonites, and inhabitants of Mt. Seir could sway how the Chronicler's readers defined themselves in relation to their neighbors to the south and east of Yehud.[77] The Chronicler's adaptation and extension of Isaiah's admonition to King Ahaz (Isa. 7:9) in 2 Chron. 20:20 may accentuate, as Peterson and Micheel have stressed, the importance which the Chronicler's audience would ascribe to prophets, including perhaps the Asaphite Levites of their own time.[78] In short, one can fully acknowl-

75. M. Noth, "Eine palästinische Lokalüberlieferung in 2. Chronicles 20," *Zeitschrift des deutschen Palästina Vereins* 67 (1944-45): 45-71; Rudolph, *Chronikbücher,* pp. 258-63; Welten, *Geschichte,* pp. 140-53; Williamson, *Chronicles,* pp. 291-93; De Vries, *Chronicles,* pp. 323-29; Mason, *Preaching the Tradition,* pp. 65-66; Davies, "Defining the Boundaries," pp. 43-45; Japhet, *Chronicles,* pp. 783-99.

76. Indeed, whether there ever was such a thing as an institution of holy war apart from the rites, beliefs, and rituals employed by those ancient Israelites involved in battle is highly uncertain.

77. In Davies' view, this is a major point of the story, "Defining the Boundaries," pp. 52-54.

78. D. L. Peterson, *Late Israelite Prophecy: Studies in Deutero-Prophetic Literature and in Chronicles,* Society of Biblical Literature Monograph Series 23 (Missoula: Scholars Press, 1977), pp. 75-76; R. Micheel, *Die Seher- und Prophetenüberlieferungen in der Chronik,* Beiträge zur biblischen Exegese und Theologie 18 (Frankfurt am Main: Lang, 1983), pp. 52-53. This line of interpretation helpfully draws attention to the lines of continuity between groups, such as the Levites, who appear in both pre-exilic and post-exilic times. But surely the point of this long story comes to more than the legitimation of one particular priestly circle or class.

edge the cultic dimension of 2 Chronicles 20, while recognizing that the significance of the text is not limited to this one dimension.

By citing former wars of YHWH, the Chronicler emphasizes their relevance for the present. The use of exhortations and a prayer in this chapter heighten this didactic effect.[79] To be sure, the battle involves very circumscribed geographical boundaries.[80] However dramatic the divine victory, the enemies of Judah are local and, in the context of the Chronicler's history, traditional. But would not the local nature of this conflict underline its pertinence for the Chronicler's post-exilic audience? It would be easy for those Judeans living in post-exilic times to view the exodus and conquest as ancient events, as part of a glorious age now lost to them, except as memories. With perhaps such an attitude in mind, the Chronicler presents an alternative point of view. The wars of YHWH are not only a relic of the ancient past, but also something of more immediate consequence. From the Chronicler's History the residents of post-exilic Judah would be reminded that the God they worshipped at the Jerusalem temple was not merely Lord of Yehud, but also the One "ruling over all the kingdoms of the nations," whom "none can withstand." Since the temple cult has become the matrix for the divine warrior's victory in battle, the Chronicler can be seen as bringing out the historical, theological, and military significance of the Jerusalem temple. The God who told the threatened Israelites to stand back while he vanquished an immense Egyptian force in the second millennium is the same God who told the threatened Judahites to stand back while he turned the Moabites, Ammonites, and Meunites against each other in the first millennium. The same God who answered the prayers of Jehoshaphat, spoken in the first temple, is available to the Chronicler's audience at the second temple. In reapplying holy war tradition, the Chronicler has accentuated the importance of the Jerusalem temple in community life. The reinterpretation and reapplication of sacral war ideology in 2 Chronicles 20 testifies not only to its vitality in the post-exilic period but also, by virtue of the very existence of the temple, its continuing relevance for the people of Judah.

79. M. Fishbane, *Biblical Interpretation in Ancient Israel* (Oxford: Clarendon, 1985), pp. 391-92.

80. Welten, *Geschichte,* p. 153.

The Use of the Zion Tradition in the Book of Ezekiel

THOMAS RENZ

The Zion tradition combines elements found in other ancient Near Eastern holy mountain beliefs with earlier Israelite traditions to affirm God's presence on Mt. Zion and to spell out what this presence entails. In the book of Ezekiel, focusing on God's presence and focusing on Zion are presented as exclusive alternatives. Ezekiel went back to the roots of the Zion tradition in ancient Near Eastern holy mountain beliefs and earlier Israelite traditions to modify and develop the tradition according to the needs of the exilic and post-exilic people of God. This essay examines this change and provides a special focus on the glory of God as an essential element in Ezekiel's message.

I. Introduction

This paper has four parts. The first defines which elements will count as pointers to the Zion tradition, while the second summarizes what is regarded to have been the function of the Zion tradition prior to the book of Ezekiel. The third part collects the evidence from the book of Ezekiel and the last attempts to evaluate the findings. The appendix contrasts and

77

compares different ways of conceptualizing the use of the Zion tradition in the book of Ezekiel.

II. What Will Count as Evidence for, or Pointers to, the Zion Tradition?[1]

The "Zion tradition" is believed to be a complex of ideological or theological motifs which came to be applied to Zion after David's conquest of the city.[2] The elements of the tradition are thought to derive from Canaanite mythology,[3] ancient Israelite traditions,[4] and Davidic royal ideology.[5]

1. Cf. J. J. M. Roberts, "Zion Tradition," Supplementary Volume to *Interpreter's Dictionary of the Bible*: 985-87; B. Ollenburger, *Zion: The City of the Great King,* JSOT Supplement 41 (Sheffield: JSOT Press, 1987); J. D. Levenson, "Zion Traditions," *Anchor Bible Dictionary* VI: 1098-1102. See also F. Stolz, "צִיּוֹן," *Theologisches Handwörterbuch zum Alten Testament* 2: 543-51; N. W. Porteous, "Jerusalem-Zion: The Growth of a Symbol," in A. Kuschke, ed., *Verbannung und Heimkehr, FS W. Rudolph* (Tübingen: Mohr [Siebeck], 1961), pp. 235-52; D. Sperling, "Mount, Mountain," Supplementary Volume to *Interpreter's Dictionary of the Bible:* 608f.; H.-J. Kraus, *Worship in Israel: A Cultic History of the Old Testament,* trans. G. Buswell from the revised German edition (Oxford: Blackwell, 1966), pp. 179ff.; H.-J. Kraus, *Theology of the Psalms,* trans. K. Crim (Minneapolis: Augsburg, 1986), pp. 78-84.

2. It has sometimes been argued that the identification of Zion with Zaphon was pre-Israelite, but the issue is thoroughly discussed in favor of Davidic origin by J. J. M. Roberts, "The Davidic Origin of the Zion Tradition," *Journal of Biblical Literature* 92 (1973): 333ff.

3. Cf. H. Schmid, "Jahwe und die Kulttraditionen von Jerusalem," *Zeitschrift für die alttestamentliche Wissenschaft* 67 (1955): 168-97, 175ff.; J. H. Hayes, "The Tradition of Zion's Inviolability," *Journal of Biblical Literature* 82 (1963): 419-26. Both emphasize the Zion tradition as a combination of Israelite and pre-Israelite traditions. Also J. Maier, *Vom Kultus zur Gnosis: Studien zur Vor-und Frühgeschichte der "jüdischen Gnosis": Bundeslade, Gottesthron und Märkabah,* Kairos: Religionswissenschaftliche Studien 1 (Salzburg: Otto Müller, 1964), pp. 43-49; W. H. Schmidt, "Jerusalemer El-Traditionen bei Jesaja," *Zeitschrift für Religions- und Geistesgeschichte* 16 (1964): 302-13, and *Alttestamentlicher Glaube in seiner Geschichte,* 2nd ed., Neukirchener Studienbücher 6 (Neukirchen: Neukirchener Verlag, 1975): 207-26; G. von Rad, *Old Testament Theology,* vol. 2, trans. D. M. G. Stalker (New York: Harper & Row, 1965), pp. 155-58; cf. his "The Tent and the Ark (1931)," *The Problem of the Hexateuch and Other Essays,* trans. E. W. Trueman Dicken (Edinburgh and London: Oliver & Boyd, 1965), pp. 103-24, in which he argues for the Canaanite origin of the tradition of the ark; H.-M. Lutz, *Jahwe, Jerusalem und die Völker: Zur Vorgeschichte von Sach. 12,1-8 und 14,1-5,* Wissenschaftliche Monographien zum Alten und Neuen Testament 27 (Neukirchen-Vluyn: Neukirchener Verlag, 1968); R. J.

Usually the "Zion tradition" is regarded as making the following claims for Zion:

1. Zion is "the highest mountain," the mountain on which God dwells (הַר אֵל *har 'ēl*), Mount Zaphon in Canaanite mythology.
2. Zion is the source of the river(s) of paradise.

Clifford, *The Cosmic Mountain in Canaan and the Old Testament,* Harvard Semitic Monographs 4 (Cambridge, MA: Harvard University Press, 1972); R. E. Clements, *Isaiah and the Deliverance of Jerusalem: A Study of the Interpretation of Prophecy in the Old Testament,* JSOT Supplement 13 (Sheffield: JSOT Press, 1980), pp. 41-48. See with different emphases J. Jeremias, "Lade und Zion: Zur Entstehung der Ziontradition," in H. W. Wolff, ed., *Probleme Biblischer Theologie, Festschrift Gerhard von Rad* (Munich: Chr. Kaiser, 1971), pp. 183-98; J. A. Soggin, "Der offiziell geförderte Synkretismus in Israel während des 10. Jahrhunderts," *Zeitschrift für die alttestamentliche Wissenschaft* 78 (1966): 179-204, esp. 182-88, 196f.; G. Fohrer, "Israels Haltung gegenüber den Kanaunäern und anderen Völkern," *Journal of Semitic Studies* 13 (1968): 64-75; E. Otto, "El und JHWH in Jerusalem: Historische und theologische Aspekte einer Religionsintegration," *Vetus Testamentum* 30 (1980): 316-29.

    4. Cf. M. Noth, "Jerusalem und die israelitische Tradition (1950)," in *Gesammelte Studien zum Alten Testament,* 3rd ed., Theologische Bucherei 6 (Munich: Chr. Kaiser, 1966), pp. 172-87. O. Eissfeldt argued in a succession of essays that a pre-Mosaic Israelite cultic tent preserved ancient Israelite traditions which were combined with Canaanite traditions first in Shiloh and then in Jerusalem. See "Jahwe Zebaoth (1950)" and "Silo und Jerusalem (1956)," in R. Sellheim und F. Maass, eds., *Kleine Schriften III* (Tübingen: J. C. B. Mohr, 1966), pp. 103-23, 417-25; "Kultzelt und Tempel (1973)" and "Monopol-Ansprüche des Heiligtums von Silo (1973)," in R. Sellheim and F. Maass, eds., *Kleine Schriften VI* (Tübingen: J. C. B. Mohr, 1979), pp. 1-7, 8-14. R. de Vaux argued that the tent and the ark of the covenant were part of two old Israelite traditions which were finally transferred to Jerusalem. See *Ancient Israel: Its Life and Institutions,* trans. J. McHugh (London: Darton, Longman & Todd, 1961), pp. 294-302. Cf. S. Olyan, "Zadok's Origins and the Tribal Politics of David," *Journal of Biblical Literature* 101/2 (1982): 177-93, 181f. Ollenburger mentions also a Princeton Theological Seminary dissertation (1968) by D. L. Eiler with the title "The Origin and History of Zion as a Theological Symbol in Ancient Israel" (*Zion,* p. 166, n. 36). See also Schmid, "Jahwe," pp. 173f., 192-97; Hayes, "Inviolability," pp. 419f.

    5. See Roberts, "Davidic Origin," "The Religio-Political Setting of Psalm 47," *BASOR* 220/21 (1975/76): 129-32, and "Zion in the Theology of the Davidic-Solomonic Empire," in T. Ishida, ed., *Studies in the Period of David and Solomon* (Winona Lake, IN: Eisenbrauns, 1982), pp. 93-108. See also the articles by Soggin, Fohrer, and Otto mentioned in n. 3; cf. Lutz, *Jahwe, Jerusalem und die Völker;* Clements, *Isaiah,* pp. 80-83. Hayes argues that David took over pre-Israelite traditions regulating Jebusite king-succession, "Inviolability," pp. 420f.

3. Zion is the place where the victory of the Creator God over the unruly (הָמָה *hāmāh*) waters of chaos is celebrated (although the conflict need not have taken place there).
4. Zion is the place where God's crushing victory over rebellious nations and their rulers (again the root הָמָה *hāmāh* is employed) at the gates of Jerusalem is celebrated.[6]
5. Zion is the place to which the nations will come as pilgrims to worship YHWH (as portrayed in Isa. 2:2-4 = Mic. 4:1-5).[7]

This list, however, has two significant shortcomings. First, it deliberately takes into account only motifs associated with divine mountains in Canaanite mythology.[8] The motifs taken over from earlier Israelite tradi-

---

6. The verb הָמָה *(hāmāh)* is used in connection with motifs from the Zion tradition in Isa. 51:15; Jer. 5:22; 6:23 (= 50:42); 31:35; 51:55; Ps. 83:3(2), המון *(hamon)* in Isa. 13:4; 29:5-8; 33:3; Jer. 47:3; 51:42; Ps. 65:8(7); 2 Chron. 20:2, 15, 24. המה *(hamah)* and המון *(hamon)* are used together in Isa. 17:12. See A. Baumann, הָמָה *(hāmāh), Theological Dictionary of the Old Testament* 3: 414-18; Lutz, *Jahwe, Jerusalem und die Völker,* pp. 48f., 60ff. המון *(hamon)* is also used 16 times in Ezek. 29–32 to refer to various armies (cf. 39:11, 15f.).

7. These motifs, apart from the last, were first listed by E. Rohland, "Die Bedeutung der Erwählungstraditionen Israels für Eschatologie der alttestamentlichen Propheten" (dissertation, Heidelberg, 1956), pp. 145ff. As presented here, the list reflects my own emphases rather than Rohland's. The fifth element was added by H. Wildberger, "Die Völkerwallfahrt zum Zion. Jes. ii 1-5," *Vetus Testamentum* 7 (1957): 62-81; idem, *Jesaja 1–12,* Biblischer Kommentar: Altes Testament 10/2 (Neukirchen: Neukirchener Verlag, 1972), pp. 75ff.; cf. also P. Grelot, "Un parallele babylonien d'Isaie lx et du Psaume lxxii," *Vetus Testamentum* 7 (1957): 319-21. The antiquity of this motif was stressed by H. Junker, "Sancta Civitas, Jerusalem Nova: Eine formkritische und überlieferungsgeschichtliche Studie zu Jes. 2," *Tierer Theologische Studien* 15 (1962): 28. Ollenburger is not convinced that the pilgrimage motif is an early and necessary part of the Zion tradition. See *Zion,* pp. 15f.

8. Roberts argues quite effectively against a Jebusite origin of the fourth motif which he connects with Davidic tradition ("Davidic Origin," pp. 337-44). Similarly W. H. Schmidt and J. Jeremias argued that the interest in "the nations of the world" presupposes a certain "monotheism" known only in Israel (see, e.g., Jeremias, "Lade und Zion," p. 189). While it is true that Israel's monotheism puts these motifs in a different context, the motif of a pilgrimage of the nations to a sacred city is not unknown outside Israel. See M. Weinfeld, "Zion and Jerusalem as Religious and Political Capital: Ideology and Utopia," in R. E. Friedman, ed., *The Poet and the Historian: Essays in Literary and Historical Biblical Criticism,* Harvard Semitic Studies 26 (Chico, CA: Scholars Press, 1983), pp. 75-115, esp. p. 111. It is likely in my view that the fifth element was developed in coming to grips with Babylonian ideology rather than

tion are not reflected here. Second, it does not reflect the historical nature of the election of Zion.[9] It seems that Israelite tradition remained conscious of the origin of the Zion tradition in David's conquest of the city and the building of the temple through Solomon.[10] This is true even if the Zion tradition did not only take up Canaanite traditions, but was a continuation of a Jebusite cult tradition.[11] YHWH has chosen to dwell in Zion at a particular time in history. Most Israelite traditions which came to be associated with Zion retain a pre-history. In spite of this pre-history, these elements have been integrated in the Zion tradition and need to be considered in this study. Zion is regarded not only as "the highest mountain," but also as the place where the ark of the covenant is located. As the latter, it is the dwelling place of "YHWH Zebaoth who is enthroned over the cherubim."[12] Consequently, the Zion tradition can manifest itself not only in the narrative elements listed above, but also in certain designations of YHWH and motifs from the ark tradition such as the cherubim.[13] In addition to

---

Canaanite mythology. One should also note that the elements listed have different references in Canaanite mythology: the first motif is related to Baal, who is told to have a temple on Zaphon, the second to El, who has a tent at the two rivers on the mountain which is also the meeting place of the gods. This mixture of motifs from Baal and El traditions is probably Israelite as well.

9. In view of Rohland's interest in the Zion tradition as one of the "Erwählungstraditionen Israels" this might seem surprising. Yet the purpose of Rohland's catalogue of motifs was to list the non-Israelite motifs connected with the Zion tradition in the Zion psalms, not necessarily to provide a comprehensive description of what Israelites came to believe about Mt. Zion. See "Erwählungstraditionen," pp. 141ff.

10. Cf. Noth's remarks regarding the absence of Jerusalem in the Pentateuch ("Jerusalem," pp. 172f.).

11. Thus, Kraus, who believes in a Jebusite origin of the Zion tradition, remarks that "in the long run the election of Jerusalem could be explained and justified only by the election of David" (*Worship*, p. 182).

12. Cf. Kraus, *Theology*, pp. 17-24. See also M. Görg, "ישׁב," *Theological Dictionary of the Old Testament* 6: 434f.

13. J. Levenson, *Sinai and Zion: An Entry into the Jewish Bible* (Minneapolis: Winston Press, 1985). B. Janowski has recently argued for the independence of the cherubim from the ark tradition. See "Keruben und Zion: Thesen zur Entstehung der Zionstradition," in D. Daniels et al., ed., *Ernten, was man sät, Festschrift K. Koch* (Neukirchen: Neukirchener Verlag, 1991), pp. 231-54. Janowski consequently would want to emphasize even more strongly the direct relationship between cherubim and the Zion tradition. For a detailed treament of the relationship between YHWH's throne and the cherubim on the one hand and between throne and ark on the other hand, see §56 "Jahwe Zebaoth, der Kerubenthroner," in M. Metzger's *Königsthron und Gottesthron: Thronformen und Throndarstellungen in Ägypten und im Vorderen Orient im dritten und*

these and other elements related to divine mountain traditions such as the identification of the sacred mountain with Eden,[14] the following elements are regarded as potential pointers to the Zion tradition because they occur frequently in connection with it:

1. The designation of YHWH as "YHWH Zebaoth."[15]
2. The designation of YHWH as "(El) Elyon."[16]

---

zweiten Jahrtausend vor Christus und deren Bedeutung für das Verständnis von Aussagen über den Thron im Alten Testament, Alter Orient und Altes Testament 15/1 (Kevelaer: Butzon & Bercker; Neukirchen-Vluyn: Neukirchener Verlag, 1985), pp. 309-51, and §56 "Thron und Lade," pp. 352-65. Metzger argues that the cherubim in the holy of holiest in the temple were standing upright and meant to guard the ark and to support the רָקִיעַ *(rqy')*. They were therefore not connected with the designation "YHWH Zebaoth who is enthroned over the cherubim." While Metzger regards it as likely that YHWH's throne was imagined as a cherubim-throne (in analogy to the Syro-Phoenician sphinx-thrones), this cherubim-throne was above the רָקִיעַ *(rqy')* and not pictured in the temple. It was only later that YHWH's throne came to be identified with the ark, against which Jer. 3:16f. polemicizes. Metzger presents also a review of scholarship on the relationship between the designation "YHWH who is enthroned over the cherubim," the cherubim in Jerusalem and the temple in Shiloh on pp. 326ff. See also M. Barker, *The Gate of Heaven: The History of Symbolism of the Temple in Jerusalem* (London: S.P.C.K., 1991), pp. 138-45. Maier points out that it is only an hypothesis that earlier Israelite traditions were as closely connected with the ark as usually assumed. He only allows that the transfer of the ark was the *presupposition* for the concentration in the "city of David" of various old Israelite traditions (*Vom Kultus zur Gnosis,* pp. 49-52). This does not make any difference for our study.

14. For which see, e.g., Barker, *The Gate of Heaven,* pp. 57-103. I do not list those elements here in detail, since they will be easily recognized along the way. The connection of temple and creation myths in later Jewish thought can be traced by consulting R. Patai, *Man and Temple in Ancient Jewish Myth and Ritual* (London: Thomas Nelson, 1947), pp. 54-104.

15. See the references in n. 4 and n. 7 and Kraus, *Theology,* pp. 17-24; cf. T. N. D. Mettinger, *The Dethronement of Sabaoth: Studies in the Shem and Kabod Theologies,* Coniectanea biblica, Old Testament 18 (Lund: Gleerup, 1982), and *In Search of God: The Meaning and Message of the Everlasting Names,* trans. Frederick H. Cryer (Philadelphia: Fortress Press, 1988), pp. 123-57. The designation is probably older than the Zion tradition, but has come to be associated with it together with the ark.

16. A designation probably taken over from the pre-Israelite cultus in Jerusalem. See G. Wehmeier, "עלה," *THAT* 2: 272-90, cols. 285-87. Cf. Schmid, "Kulttraditionen," pp. 175-78; Mettinger, *In Search of God,* p. 122. It seems less likely that with the designation "Elyon" YHWH took over also a Jebusite sanctuary. See de Vaux, *Ancient Israel,* pp. 310f. The same is true for the assumption that David took over Jebusite priest personnel. See de Vaux, *Ancient Israel,* p. 374; Olyan, "Zadok's Origins."

3. The association of YHWH with cherubim.[17]
4. The characterization of YHWH as "king."[18]
5. YHWH's *kabod,* "the glory of the Lord."[19]
6. YHWH's footstool.[20]

There are other expressions and ideas which are known mostly in close connection with the Zion tradition, but they are used too infrequently in the Old Testament to allow us to draw any conclusions from their absence in Ezekiel, e.g., the designation of God as rock of salvation,[21] and the idea of YHWH's rest or resting place.[22]

In sum, the Zion tradition comprises a variety of elements which were not originally connected with Zion, but now find their point of reference in Zion. The creation of the Zion tradition consequently was not a *creatio ex nihilo,* but rather the creation of a focal point and integrating moment in Zion for a variety of pre-existing motifs and traditions.[23] This may create the impression that the whole of pre-exilic Israelite beliefs is subsumed under the Zion tradition, yet this is not the case. It needs to be

17. Cherubim are associated with vegetation and with movements of the deity. There seems to be no connection between these two ideas and only the latter is relevant here (cf., however, Ezek. 28:14-16). See D. N. Freedman and M. P. O'Connor, "כרוב," *Theological Dictionary of the Old Testament* 7: 307-19. Cf. M. Haran, *Temples and Temple Service in Ancient Israel: An Inquiry into the Character of Cult Phenomena and the Historical Setting of the Priestly School* (Oxford: Clarendon Press, 1978), p. 254; T. H. Gaster, *Myth, Legend & Custom in the Old Testament: A Comparative Study with Chapters from 'Folklore in the Old Testament' by Sir James Frazer* (New York: Harper & Row; London: Duckworth, 1969), p. 48. See n. 13.

18. See Ollenburger, *Zion,* passim. E.g., Ps. 68:25-30; Ps. 132.

19. See especially Ps. 63:3(2) and 1 Sam. 4:21f., as well as Ps. 24:8-10.

20. Mentioned in Ps. 99:5; 132:7; Isa. 66:1; Lam. 2:1; 1 Chron. 28:2; cf. H.-J. Fabry, "הדם," *Theological Dictionary of the Old Testament* 3: 325-34.

21. See Ps. 89:26; 95:1; cf. Deut. 32:15; 2 Sam. 22:3, 17 (= Ps. 18:2, 46); Isa. 17:10. Both "rock" and "salvation" are common terms in praise of YHWH even separately from one another. It seems unlikely that the combination of terms was distinctive to the Zion tradition. See, however, D. Eichhorn, *Gott als Fels, Burg und Zuflucht: Eine Untersuchung zum Gebet des Mittlers in den Psalmen,* Europäische Hochschulschriften 23/4 (Frankfurt: Peter Lang, 1972); Ollenburger, *Zion,* pp. 77f.

22. See Pss. 95:11; 132:8; Isa. 66:1; cf. 1 Chron. 28:2. Cf. V. A. Hurowitz, *I Have Built You an Exalted House: Temple Building in the Bible in the Light of Mesopotamian and Northwest Semitic Writings,* JSOT Supplement 115 (Sheffield: JSOT Press, 1992), pp. 330f.

23. That this was an Israelite process is argued in Jeremias, "Lade und Zion," especially pp. 193f.

pointed out that Zion was not the only focal point of Israelite beliefs. Other focal points were certainly the Exodus and the Sinai covenant tradition. It is argued below that the Davidic covenant tradition can also be distinguished from the Zion tradition and it seems not advisable to incorporate holy war motifs completely into the Zion tradition. On the other hand, the attempt to associate with the Zion tradition only those elements which are not found elsewhere in Israelite thought and belief may distort seriously our picture of the beliefs people held in association with Zion.[24]

Finally, it should be pointed out that in my view the affirmation of an inherent and unconditional inviolability of Zion need not have been an essential part of the tradition,[25] i.e., a denial of Zion's inviolability need not imply a denial of the Zion tradition as such. In any case, however, it seems that the assumption that Zion is an especially protected place is the inevitable conclusion from the premise that God is present in the city.

III. What Was the Function of the Zion Tradition?

The Zion tradition is sometimes regarded as the theological expression and instrument of Davidic politics.[26] Yet, while it could certainly function in this way, it is by no means clear that it was designed as such. The Zion tradition is concerned with YHWH's responsibility for the maintenance of the cosmic and historical order of his creation. The Davidic covenant tra-

---

24. The attempt to describe a pre-exilic "Zionology" may be compared with the attempt to describe an early Christian "soteriology." It cannot be done in isolation from other considerations (in the latter case, for example, christology and pneumatology), but the result can be identified as a distinct set of beliefs.

25. Cf. Ollenburger, *Zion*, pp. 16f.; Clements, *Isaiah*, pp. 84f., 88. Contrast Hayes who concludes that the invulnerability of Jerusalem is a pre-Davidic or non-Israelite tradition ("Inviolability," p. 426), and Kraus who argues that the motif of "the unconquerable city of God" was already part of the old Jebusite tradition (*Theology*, pp. 81f.).

26. See esp. Soggin, "Synkretismus," and Fohrer, "Israels Haltung"; cf. Clem ents, *Isaiah*, p. 88, "Overall therefore we can best regard the Zion psalms as giving voice to a particular aspect of the Jerusalem royal ideology." Otto, "El und JHWH," criticizes this as being too simplistic and contends that Davidic politics are not so much the cause as the consequence of the theology which developed after the conquest of Jerusalem. From a different angle Jeremias ("Lade und Zion," pp. 185f.) argues that the Davidic tradition would have been "unthinkable" without David's transfer of the ark to Jerusalem.

dition is concerned with the way by which YHWH's governance is translated into human government. Both traditions affirm Zion as the center of government, yet while the Davidic tradition seems to be dependent on the Zion tradition (cf. Ps. 2:7; 1 Kings 11:32, 36), the Zion tradition can be imagined without the Davidic tradition.[27] In other words, while it is part of the Davidic covenant tradition to affirm that YHWH has elected the Davidic dynasty to rule on his holy hill, it does not seem to be a necessary part of the Zion tradition that there is a Davidic king ruling in Zion. The dependence of the Davidic tradition on the Zion tradition explains that the two traditions are sometimes closely related to one another (so especially in Ps. 132). The priority and sufficiency of the Zion tradition is, however, evident in those psalms which give strong expression to the Zion tradition without any reference to Davidic kingship (see Pss. 46, 48, and 76).[28] The Zion tradition with its emphasis on YHWH's kingship and his role as defender of Zion and of order could even be used as the basis for a critique of the royal court. "Zion" is therefore to be regarded as a theological symbol first of all. The Zion tradition calls for subordination to and trust in YHWH. This could be translated by Davidic kings into subordination to Zion and the human king reigning on Zion, but it could also be held against a Davidic king.[29]

It seems therefore appropriate to put more emphasis on the theological or cultic function of the Zion tradition. The integration of mythological motifs certainly served to underline the supremacy of YHWH. Whether, as Eckhard Otto has suggested, this was primarily done to facilitate the conversion of the Canaanite inhabitants of Jerusalem to the Yahwistic faith,[30] or, because it was a way to prevent Israelites looking for religious alternatives, is now difficult to determine. The Zion tradition in any case provided a fixed reference point for the reinterpretation of ancient myths and a focal point for the worship of YHWH as creator and king. Of course, Jerusalem (Zion) thereby assumed the qualities of a

27. This is, of course, one of the reasons why it has been argued that there was a Jebusite Zion tradition prior to the conquest of the city by David.

28. Cf. Ollenburger, *Zion,* pp. 59-66.

29. See Ollenburger, *Zion,* passim, especially chapter 4, pp. 81-144.

30. Otto, "El und JHWH." I do not find Milgrom's argument in "Religious Conversion and the Revolt Model for the Formation of Israel," *Journal of Biblical Literature* 101/2 (1982): 169-76 against the existence of religious conversion before the second temple period convincing. Cf. C. van Houten, *The Alien in Israelite Law,* JSOT Supplement 107 (Sheffield: JSOT Press, 1991), pp. 59-61.

mythical space.[31] The Zion tradition then served also to explicate what the presence of YHWH "who dwells over the cherubim" means for Zion. In sum, it seems that the Zion tradition was a way of thinking about God and to do so in connection with a specific place which is thereby validated as the dwelling place of God, the place where human beings can experience God.

IV. Evidence for Use of the Zion Tradition in the Book of Ezekiel

Although the term "Zion" is never used in the book of Ezekiel, motifs usually associated with the Zion tradition are frequently used in the book, and the temple in Jerusalem is obviously regarded as YHWH's sanctuary with all the consequences this would entail for the significance of this place. The uses of the Zion tradition are grouped in four categories: (A) the use of the tradition in statements about the temple and the city of Jerusalem to be destroyed by the Babylonians; (B) the use of the tradition in statements about the restoration, especially concerning the new sanctuary required in and promised for the restoration period; (C) the use of the tradition to make statements about the God of Israel; (D) other uses of the Zion tradition.

A. Concerning the Temple and the City of Jerusalem

In an oracle in which the message of the first series of sign acts is summarized, the following is said about Jerusalem:

> "This is Jerusalem: I have set her in the center of the nations, with countries all around her. And she has rebelled against my ordinances, becoming more wicked than the nations, and against my statutes more than the countries all around her. Yes, they have rejected my ordinances and my statutes — they have not followed them" (5:5-6).[32]

31. See B. S. Childs, *Myth and Reality in the Old Testament* (London: SCM Press, 1960), pp. 83-93, for the concept of mythical space. Cf. Barker, *The Gate of Heaven,* pp. 58-65.
32. The translations given in this paper are based on RSV and NRSV, but reflect my own exegetical decisions and preferences.

These verses confirm the tradition of Jerusalem as the center of the earth.[33] As the center of the earth, Zion should be the place from which order is established and maintained in the world. Yet instead rebellion against God's ordinances is found at the very heart of his reign. This must have serious consequences:

> "Therefore thus says the Lord GOD: Because you are more turbulent than the nations that are all around you — you have not followed my statutes or kept my ordinances; you have not even acted according to the ordinances of the nations that are all around you! — therefore thus says the Lord GOD: I myself am against you; I will execute judgements in your midst in the sight of the nations and I will do with you what I have never done before and will never do again because of all your abominations" (5:7-9).

The Zion tradition had proclaimed that the raging (יֶהֱמוּ *yehĕmû*) of the chaotic waters (Ps. 46:4), the tumulting (הָמוּ *hāmû*) of the nations (Ps. 46:7) can do no harm to the city of God.[34] Yet the book of Ezekiel claims that the turbulence of the inhabitants of Jerusalem (המנכם) is greater than any turbulence originating from the nations. Peace can therefore no longer be guaranteed, the sanctuary is defiled, and YHWH is no longer the protector of the city:

> "Therefore, by my life, says the Lord GOD, I swear: because you have defiled my sanctuary with all your detestable things and with all your abominations, therefore I for my part will cut short; my eye will not show pity, and even I will not spare" (5:11).

The allusions to the Zion tradition in this oracle underline the seriousness of Israel's rebellion and serve to justify YHWH's judgment against her. She of all nations, at the center of the world, should have heeded the ordi-

---

33. A similar claim was made for Nippur *(mar-kas šame u erṣeti)* which is in close vicinity to the place where Ezekiel was located. See *The Chicago Assyrian Dictionary,* vol. *M1*, p. 283. I have not included the claim that Zion was at the center of the earth in the list above, because there is no clear biblical evidence for this belief outside Ezekiel. However, the fact that this was a widespread part of ANE beliefs about sacred places and that it is frequently applied to Jerusalem in later Jewish and Christian literature makes it likely that the motif of Jerusalem being at the center of the earth was part of the Zion tradition. See, e.g., Levenson, *Sinai and Zion*, pp. 115ff.

34. In English translations vv. 3 and 6. Cf. n. 6 for the use of המה and המון in connection with the Zion tradition.

nances of the creator. Yet Israel has not even acted according to the ordinances of the nations, i.e., the nations are here presented as relatively "orderly" compared to Jerusalem's rebellious raging against the creator. YHWH's willingness to subdue the turbulent chaos, as affirmed by the Zion tradition, must now lead him to turn against Jerusalem herself.

The second passage to be considered is in chapter 7 which pronounces the end upon "the four corners of the earth" (v. 2).[35] In vv. 11-14 המון is employed again, now to refer to the masses who amass wealth and thereby bring themselves under the wrath of God.[36] The following verses announce that all the silver and gold will fall to the nations. Everything abused by Israel will be given to the nations for use.

> "One's beautiful ornament in which one took pride, they made their abominable images, their detestable things out of it; therefore I will turn it into an unclean thing for them. And I will hand it over to strangers as plunder, and to the most wicked of the earth as spoil; and they shall desecrate it" (7:20-21).

This is even true for the sanctuary itself which has been defiled by Israel (cf. 23:38f.):

> "I will turn my face from them, and they shall desecrate my treasured place; vandals shall enter her and desecrate her, and make a desolation. Forge the chain! Because the land is full of bloody crimes and the city is full of violence, I will bring the worst of the nations to take possession of their houses; I will put an end to the arrogance of the strong, and their holy places shall be desecrated" (7:22-24).

Jerusalem is no longer secure from the nations. Maybe we can deduce the reason for this removal of the special status as protected city from the use of the plural (מְקַדְּשֵׁיהֶם *m^eqadšêh^em*) in v. 24 (cf. 21:7 [2]).[37] Israel had no

---

35. While the chapter speaks only about the land of Israel, the phrase most probably means the whole earth (cf. Isa. 11:12; Job 37:3; 38:13). The judgment upon Jerusalem is described in cosmic terms.

36. Note the onomatopoetic force of המה in these verses (cf. Joel 4:14 [3:14]).

37. Note the peculiar vocalization as piel participle which is not reflected in the ancient versions. Greenberg, *Ezekiel 1–20,* Anchor Bible 22 (New York: Doubleday, 1983), p. 55, suggests that the vocalization is "a later deliberate distortion, perhaps intended to convey the sense 'those [places] they [not God!] sanctify.'" In 21:7 (2) the usual plural form of the noun is used.

longer singled out Jerusalem as "the holy place"; as a consequence
YHWH will no longer single out Jerusalem for protection.[38] It is not entirely clear whether the unusual צְפוּנִי (ṣᵉpuni; "my treasured place") in
v. 22 refers to the city or to the land.[39] It seems, however, likely that the
allusion to צָפֹן (ṣapon; "Zaphon," "North") was not missed. Yet the place
which God still treasures is no longer the place where people are "treasured" against the onslaught of the nations.[40] The validity of the Zion tradition with regard to the special significance of Zion is put into question,
first by the behavior of the people, then by the one who is supposed to
dwell there.

The question whether God dwells in Zion is dealt with in more detail
in the first temple vision in chapters 8–11. The vision makes it explicit
that YHWH will remove himself from the Israelites, because they have removed themselves from him through their "abominations" (cf. 8:6).[41]
Judgment will affect the sanctuary no less than the city as a whole, and it
even has to begin in the sanctuary (9:6). Thus the special role of Mt. Zion
is indirectly confirmed. What used to be the center from which God's order was established is now the center of chaos and consequently will be
the center of judgment in the restoration of order. The "abominations" pictured in the vision are the worse for being committed near YHWH's sanctuary. The supreme punishment is therefore the gradual departure of the

38. The breakdown of the distinction between the sacred and the profane (cf.
22:26) and the combination of YHWH worship with idol worship (cf. 23:38f.) are seen
in the book of Ezekiel as among the most significant violations, which is why the
maintenance of this distinction plays such a significant role in chapters 40–48.

39. The Targum renders v. 22: "And I will make My Shekinah depart from
them, because they have profaned the land of the abode of My Shekinah, and wicked
ones shall enter it and profane it" (S. H. Levey, *The Targum of Ezekiel,* The Aramaic
Bible 13 (Edinburgh: T. & T. Clark, 1987), p. 34. Note that Levey's translation makes
the Judeans rather than the invaders (RSV) the agent of the profaning. The Aramaic allows both, as does the Hebrew.

40. Note that in all three instances in which the root צפן is used with reference
to God's "treasuring" of his people connections to the Zion tradition can be drawn. In
Ps. 27:4f. the shelter in which God hides his people is the temple; in Ps. 31:21 (20) reference is to God's presence (פָּנֶיךָ; paneyka); and in Ps. 83:3f. (2f.) God's people are referred to as "your protected ones" in the face of the tumult of the nations.

41. It is not clear whether in 8:6 the people are the implicit subject ("removing
themselves from my sanctuary") or YHWH ("driving me away from my sanctuary").
The former has been favored by recent commentators (e.g., Zimmerli, 1: 218, 238;
Greenberg, 168f.; Allen, 1: 120). Again the idea would be that Israel no longer privi-
leges the sanctuary, but worships at an altar outside the temple.

glory of YHWH from the temple (divided into three stages narrated in 10:4-5, 18-19). With this departure of the glory of YHWH from Jerusalem, Zion ceases to be the place the Zion tradition claims it was.[42] In direct refutation of claims made in Jerusalem, YHWH declares that rather than the exilic community being far from him, it is Jerusalem which is far from him. To the exiles, however, he has become "a sanctuary to some extent" (11:16).[43] Possession of the land is no longer accepted as the sacramental token of God's favor. The fundamental issue is idolatry. The exiles will inherit the land and remove the "abominations" (11:17f.), those who practice idolatry, however, are doomed for destruction (11:21). Thus, Jerusalem's sanctity is connected with and dependent on the worship practiced in the city.

The historical nature of Jerusalem's sanctity is pointed out in chapter 16 which declares to Jerusalem: "Your origin and your birth are of the land of the Canaanites; your father was an Amorite, and your mother a Hittite" (16:3; cf. v. 45). Jerusalem's special position is entirely due to her relationship with YHWH. The consequence drawn from this is that when the relationship between Jerusalem and YHWH is broken, Jerusalem loses her special position as the place of God's presence. Since Jerusalem has behaved worse than Sodom and Samaria, she has put herself on the same (or a lower) level as these cities. Her restoration after the judgment can therefore only be a restoration alongside the restoration of Sodom and Samaria (16:53), both of which will be full beneficiaries of the new covenant

42. Remember that, in the words of Levenson, "the most central aspect of the cosmic mountain, that which implies the others, is the presence of God or the gods" (*Sinai and Zion,* p. 137). Cf. Ollenburger, *Zion,* p. 23.

43. מְעַט in לְמִקְדָּשׁ מְעַט *(lᵉmiqdāš mᵉaṭ)* could be understood as qualifying מִקְדָּשׁ adverbially either in temporal or spatial respect. Elsewhere the adverb refers to degree rather than time (2 Kings 10:18; Zech. 1:15). See already G. A. Cooke, *The Book of Ezekiel,* International Critical Commentary (Edinburgh: T. & T. Clark, 1936), p. 125; cf. more recently W. Zimmerli, *Ezekiel 1,* trans. R. E. Clements (Philadelphia: Fortress Press, 1979), p. 262; *Hebräischer und Aramäischer Lexikon zum Alten Testament,* 578; and B. K. Waltke and M. O'Connor, *An Introduction to Biblical Hebrew Syntax* (Winona Lake, IN: Eisenbrauns, 1990), p. 663. Greenberg, *Ezekiel 1–20,* p. 190, and following him L. Allen, *Ezekiel 1–19,* Word Biblical Commentary 28 (Dallas: Word Books, 1994), p. 128, note the appositional use of מְעַט in the expression עֵזֶר מְעַם *('ēzer mᵉaṭ;* "a little help") in Dan. 11:34 and translate "a little sanctuary" (cf. LXX: ἁγίασμα μικρόν). For a theological discussion of the phrase see P. Joyce in John Barton and David Reimer, eds., *After the Exile: Essays in Honour of Rex Mason* (Macon, GA: Mercer University Press, 1996).

to be made with Jerusalem (16:61).[44] It is remarkable that even though cultic sins play a significant role in the chapter, no use is made of the Zion tradition in this history of Jerusalem. In contrast, chapter 20 which narrates the history of Israel from an exilic perspective (contrast 20:1-3 with 16:1-3) skips the entire part of the history related to the possession of the land and to Zion, yet culminates in a vision of acceptable sacrifice "on the high mountain of Israel" (20:40; see below). This points to a re-creation rather than restoration of the Zion tradition. The exiles inherit the land as if they had never been in possession of it.

To summarize, talk about the sanctuary in the book of Ezekiel serves especially to underline that God is offended not only by idol worship as such, but also by the fact that idol worship took place close to his own sanctuary (see especially ch. 8) and by people who at the same time would worship idols and come into his sanctuary (cf. 23:38f.). The demand to the exiles was consequently to rely no longer on the sanctuary in Jerusalem which was to be desecrated (24:21), but rather to accept "the little sanctuary" (11:16) YHWH has become to them instead in exile. The sanctuary in Jerusalem no longer gave access to YHWH, yet it seems that the Zion tradition has been dissolved temporarily rather than demolished in principle. While the temple in Jerusalem was no longer a guarantee of God's presence for Israel, in the oracles concerning the nations the temple is still called "my sanctuary" by YHWH and triumph over its profanation will draw his judgment upon a people (25:3).

B. Concerning the Restoration and the New Sanctuary

The only purpose left for the old YHWH sanctuary in Jerusalem was to reveal Israel's and the nation's contempt for YHWH in their contempt for the sanctuary. Significantly, the new sanctuary is never described as a continuation of this old sanctuary which has been desecrated in three ways: firstly by the sin of Israel, secondly by YHWH's abandonment of it, and thirdly by its destruction. The old sanctuary is not rebuilt and resacralized. There is never any doubt about the need for a new sanctuary. The divine presence does not fully manifest itself in exile. While Israel enjoys a measure of divine near-

---

44. Translating וְלֹא מִבְּרִיתֵךְ *(wᵉlōʾ mibbᵉrîtēk)* as "not outside your covenant"; cf. NEB; W. H. Brownlee, *Ezekiel 1–19,* Word Biblical Commentary 28 (Waco, TX: Word Books, 1986), p. 242.

ness even in exile, it is a reduced presence they have to content themselves with while in exile (see again 11:16). There is no suggestion that even a temporary dwelling for God should be built in Babylonia.[45] There exists no alternative to a return to the former homeland. Yet, contrary to what one might expect, Zion will not be the center from which the land is reordered and restored. The presence of God "upon a very high mountain" will be the final result of restoration, not its means. It is therefore not earlier than 37:26-28 that the new sanctuary is mentioned.[46]

> "I will make a covenant of peace with them; it shall be an everlasting covenant with them. I will place them and multiply them, and will set my sanctuary in their midst for evermore. My dwelling place will be over them; and I will be God for them, and they will be a people for me. The nations will realize that I the LORD sanctify Israel, when my sanctuary is in their midst for evermore."

Israel's restoration (or better: the re-creation of Israel) is completed with YHWH's presence among his people in his sanctuary, which he himself "gives" to his people.[47] The following chapters are no longer concerned with the process of re-creation, but with describing and safeguarding the new reality.[48] The Zion tradition is more prominent in these chapters than in any of the preceding ones.[49]

In the vision narrated in 40:1ff. Ezekiel is set down "upon a very high mountain" with a view on the temple complex, "a structure like a city" (40:2). The presence of a guide with "a line of flax and a measuring reed" in his hand (40:3; cf. Zech. 2:5-9) indicates that the vision in chap-

45. See P. R. Ackroyd, *Exile and Restoration: A Study of Hebrew Thought of the Sixth Century B.C.* (London: SCM Press, 1968), pp. 31ff., for a discussion of worship in the exilic situation.

46. LXX and Targum have been less patient and read the singular for "mountain heights" in 34:14, thus interpreting it in terms of the sanctuary on Mt. Zion.

47. Cf. Ps. 78:68 and see Hurowitz, *I Have Built You an Exalted House,* pp. 332-34, for the notion of gods as builders of temples and cities.

48. Cf. J. Galambush, *Jerusalem in the Book of Ezekiel: The City as Yahweh's Wife,* Society of Biblical Literature Dissertation Series 130 (Atlanta: Scholars Press, 1992), pp. 148ff.

49. Cf. J. Levenson's comprehensive study of the traditions behind Ezek. 40–48 in the first part of his *Theology of the Program of Restoration of Ezekiel 40–48,* Harvard Semitic Monograph 10 (Missoula, MT: Scholars Press, 1976), pp. 5-53. The Zion tradition informs of course also chapters 38–39 concerned with a new assault of the nations (see below).

ters 40–42 is about surveying a building site, which can be, and in this instance certainly is, a highly theological task.[50] The architectural design of the temple embodies the holiness of God. A sacred space is delineated with holiness in different gradations. The idea that buildings can testify to the nature of God is known within the context of the Zion tradition as well (see Ps. 48:12-14), yet the focus there is on God's deliverance which people are reminded of by looking at the stronghold Zion. Here the focus seems to be exclusively on holiness and the grandeur of the structure.

Chapters 43–46 are a revelatory temple tour like chapters 8–11 to which they form a positive counterpart.[51] While in chapters 8–11 the glory of God was leaving the temple, chapters 43–46 describe how YHWH takes possession of his new home and how thereby the temple complex of chapters 40–42 comes alive. In what must have been "the crown and consummation of Ezekiel's life's work"[52] Ezekiel, placed in the inner courtroom, sees the glory of God filling the temple and hears a voice declaring:

> "Son of man, the place of my throne and the place for the soles of my feet, where I will dwell in the midst of the people of Israel for ever — never again shall the house of Israel defile my holy name, neither they, nor their kings, by their whoring, and by the corpses of their kings, their "high places." When they placed their threshold by my threshold and their doorposts beside my doorposts, with only a wall between me and them, they were defiling my holy name with their abominations which they committed, so I have consumed them in my anger. Now let them keep away from me their idolatry and the corpses of their kings, and I will dwell in their midst for ever" (43:7-9).

The glory of God is once more in a sanctuary which can be defined in line with the Zion tradition as "the place of my throne and the place for the soles of my feet" (43:7).[53] Yet now, YHWH is determined to stay (cf.

50. This motif has roots in ancient Near Eastern iconography and texts. See Hurowitz, *I have built you an exalted House,* pp. 326f., where with reference to *Enuma Elish* IV 141-46 and Job 38:4-7 he points out (on p. 327) that the "surveying of a building site has been borrowed in the Mesopotamian and biblical traditions as a motif in creation stories."

51. Cf. D. I. Block, *The Book of Ezekiel,* New International Commentary on the Old Testament (Grand Rapids: Eerdmans, 1998). The connection with the two previous visions of the glory of God is made explicit in 43:3.

52. Levenson, *Theology,* p. 10.

53. Cf. H.-J. Fabry, "הדם," *Theological Dictionary of the Old Testament* 3: 325-34, esp. pp. 332ff.

44:1-4). The whole temple area is constructed in a way which will remove all possible defilements as far from YHWH as possible. In this way the structure of the temple complex reflects Israel's former sinful behavior.

> "You, son of man, describe the temple to the house of Israel. They are to measure the pattern, that they may be ashamed of their iniquities. When they are ashamed of all that they have done, make known to them the design of the temple, its arrangement, its exits and its entrances, yes its whole design and all its ordinances, its entire design and all its laws; and write it down in their sight, so that they may observe its entire design and all its ordinances — they shall follow them" (43:10f.).

To safeguard this holiness the altar and the offerings brought on the altar become very important (43:13-27). Furthermore, the gradations of holiness pertaining to the buildings and courts find expression also in different grades of holiness in the human sphere.[54] The organization of the temple personnel and the conditions for entrance of the sanctuary are strictly regulated.[55] Israel's ruler has an exalted and privileged position (even in the cult, see, e.g., 45:17!), yet in this theocracy he seems to be subordinated to the priests in the final analysis. Thus, jurisdiction is in the hands of the priests (44:24). The religious center of the land on the one hand and the political capital on the other hand are clearly distinguished with greater prominence given to the sacred center (ch. 45).[56]

Chapters 47–48 work out the relationship between the new sanctuary and the land. Here the Zion tradition provides the idea of a sacred stream which issues from the sanctuary and is an instrument of regeneration and transformation for the land.[57] The marvellous trees on either side of the river (47:7, 12) recall the Eden narrative.[58] Such a combination of Eden and Zion traditions is also seen in chapters 28 and 31 (see below).

54. I. M. Duguid speaks of a "buffer zone" mentality." See *Ezekiel and the Leaders of Israel* (Leiden: Brill, 1994), p. 129. Cf. also P. P. Jenson, *Graded Holiness: A Key to the Priestly Conception of the World,* JSOT Supplement 106 (Sheffield: JSOT Press, 1992).

55. Cf. Duguid, *Ezekiel,* pp. 75-90.

56. Cf. Duguid, *Ezekiel,* pp. 25-33, 40-43, 50-55.

57. Cf. Barker, *The Gate of Heaven,* pp. 86-89. Again, a similar claim had been made for Nippur, the sacred Babylonian city close to Ezekiel. See *ANET,* pp. 573ff.

58. Levenson, *Theology,* p. 32, suggests that Ezekiel's "stress on Eden traditions in his description of Zion is a way of reorientating the hopes of his audience from the east, where Eden had been thought to lie, to the west, the direction of Israel's future." Cf. Gaster, *Myth, Legend & Custom,* pp. 24ff.

The last verses of the book (48:30-35) underline the importance of the new city to which is given a new name which summarizes the characteristic feature of this new city: "YHWH is there" (יְהוָה שָׁמָּה *yhwh šāmmāh*). The new name maybe hints at "Jerusalem" (יְרוּשָׁלַ͏ִם *yĕrušalaim*), but the whole of chapters 40–48 mentions neither Jerusalem nor Zion by name and it has therefore been suggested that the writer of these chapters had another city in mind (e.g., Shechem for its position in the middle of the land). This is unlikely, yet it seems that the writer deliberately avoided using the term "Zion" and thereby mutes any suggestion of an inherent sanctity of this place. In fact, the vision could find fulfillment somewhere else. It is not the place which is important, but the presence of YHWH and the consequences this presence entails.[59]

C. Concerning the God of Israel

The Zion tradition did not locate the presence of God exclusively in Jerusalem. Yet Jerusalem was thought to be the place chosen to be the resting place of the glory of God, the center of YHWH's government, the place where his (earthly) palace and throne are. Thus, to see the glory of God in a vision outside Jerusalem and even outside the land of Israel would have been disturbing. The opening vision of the book of Ezekiel reports such a disturbing vision. It is a vision of God's glory, his throne and his heavenly chariot made up of living creatures similar to such creatures as stood in front of holy places and before the portals of Babylonian and Assyrian palaces. In chapter

---

59. Note that at least in the Christian era it was possible for some religious groups to transfer the complete Zion tradition to a different location. See N. I. Ndiokwere, *Prophecy and Revolution: The Role of Prophets in the Independent African Churches and in Biblical Tradition* (London: S.P.C.K., 1981). Cf. Appollonius's remarks about Montanus quoted in Eusebius, *Historia Ecclesiastica,* Book V, xviii, 1-2, Loeb Classical Library, *The Ecclesiastical History with an English Translation by Kirsopp Lake,* vol. 1 (London: Heinemann; Cambridge: Harvard University Press, 1959), pp. 486f.: "It is he who taught the annulment of marriage, who enacted fasts, *who gave the name of Jerusalem to Pepuza and Tymion,* which are little towns in Phrygia, and wished to hold assemblies there from everywhere . . ." (my emphasis). This might have been facilitated, however, by the prominence of the concept of a "New Jerusalem" in the New Testament, a concept which, however, seems to have been developed prior to the New Testament (see Porteous, "Jerusalem-Zion," pp. 251ff.). More specifically, P. Walker pointed out that the Montanists were probably influenced by the use of the "New Jerusalem" concept in the letter to Philadelphia in Revelation 3:7-13.

1 they are not yet identified as "cherubim,"[60] they are only identified as such retrospectively in 10:15, 20. By not yet identifying the "living creatures" in chapter 1 as "cherubim," the text seems to preserve the connection to Babylonian winged creatures (guardians of sanctuaries and palaces) as well as to the throne of God in Jerusalem. By pointing out that the Babylonian guardians are in fact subordinated to YHWH and form his throne, the text underlines that YHWH is in full control of the events to be described. While a description of YHWH's throne outside the land of Israel is surprising, it is only in chapter 10 that the divine throne becomes a divine chariot which stands in direct opposition to the Jerusalemite sanctuary. The vision at the Chebar canal could be interpreted as an expression of God's heavenly throne which does not necessarily stand in contrast to God's earthly throne in Jerusalem. The emphasis in chapter 10 is, however, directly on the mobility of God's presence. Cherubim are used not to fix God's throne in Jerusalem, but to form the chariot with which YHWH is free to come and go to Jerusalem (or, indeed, any other place) as he chooses.[61]

A positive affirmation of an earthly place of God's throne is to be found only in the last temple vision, which takes up Zion language by speaking about YHWH's footstool (43:7; see above). This verse along with others which guarantee God's future presence among the people returned from exile (cf. 37:27) knows of a time when the people of Israel will again live at the "navel of the earth" (38:12; cf. Judg. 9:37).[62] This reveals that God's presence is not spiritualized in the book of Ezekiel. There is no transition from a Jerusalem-bound to a universal deity. YHWH is affirmed in the book of Ezekiel to be a universal God, but he is also a God who will again take residence in the land of Israel. Thus, Haran's statement that

---

60. The Targum, however, makes this identification already in ch. 1. For "cherubim," see n. 14.

61. There seems to be an uneasy relationship in this chapter between the main narrative telling of God's glory leaving the temple and an emphasis on God's mobility (9:3a!). See F. L. Hossfeld, "Probleme einer ganzheitlichen Lektüre der Schrift, Dargestellt am Beispiel Ez 9–10," *Theologische Quartalschrift* 167 (1987): 266-77, esp. pp. 272ff.; cf. his "Die Tempelvision Ezek. 8-11 im Licht unterschiedlicher methodischer Zugänge," in J. Lust, ed., *Ezekiel and His Book: Textual and Literary Criticism and Their Interrelation,* Bibliotheca ephemeridum theologicarum lovaniensium 74 (Leuven: Leuven University Press, 1986), pp. 151-65. A major weakness of Hossfeld's solution seems to me that he does not relate his findings to the evidence in chs. 40–48.

62. Cf. Gaster, *Myth, Legend and Custom,* p. 428.

[t]he omission of the ark in Ezekiel's prophecy can easily be explained by the simple fact that by this time the ark no longer existed. . . . It can also be explained by the cosmic background of Ezekiel's vision, for the chariot which he sees wanders about the sky.[63]

is partly true, partly misleading. The best explanation of the omission of the ark still seems to be the assumption that the ark no longer existed.[64] If a rhetorical explanation is sought, it is not so much "the cosmic background of Ezekiel's vision" which does not allow speaking about the ark, but the emphasis laid in the book on the priority of God rather than the tangible signs of his presence. God will not return to Zion or the ark of his covenant, because Zion is a holy place and the ark a guarantee of his presence, but Zion will again be a holy place (if Zion it will be), because God will return to Zion. The best way to make sure that the priorities are right, seems to have been not to mention Zion at all in the restoration program.

Surprisingly maybe, two designations of God often used in connection with the Zion tradition are completely absent from the book: "(El) Elyon" which is used frequently in the Psalms (it occurs, however, only twice in Isaiah, once in Jeremiah), and "YHWH Zebaoth" (sixty-two times used in Isaiah, eighty-two instances in Jeremiah).[65] Especially the absence of the designation "YHWH Zebaoth" can hardly be accidental, even more so as it has been observed that "YHWH Zebaoth" is often used in connection with specific formulas which are used in the book of Ezekiel as well, however with the designation "Adonai YHWH," which is not very common outside the book of Ezekiel (Ezekiel accounts for 217 out of 283 occurrences of the designation). Thus, formulas such as כה אמר יהוה צבאות *(koh 'amar yhwh ṣᵉbā'ōt)* have been substituted in the book of Ezekiel through the corresponding formula with אדני יהוה *(ᵃdonay yhwh)*, i.e., in this case through כה אמר אדני יהוה *(koh 'amar ᵃdonay yhwh).*[66] In a wide-ranging examina-

---

63. Haran, *Temples and Temple Service in Ancient Israel,* pp. 249f.

64. Note that the ark is not mentioned either in the list of temple vessels transported to Babylon (2 Kings 25:13-17; Jer. 52:17-23).

65. The designation "Zebaoth" remains prominent in post-exilic prophetic literature: Haggai (14), Zechariah (53), and Malachi (24). Also in Ezekiel, YHWH is never designated מלך *(melek)* "king" (used in Isaiah four times, in Jeremiah once), but he is said in 20:33 to "rule" (מלך *mālak*) the future Israel.

66. F. Baumgärtel, "Zu den Gottesnamen in den Büchern Jeremia und Ezechiel," *Verbannung und Heimkehr, FS W. Rudolph,* pp. 1-29. Baumgärtel's attempt to eliminate all free uses, i.e., uses outside formulas, of יהוה צבאות *(yhwh ṣᵉbā'ōt)* and

tion of the two designations Baumgärtel suggested cautiously that for Ezekiel the designation "YHWH Zebaoth" was so much bound up with the ark in the temple that it became impossible for him to designate YHWH as "YHWH Zebaoth (who is enthroned over the cherubim)" after the destruction of the temple and the disappearance of the ark. Only after the exile, when the designation "YHWH Zebaoth" had become independent of the ark, was it possible to speak again of YHWH as "YHWH Zebaoth." It was not so much the disappearance of the ark as such which caused Ezekiel to abandon the use of "YHWH Zebaoth," since the same problem would have arisen for Jeremiah, but the close relationship between the designation "YHWH Zebaoth" and the affirmation of God's presence on Mt. Zion. The designation "YHWH Zebaoth" (and probably also "El Elyon") characterizes YHWH as being present on Mt. Zion. It is precisely in this area that Jeremiah and Ezekiel offer different perspectives. Jeremiah proclaims that "Jerusalem and Judah so angered YHWH that he expelled them from his presence" (Jer. 52:3); Ezekiel proclaims that Jerusalem and Judah so angered YHWH that he left the place and destroyed the city. For Jeremiah (and Isaiah) focusing on Zion was a way of focusing on YHWH and Zion was still a holy place:

> "Remember the LORD from afar, and let Jerusalem come into your mind: 'We are put to shame, for we have heard reproach; dishonor has covered our face, for aliens have come into the holy places of the LORD's house'" (Jer. 51:50b-51).

Yet for Ezekiel focusing one's mind on Jerusalem could distract from or even become a substitute for focusing on YHWH himself. Again the safest option seems to have been to avoid designations which characterize YHWH in terms of his presence on Mt. Zion.

D. Other Uses of the Zion Tradition

In chapters 28 and 31 the Eden traditions are connected with the Zion tradition. This seems to be an obvious step considering the features which the two traditions have in common such as "fabulous mineral wealth, great beauty, a miraculous stream, perhaps trees of greater than botanical

---

אדני יהוה (ǎdonay yhwh) in prophetic literature (apart from Proto-Isaiah) as secondary is, however, less convincing.

significance, and certainly the unmediated accessibility of God."[67] Yet the connection is spelled out more clearly in the book of Ezekiel than anywhere else (cf. Isa. 51:3).[68] In 28:11-15 the king of Tyre is portrayed as having lived "in Eden, the garden of God" (v. 11), "on God's holy mountain" (v. 14). Levenson has argued that the description of the ruler of Tyre is taken from the description of Zion in earlier literature (cf. also Ezek. 16:14).[69] The Zion tradition is here freely used to underline beauty, wealth, abundance, and privilege found in Tyre. With this relationship between Zion and Eden established, the connection to the Zion tradition is easily made, when in 31:1-9 again Eden language is used, now in an oracle concerned with Pharaoh king of Egypt, especially if one recognizes that the forest language used here as well was earlier employed in a thinly veiled oracle against Jerusalem (21:1-5 [ET 20:45-49]). The difference in the use of Zion and Eden traditions in chapters 28 and 31 on the one hand and chapters 40–48 on the other hand is of course that Tyre and Egypt represent "Paradise Lost," whereas the new sanctuary will represent "Paradise Regained." Rhetorically, the purpose of this use of Zion and Eden traditions seems to be to redirect Israel's hopes away from Tyre and Egypt, to the theological reality YHWH will create in the future, without actually denying the former attractiveness of Tyre and Egypt. Yet it does more than that. Use of these traditions is not only made in chapters 28 and 31 to emphasize Tyre's and Egypt's loss of Edenic qualities, but also to underline that even Tyre and Egypt could boast these qualities only due to YHWH's provision, a point made with regard to Jerusalem most explicitly in chapter 16.[70]

67. Levenson, *Theology,* p. 31. It is less clear than Levenson indicates that the Zion tradition actually contained all these elements, but one may infer this from the occurrence of these motifs in related divine mountain traditions. See esp. Clifford, *The Cosmic Mountain,* passim.

68. Levenson, *Theology,* argued that the presence of "Gihon" in Genesis 2:13 suggests that the connection was made prior to Ezekiel. The name "Gihon" ("the Gusher" or "the Bubbler") could have been widespread enough to warrant caution regarding an original connection between the Paradise river and the spring in Jerusalem. On the other hand some texts suggest that the Gihon in Jerusalem had more than natural significance for the Jerusalemites (see 1 Kings 1:32-45; Isa. 7:3-9; Ps. 46:5?).

69. Levenson, *Theology,* pp. 26f.

70. This is maybe further underlined through the emphasis on precious stones in 28:13 (cf. 27:22). Although Gaster claims that the description of Paradise as "a land of gold and gems" is characteristic for the folklore of many peoples (*Myth, Legend & Custom,* p. 28, thus, e.g., in the Mesopotamian Epic of Gilgamesh), it must be noted in

V. The Zion Tradition and the
Book of Ezekiel: Conclusion

The Zion tradition makes it possible to speak forcefully about the relationship between God's presence and a people's protection, between God's provision and a people's abundant wealth. From beginning to end the Zion tradition remains valid in the book of Ezekiel as a description of the consequences of God's presence for a people. With the emphasis in the book on God and Israel's dependence on the provision of God, the Zion tradition could hardly have been avoided. Yet, Ezekiel does not even shrink from utilizing the tradition in speaking about Tyre and Egypt.[71] In so far as the Zion tradition claims that the wealth and protection of Jerusalem are related to the presence of God in that place the Zion tradition was not demolished in the book of Ezekiel. In so far as the Zion tradition claims that God will always and under any circumstances be present in Zion, the tradition is rejected in the book. It is not clear whether such a claim was actually always made. It might thus be wise to speak of "Zion traditions" in the plural. The book of Ezekiel does not attempt to deny the Zion tradition, but to give it a specific interpretation, either by putting emphasis on the possibility of God abandoning Jerusalem (if this was regarded as a possibility, which was not spelled out explicitly), or by introducing a condition not known before. A similar uncertainty exists with regard to the relationship between the Zion tradition and politics. It is not entirely clear

---

the Old Testament precious stones provide also the link between the garden of Eden and Israel's sanctuary. See G. J. Wenham, "Sanctuary Symbolism in the Garden of Eden Story," in *Proceedings of the Ninth World Congress of Jewish Studies* (Jerusalem, 1986), pp. 19-25, esp. p. 22; reprinted in R. S. Hess and D. T. Tsumura, eds., *"I Studied Inscriptions from before the Flood": Ancient Near Eastern, Linguistic and Literary Approaches to Genesis 1–11,* Sources for Biblical and Theological Study 4 (Winona Lake, IN: Eisenbrauns, 1994), pp. 399-404. Note especially the שֹׁהַם (*šōham*) stone (Ezek. 28:13) which appears apart from Job 28:16 only in the context of Eden and the sanctuary. Cf. in the hymn to Enlil at Nippur: "The city is filled with splendour . . . the foundations (of the sanctuary) are made of lapis lazuli" (Weinfeld, "Zion and Jerusalem," p. 111).

71. Although divine mountain traditions were known in Babylonia as well (note especially the claims made for Nippur pointed out in previous footnotes), they are never applied to Babylonian locations in the book of Ezekiel. It seems that the application to Tyre and Egypt could be made only together with the claim that they are as doomed as Jerusalem. Ezekiel did not want to create an alternative focal point for the beliefs of the exiles in Tyre, Egypt, or any Babylonian location.

how political ideology was related to the Zion tradition before the exile, yet in the vision of the future the political is clearly distinguished from and subordinated to the religious.[72]

It is noteworthy in any case that the Zion tradition does not seem to provide a basis for restoration. If Zion will be restored and God will again dwell on Zion, then this will have the consequences spelled out in the Zion tradition, but the Zion tradition cannot guarantee that God will dwell on Zion. Here, the freedom of God is affirmed over, and maybe even against, the Zion tradition. In some respects, one can claim that the Zion tradition functions in a descriptive way rather than authoritatively. While it is affirmed that the raging of the nations against Zion will not succeed in the future (chapters 38–39), it did succeed in the past (7:24). It is thus not the Zion tradition which guarantees Israel's protection, but YHWH's presence and his determination to protect his people. Like "the staff of reed" Egypt (29:6), the Zion tradition provided a danger to Israel, as soon as trust in Zion became an alternative to trust in YHWH. Yet, when YHWH is the center of Israel, the Zion tradition is well capable of explaining what this might mean for a people.

Appendix: Possible Ways of Conceptualizing the Use of the Zion Tradition in Ezekiel

A. Through a Distinction between Basic Affirmations and Related Beliefs

One way of conceptualizing the use of the Zion tradition in the book of Ezekiel is to distinguish within the Zion tradition a kernel consisting of basic affirmations from related beliefs which were developed out of the basic affirmations. One could surmise that popular belief interpreted the basic affirmations positively, while in Ezekiel the same basic affirmations are related to negative consequences for Jerusalem, e.g.,

72. Note that the world created in chs. 37ff. culminates in something more akin to a closed paradise than an empire. This is in contrast to, e.g., Isaiah 40–55, which has been explored under the aspect of nationalism by D. C. T. Sheriffs, "'A Tale of Two Cities' — Nationalism in Zion and Babylon," *Tyndale Bulletin* 39 (1988): 19-57.

basic affirmation	related positive belief	related negative belief
God subdues chaos	fighting against the nations	fighting against Zion
Zion is the center	of YHWH's protection	of YHWH's judgment

B. Through an Understanding of the Zion Tradition as a Set of Beliefs Which Came into Conflict with One Another

A different way of conceptualizing Ezekiel's use of the Zion tradition is to assume that in Ezekiel's view the Zion tradition was no longer capable of presenting a coherent worldview due to Jerusalem's disobedience to her creator and protector. Thus, the Zion tradition came to affirm conflicting statements. Some statements had to be given up to uphold others, e.g.,

YHWH, is present on Zion, the divine mountain	and	YHWH, the creator of the cosmos, subdues chaos
YHWH protects Zion	and	YHWH protects order

Since YHWH cannot protect order and Zion at the same time, a decision has to be made. In Ezekiel it is affirmed that YHWH would rather protect order than Zion, that he would continue to subdue chaos even at the cost of destroying Jerusalem.

C. Through an Understanding of the Positive Statements about Zion as Conditional on the People's Fellowship with God

This understanding would highlight the historical nature of YHWH's election of Zion (cf. especially Ezek. 16) and the affirmation that only acceptable worship provides access to YHWH. As long as acceptable worship was offered "on the highest mountain," the Zion tradition retained its full validity, yet after the desecration of this holy place through idolatry, the Zion tradition was no longer a reliable guide to reality. One would not necessarily have to assume that the conditionality of the Zion tradition was a feature unknown before Ezekiel, but according to this conceptualization the conditionality would have become more emphasized with Ezekiel.

D. By Regarding the Zion Tradition as a Flexible Instrument Which in Different Hands Can Do Many Things to Many People

The closest parallel might be the temple itself: an edifice which could tell many wonderful things about YHWH or just be "a den of thieves," a place where one could approach God in worship or offend him most effectively through idolatry. According to this model, the Zion tradition is a vehicle for truth rather than "absolute" truth itself (i.e., truth unrelated to a specific context). This option might be closest to option (C) indicating that the Zion tradition is true only in a given set of circumstances, but it makes room also for the insight of option (B) that particular beliefs related to the Zion tradition might come in conflict with one another and ultimately cause the breakdown of the Zion tradition as a coherent set of beliefs, and it finally allows to affirm the conviction expressed with option (A) that there remain some basic truths which no amount of mishandling can falsify. It seems that in Ezekiel's view these basic truths are truths about YHWH rather than truths about Zion. To express those truths about YHWH Ezekiel activates certain parts of the Zion tradition, while other parts of the tradition remain inactive.

Zion in the Songs of Ascents

PHILIP E. SATTERTHWAITE

The Songs of Ascents, which share the same title and have numerous other features in common, are also linked by a unifying theme — YHWH's restoration of Zion. The Songs of Ascents, most likely a pilgrim collection, have been structured as a series of prayers on different aspects of this theme. The collection as a whole re-affirms YHWH's choice of Zion and David, but is also notable for the variety of moods it expresses: commitment to the God who has chosen Zion may be a source of hope and joy, but it can also provoke hostility from outsiders and bring doubt and anguish for those who long to see Zion restored.

I. Introduction

The Songs of Ascents (Pss. 120–134), marked out as a separate group in the Psalter by the title which stands at the head of each of them (המעלות שיר, "A Song of Ascents"), have in common a number of other features which might suggest that they are a literary, or at least a redactional, unity.[1] Apart from Psalm 132 they are all roughly the same length. They

---

1. E. Beaucamp has helpfully summarized these features in his commentary on the Songs of Ascents in *Le Psautier, Vol. 2, Ps 73–150* (Paris: Gabalda, 1979), pp. 233-

105

share certain linguistic features:[2] unfamiliar words or spellings of words;[3] unusual phrases;[4] distinctive and/or frequent uses of some particles,[5] prepositions,[6] and adverbs.[7] They share certain poetic techniques: the use of key-words;[8] "terrace patterns" (in which an element at the end of one line is taken up by the beginning of the next line, and sometimes occupies the whole of the next line);[9] and the linking of successive lines by beginning them with the same word or phrase.[10] Linkages between lines have to

---

55, esp. pp. 239-47. His article, "L'unité du recueil des montées. Psaumes 120–134," *Studii Biblici Franciscani* 29 (1979): 73-90, is a slightly altered version of pp. 239-55 of his commentary.

2. Beaucamp, *Le Psautier,* pp. 239-40. See also the table of "Unusual Linguistic Features in the Songs of Ascents," in L. D. Crow, *The Songs of Ascents (Psalms 120–134): Their Place in Israelite History and Religion,* Society of Biblical Literature Dissertation Series 148 (Atlanta: Scholars Press, 1996), pp. 148-49.

3. E.g., שחברה־לה (Ps. 122:3); אזי (Ps. 124:3-5); משך (Ps. 126:6); שנא (Ps. 127:2).

4. E.g., אצמיח קרן (Ps. 132:17); יציץ נזרו (Ps. 132:18); שבטי־יה (Ps. 122:4); עון as the object of שמר, and in the phrase והוא יפדה את־ישראל מכל עונתיו (Ps. 130:8).

5. E.g., affirmative כי (Pss. 120:7; 122:5; 125:3; 128:2, 4; 130:4, 7; 132:14; 133:3); הנה (Pss. 121:4; 123:2; 127:3; 128:4; 132:6; 133:1; 134:1); ־ש has almost entirely replaced אשר in the Songs of Ascents (־ש occurs at Pss. 122:4; 123:2; 124:1, 2, 6; 129:6, 7; 133:2, 3; אשר at Pss. 127:5; 132:5).

6. E.g., ל used for the ethic dative (Pss. 120:6; 122:3; 123:4; 132:12, 13).

7. E.g., רבת (Pss. 120:6; 123:4; 129:1, 2).

8. This is true at the level of the individual Psalms of Ascents: e.g., שמר in Psalm 121; שלום in Psalm 122; חנן in Psalm 123; the puns on בן/בית/בנה in Psalm 127; ברך in Psalm 134. It is also true across the entire collection, to the extent that L. J. Leibreich was able to suggest that the collection as a whole has been influenced by the language of the priestly blessing in Numbers 6:24-26; see "The Songs of Ascents and the Priestly Blessing," *Journal of Biblical Literature* 74 (1955): 33-36.

9. E.g., לשון רמיה (Ps. 120:2-3); שכן (Ps. 120:5-6); שלום (Ps. 120:6-7); ינום (Ps. 121:3-4); ירושלם (Ps. 122:2-3); פח (Ps. 124:7a/b); הגדיל יהוה לעשות עם (Ps. 126:2-3); in Psalm 126:5-6 the two halves of v. 5 are successively developed by the two lines of v. 6; שוא (Ps. 127:1-2); יפדה and פדות (Ps. 130:7-8). For a treatment of the characteristic uses of terrace patterns, see W. G. E. Watson, *Classical Hebrew Poetry. A Guide to its Techniques,* JSOT Supplement 26 (Sheffield: JSOT Press, 1984), pp. 208-13.

10. E.g., לולי (Ps. 124:1-2); אזי (Ps. 124:3-5); אז (Ps. 126:2); אם־יהוה לא (Ps. 127:1a/b); וראה (Ps. 128:5-6); רבת (Ps. 129:1-2); ירד . . . כשמן and שירד . . . כטל (Ps. 133:2-3). Some of these cases are examples of "staircase parallelism" (see Watson, *Classical Hebrew Poetry,* pp. 150-56).

a considerable extent displaced parallelism within the line as a generator of poetic movement in the Songs of Ascents.[11]

Further shared features may be noted: while some of the Songs seem at first sight to fit into recognized psalm-genres, they turn out, on closer examination, to diverge from these genres in significant ways.[12] Some of the Songs have a dialogic structure, or mix singular and plural voices (Pss. 121, 122, 123, 128, 134). If one considers the arrangement of the Songs of Ascents, the geographical shift towards Jerusalem in the opening three (Pss. 120–122), taken along with the increasingly clear focus on worship in the temple in the last three (Pss. 132-34), suggests an attempt to underscore a leading theme by means of structure. The six "repeated formulae" identified by Crow have a similar effect.[13] Both Eerdmans and Beaucamp have suggested that the Songs only make full sense when read in succession, a point which this essay also aims to demonstrate.[14]

Finally, and following on from this, it will be argued that the strongest unifying feature in the Songs of Ascents is a shared theme. This may be summed up as: "The Restoration of Zion: YHWH's Purposes for Her." Not that this theme is made explicit in all the Songs of Ascents, but that it defines the underlying issue which all the Songs in different ways address. Linked to the portrayal of Zion as a focus of YHWH's purposes is a view of the community which gathers in Zion to worship YHWH as "Israel."[15]

11. Beaucamp, *Le Psautier,* p. 242. This point should not be exaggerated: Pss. 121:3, 5; 122:5, 7 are all clear examples of poetic parallelism.

12. Beaucamp, *Le Psautier,* p. 244. This is a point which also emerges from L. C. Allen's discussions of the genre of the individual Songs: see his comments on each of the Songs under "Form/ Structure/Setting," in *Psalms 101–150* (Waco: Word, 1983).

13. *Songs of Ascents,* pp. 130-31. For Crow's position see discussion below.

14. B. D. Eerdmans, *The Hebrew Book of Psalms,* Oudtestamentische Studiën 4 (Leiden: Brill, 1947), pp. 548-71, esp. 555-56, and cf. Beaucamp, *Le Psautier,* p. 243: "le sens enfin de chaque morceau s'éclaire par la place qu'il occupe dans le recueil."

15. The term ישראל is used in two main senses in the Songs of Ascents. Firstly, the term at times denotes a group which has gathered on Zion to worship, who are using these Songs in their worship and are directly addressed by this term (Pss. 124:1; 129:1; 130:7; 131:3); these worshippers are presumably representative of a larger number who acknowledge Zion as YHWH's chosen "resting-place" (Ps. 132:14) and David's descendant as his chosen king (Ps. 132:11, 17-18). Secondly, at Ps. 122:4 Israel is identified as "the tribes of Yahweh" who (at an earlier period) all came to worship on Zion. There are a number of other passages where it is not clear whether the narrower definition (those who worship on Zion) or the wider ("tribes of Yahweh") applies (Pss. 121:4; 125:5; 128:6; 130:8). If one takes these references together, they suggest a view of those who

What follows is an attempt, firstly, to probe the apparent unity of the Songs of Ascents more deeply; and, secondly, to present a reading of the Songs of Ascents which examines how Zion is presented in them, focusing on the differing moods and emotions expressed by those whose allegiance is to the God who "has chosen Zion" (Ps. 132:13).

II. Literary-Critical Issues in the Songs of Ascents

The basis of this essay is the view that the Songs of Ascents form a diverse but coherent whole, addressing different topics, using a number of different images, and reflecting different perspectives and moods, but all setting out aspects of one main theme and all in different ways enjoining devotion to Zion and to the God who has made Zion his dwelling-place. The reading of the Songs of Ascents offered in Section IV supports this view.

But what is the literary history of this collection? If it is a "coherent whole," what is the nature of this coherence? In particular, were the Songs composed in one historical context, and always intended to stand together as a collection? Or do some of the Songs derive from a different context (in which case the surface unity of the collection has been brought about by a subsequent redaction)? It is worth exploring this question further, in order to clarify the approach to the Songs of Ascents underlying this essay. The recent study by Crow helpfully pulls together many of the arguments advanced by those who have argued for the presence of redactional layers in the Songs of Ascents, and forms a useful starting point.[16] Crow's theory may be summarized as follows:

(i) The nucleus of the Songs of Ascents was a collection of psalms (Pss. 120; 123:1-4b; 124:1-7; 125:3-5a; 126; 127; 128:1-4; 129:1-4, 6-8; 130:1-6; 131:1-2), north Israelite in origin, which addressed the concerns of individuals or at the most those of small communities or towns. These included injustices suffered by individuals or a small group, family welfare, fertility, the prosperity of one's town, and so on.[17] The latest parts of this collection must be dated to the late sixth century B.C.[18]

---

worship on Zion as both the remnant of a once larger entity and potentially the nucleus of a larger restored Israel. This point is taken up in the Conclusion.

16. For bibliographical details, see n. 2.

17. *Songs of Ascents,* pp. 145-54. See, for example, the treatments of Pss. 124, 126, 127, and 128 in the chapter "Exegesis of the Songs of Ascents," pp. 29-128.

18. *Songs of Ascents,* pp. 152-54, 167-69.

(ii) In this nucleus there is no anticipatory stance toward war, at least none which ascribed any theological or political significance to Zion.[19] The copious references to Zion which are now such a distinguishing feature of the Songs of Ascents are due to a subsequent redaction. This involved, on the one hand, the insertion into the original nucleus of six formulae which recur throughout the collection ("Maker of heaven and earth," Pss. 121:2; 124:8; 134:3; "from now on and for ever," Pss. 121:8; 125:2; 131:3; "let Israel say," Pss. 124:1; 129:1; "peace on Israel," Pss. 125:5; 128:6; "YHWH bless you from Zion," Pss. 128:5; 134:3; "let Israel hope in YHWH," Pss. 130:7; 131:3);[20] and, yet more significantly, the addition of five whole psalms, 121 and 122 at the beginning, 132–134 at the end.[21] These additional psalms made the themes of Zion and David the new focus of the collection; not merely by their content, but also by the movement from diaspora to Zion which they imposed upon the whole collection.

(iii) The effect of this redaction was to "nationalize" the personal or municipal concerns of the nucleus, to tie hopes for local prosperity to the welfare of Zion.[22] The main aim of the redactors was to address an appeal for loyalty to Zion particularly to those of northern Israelite descent, by suggesting that the best way for them to achieve their personal or communal goals was by seeking Jerusalem's well-being. This aim is perhaps most explicit in Psalm 133; but it is also implicit in the use of a "northern" nucleus as the basis of a collection which now urges devotion to (southern) Zion.[23]

(iv) Thus Crow accepts the view that the Songs of Ascents were a "pilgrim collection." In contrast to some previous approaches, however, the main plank of Crow's argument is not the ambiguous heading שׁיר המעלות but the content of the Songs.[24] He makes the further suggestion that the (southern) redactors "sometimes made use of local religious traditions to support centralisation of power."[25]

19. *Songs of Ascents*, p. 153.
20. *Songs of Ascents*, pp. 130-43.
21. *Songs of Ascents*, pp. 143-45.
22. *Songs of Ascents*, pp. 182-86.
23. Crow believes that northern traditions were similarly used in some of the psalms added as part of the Zion redaction, most notably Psalm 132. On this, see also G. A. Rendsburg, *Linguistic Evidence for the Northern Origin of Selected Psalms*, SBLMS 43 (Atlanta: Scholars Press, 1990), pp. 87-93, who argues for the northern provenance of Pss. 132 and 133.
24. *Songs of Ascents*, p. 182; see also pp. 1-27 for Crow's discussion of previous interpretations of the title.
25. *Songs of Ascents*, p. 187.

There is much of value in this thorough and detailed study. Many of Crow's conclusions seem plausible. There probably are "northern" linguistic usages in the Songs.[26] The effect of the collection in its final form is indeed to link the personal and the national. It is right to highlight the role of the six formulae, which play an important part in shaping the ideology of the collection as a whole. Finally, Crow's view of the aims of those responsible for the collection may well be correct.

More doubtful is Crow's reconstruction of an earlier nucleus in which Zion and David figured not at all. Questions may be raised, firstly, concerning Crow's literary-critical criteria for isolating and removing the phrases he identifies as redactional. Meter, for example, is a matter on which more than one view is always possible.[27] In some cases, the removal of phrases as redactional seems to destroy literary artistry: an example is the phrase יאמר־נא ישראל ("let Israel say") in Psalm 124:1-2 and Psalm 129:1-2.[28]

Second, is it true that the psalms Crow identifies as constituting the northern nucleus of the collection are only concerned with individual and local issues? "Israelite" issues seem to run through some of the "nucleus" psalms, too.[29] One example, Psalm 126, is dealt with at some length and other examples more briefly.

26. *Songs of Ascents,* pp. 160-62.

27. Cf. Beauchamp, *Le Psautier,* p. 241: ". . . on ne peut supposer, en ce qui concerne la longueur des vers, des normes rigides de composition. L'argument du rhythme, en conséquence, ne saurait être allégué qu'avec bien des réserves. . . ."

28. Crow does not make it entirely clear whether or not he regards this phrase as redactional: his table "Summary of Nucleus and Redactional Materials in the Songs of Ascents" (p. 146) describes all of Psalms 124:1 and 129:1, without qualification, as *pre*-redactional verses; but on p. 141 he finds it likely that all six of the repeated formulae belong to the Jerusalemite redaction. On aesthetic grounds I find this second alternative hard to accept, at least if the implication is that יאמר־נא ישראל (or perhaps the whole of Pss. 124:1 and 129:1?) can easily be detached from their present position. The beginnings of both Ps. 124 and Ps. 129 have a similar structure, using repeated phrases to build up to a "punch-line," respectively אזי חיים בלעונו (Ps. 124:3, extended into vv. 4-5) and גם לא־יכלו לי (Ps. 129:2). In my view the phrase יאמר־נא ישראל is necessary (among other reasons) to delay this "punch-line" and thus build appropriate tension (Watson, *Classical Hebrew Poetry,* pp. 153-54, identifies the building of tension as one of the functions of "staircase parallelism").

29. In the following discussion I use the terms "Israel" and "Israelite" with same range of meanings that the term ישראל has in the Songs of Ascents (see n. 15): "Israelite issues" are issues relating, in the first instance, to the concerns of the entire community which worships on Zion and recognizes YHWH's choice of Zion, but relating, secondarily, to the concerns of a potentially larger Israel.

Crow regards Psalm 126, all of which he allocates to his earlier nucleus, as a prayer made by an Israelite community (not Zion) in the light of what they saw as a previous reversal in Zion's fortunes. The prayer simply concerned rains and fertility, and the "reversal of fortune" (v. 4) which would match that recently experienced by Zion (v. 1) would be good crops.[30] Crow thinks it likely that the reversal of Zion's fortunes referred to in v. 1 is not the return from exile in Babylon, though he does not completely rule out this possibility.[31] He is in any case clear that, whatever is denoted by v. 1, the concerns of the community among whom Psalm 126 originated were exclusively agricultural. Accordingly, the language of v. 4 (wadis running with water) and vv. 5-6 (sowing and reaping) is to be taken at face value: "the psalm is primarily that of individual Israelite landowners, whose fate is almost wholly determined by whether crops will be abundant or scarce."[32]

This is hard to accept. In order to explain how the speakers in Psalm 126 could rejoice in Zion's restoration while not belonging to Zion, Crow argues that they "felt themselves to have a claim on" Zion's prosperity.[33] But one surely has to go further than that: vv. 1-3 imply an *identification* of the speakers with those who experienced Zion's "reversal of fortune." Would the nations say of the speakers "YHWH has done great things for them" (v. 2; a claim the speakers acknowledge as true in v. 3) if the speakers were simply spectators of Zion's restoration, albeit with some stake in Zion's fortunes? By implication, then, these same speakers ask in v. 4 that they may again experience such a reversal of fortunes, one at which the nations will again marvel.[34] Good crops were, of course, important for an-

30. *Songs of Ascents,* pp. 59-66, 153, 165-67.

31. *Songs of Ascents,* p. 61, n. 47, p. 65, and especially p. 153: "Psalm 126 is a petition that agricultural prosperity extend, not just to Zion, but to the present community as well."

32. *Songs of Ascents,* p. 64. Crow argues, further, that the connection of weeping and fertility in vv. 5-6 may suggest a fertility rite like the weeping for Tammuz referred to at Ezekiel 8:14 (pp. 165-66). This could provide support for the view that fertility and crops are the main focus of the psalm, and also for the view that the nucleus psalms at points reflect non-Jerusalemite religious practices (a point Crow also makes in connection with Psalm 123, where he argues that female participation in worship and the use of female imagery for God are "almost certainly" not Jerusalemite usages [pp. 50-51]).

33. *Songs of Ascents,* p. 65.

34. Crow argues against the identification of the speakers of Ps. 126 with those who experienced Zion's restoration on the grounds that the speakers would not then

cient agrarian societies: but surely these verses imply a rather more momentous reversal of fortunes, and one that might extend to Israel as a
whole? The language of sowing and reaping in vv. 5-6 may, in fact, be
taken as a synecdoche for further restoration of Zion's fortunes. If one is
able to sow and reap, that implies occupancy of land: hence "sowing and
reaping" can be symbolic of YHWH's blessing Israel as a whole, this connection being made several times in the Old Testament.[35] So here, while
Psalm 126:5-6 likely enough does have real sowing and reaping partly in
view, the particular form here given to the *topos* (sowing in *tears* and
reaping in *joy*) is also an intelligible means by which to express the hope
that Israel's perseverance under unfavorable circumstances will result in
YHWH's blessing. The scope of these verses is national (to the extent that
the Israel of the Songs of Ascents is a nation), not local.

Similar arguments may be advanced concerning the suggestion that
Psalms 124 and 129 were in their original forms the prayers of, respectively, a group and an individual experiencing enmity, and did not have Israel as a whole in view. The language of these psalms could equally well
be used to describe Israel's history.[36]

Lastly, it is hard to believe that Psalm 127 can speak of a house in
whose building YHWH must be involved and of a city which YHWH
must watch over without any reference being intended to the temple, or to
Jerusalem.[37] The suggestion that Jerusalem and the temple are in view is
reinforced by the fact that the pun on בנה ("build") בית ("house," "temple") and בן ("son") found in Psalm 127 also occurs at 2 Samuel 7 and
1 Kings 8 (especially vv. 13-20), which both relate to the building of Solomon's temple.

In general, there is no need to follow Crow in polarizing and set-

---

still pray for restoration: "verses 1-3 [refer] to a restoration of Zion's prosperity . . . in
the past, not the future; and it is not stated that this situation has changed" (*Songs of
Ascents,* p. 65). I would turn this argument on its head: the fact that the speakers need
to make the prayer in v. 4 is itself evidence that the situation *has* changed, and, hence,
that it is a *further* divine intervention that they have in view.

35. Compare the variations on the theme of "sowing and eating" at Deut. 6:11;
28:33; Josh. 24:13; Jer. 29:5; Amos 5:11; 9:14; Zeph. 1:13. Ps. 128:2 applies this idea
(which, in its positive form, may be stated as: obedience brings blessing = enjoying the
fruits of one's labor) at an individual level.

36. Contra Crow, *Songs of Ascents,* pp. 81-85, 155; K. Seybold, *Die Wallfahrtspsalmen. Studien zur Entstehungsgeschichte von Psalm 120–134* (Neukirchen-Vluyn:
Neukirchener, 1978), pp. 27-29. See the comments on Psalms 124 and 129 below.

37. Contra Crow, *Songs of Ascents,* pp. 68-71.

ting over against each other different parts of the Songs of Ascents. Those parts which he assigns to a northern nucleus can be read in such a way that their themes and concerns are fully compatible with those parts which he attributes to a later redaction.[38] It is ultimately impossible to be certain about the history of this collection. Some of the Songs may have existed before the collection came into being (Pss. 122, 127, or 132–134, perhaps), but it seems to me equally possible that all the Songs were composed at roughly the same time, in response to one historical context. It may well be that the Songs were always designed to stand together as a series of prayers on aspects of a common theme.[39] Certainty, as stated, is impossible, but this seems to me as plausible a view as any other.[40]

Accordingly, the Songs of Ascents can be regarded as displaying a more thoroughgoing coherence and unity than might seem plausible if the Songs of Ascents were clearly a redacted collection. This is reflected, for example, in the suggestion in Section IV concerning the use of different grammatical voices both to link Songs and to mark disjunctions between them (the Songs of Ascents at different points use all the persons: first, second, and third; and singular and plural). The same applies to my arguments concerning the sequence of emotions expressed in the collection. Given this view of the likely origins of the Songs of Ascents, it seems reasonable to treat these aspects as significant; it would be less reasonable to do so given a view of the origins of the collection such as Crow's.

A similar integrative approach may be applied to other features of the Songs of Ascents. Thus, references to "we" or "you" (plural) in the

38. Similar points can be made with regard to the analysis offered by Seybold, *Die Wallfahrtspsalmen.* Though Seybold's analysis differs from Crow's on points of detail, his view of the redactors' general intentions is rather similar to Crow's.

39. This is the view of Beaucamp: "[Ces cantiques] constituent, dès le départ, un tout unifié; aucune des pièces, figurant là, ne paraît avoir existé indépendamment des autres; et toutes semblent avoir été crées pour entrer dans le recueil" (*Le Psautier,* p. 243).

40. The presence of northern linguistic elements in a collection which, taken as a whole, is clearly pro-Zion cannot be used as an argument that the collection is composite. An alternative explanation might be that the Songs were composed by an Israelite of northern descent who had come to accept the primacy of Jerusalem and David, and was acting as propagandist for this viewpoint. Compare the somewhat similar approach of Rendsburg, *Linguistic Evidence,* pp. 90, 93 (on Pss. 132 and 133). Crow (*Songs of Ascents,* pp. 160-61) notes that ‏שֶׁ‎ occurs in (what are in his view) redactional materials as well as in his nucleus.

Songs of Ascents can always be interpreted as denoting a group that may plausibly be termed "Israel" (as represented by those who have gathered in Zion to worship). Similarly, the frequent juxtaposition in the Songs of Ascents of first singular and first plural voices (as in Pss. 122, 123, 129, 130, and 131) may be seen as part of a wider tendency in these psalms to relate the experiences of individual Israelites to the fortunes of Israel as a whole (in the Songs of Ascents, it seems to me, individuals usually speak with an awareness that they are part of a wider "Israel").[41] On a different level, if similar images occur in separate psalms, one should ask if they are connected.[42] Lastly, the "repeated formulae" and other lines or half-lines sometimes seen as redactional can in general be shown to fit their contexts well: at more than one point they seem to provide the necessary completion of a developing train of thought.[43]

III. Possible Historical Backgrounds

The preceding section has argued for a high degree of literary coherence in the Songs of Ascents, but has said little about possible historical contexts in which the collection may have originated.

It is likely that the Songs of Ascents, as has been argued by a number of scholars, form a pilgrimage collection.[44] That is, they were used, most likely in Jerusalem, perhaps in the course of a procession to the temple, during a festival when the worshippers would include a significant proportion of people who had travelled from outside Jerusalem to be there. The title Songs of Ascents would, on this understanding, refer in the first instance to a procession up to the temple,[45] with perhaps a secondary allusion to the fact that many had "come up" to Jerusalem from further afield,

41. The simile in Psalm 123, in which Israel waiting for YHWH to intervene is likened to slaves/maid waiting for master/mistress, has a similar effect of mingling individual and collective language. Compare also those passages where the blessing of the God of Israel is invoked on individuals, addressed in the second person (Pss. 121:3-4; 128:5-6; 134:3).

42. Examples would be images of sowing and reaping in Pss. 126, 128, and 129; and the references to watchmen in Pss. 127:1 and 130:6.

43. See the detailed comments in Section IV on Pss. 124:8; 129:5; 130:7-8; 131:3.

44. See the survey in Crow, *Songs of Ascents,* pp. 23-25.

45. The possible alternative rendering "Songs of Steps" is also compatible with this.

for whom this procession would represent the concluding stage of a longer journey. As pilgrimages are, in an obvious way, focused on the place of pilgrimage, a theme such as "The Restoration of Zion" would be highly appropriate for a pilgrimage collection.

Why "The *Restoration* of Zion"? This aspect, of course, is most clearly expressed at Psalm 126:4: "Restore our fortunes, YHWH" (cf. v. 1). But it is also plain elsewhere in the Songs of Ascents that Zion, and those who worship YHWH on Zion, are in straitened circumstances. Psalm 125 appears to sketch a situation in which part of the land of Israel is under enemy occupation, and the appeal in Psalm 132:1 to "remember David" suggests that David's descendant now rules over a weakened and reduced kingdom, or perhaps no longer has a kingdom to rule over.

The collection could have originated in the post-exilic period.[46] The reference in Psalm 126:1 to a time when "YHWH restored the fortunes of Zion" could denote return from the Babylonian exile.[47] The circumstances described in Psalms 120 and 125 could well be those of the post-exilic period. Psalm 127 could be interpreted as speaking about the post-exilic *re*building of temple and city. More generally, the note of longing for YHWH to intervene which runs through several of the Songs of Ascents (Pss. 120, 123, 126, 130–132) would suit the post-exilic period well. Some have felt that the historical context evoked by the Songs of Ascents (and by Psalms 123 and 125 in particular) is reminiscent of the situation described in the book of Nehemiah:[48] some significant rebuilding has been accomplished, but enemy rule is still to be reckoned with, and there are hostile neighbors.

None of the above arguments are decisive, however. שוב שבות is an ambiguous expression: the reference to return from captivity which is clear in some of the uses of the phrase may be a secondary development in

46. As argued, for example, by Seybold, *Die Wallfahrtspsalmen,* p. 75; Crow, *Songs of Ascents,* pp. 169-74.

47. So, e.g., Allen, *Psalms 101–150,* ad loc.

48. A point made as early as [Anon], "The Songs of Degrees," *Journal of Sacred Literature* 6 (n.s.) (October 1854): 39-53. Among the more convincing parallels between the Songs of Ascents and the book of Nehemiah suggested by this author are the following: mockery by enemies (Ps. 123:4; Neh. 2:19; 3:33-37 [Eng 4:1-5]); the three-fold division between righteous Israelites, their enemies, and Israelites who are implicated along with these enemies (Ps. 125:5; Neh. 6:17-19); recognition by outsiders that YHWH has been at work in Israel (Ps. 126:2; Neh. 6:16); rebuilding work that continues from dawn till evening, under the protection of watchmen (Ps. 127:1-2; Neh. 4:3 [9], 15-17 [21-23]; cf. the reference to watchmen at Neh. 7:3).

the usage of a phrase which at an earlier stage could denote other "reversals of fortune."[49] The references in Psalm 125 could, for example, be to the seventh-century Assyrian occupation of Judah: as Beaucamp notes, "rien ne ressemble à une guerre comme une autre guerre, à une destruction comme une autre destruction."[50] He suggests that the original pilgrims who sang the Songs of Ascents were survivors of the northern tribes, recently liberated from Assyrian domination at the time of Josiah, and awaiting a further revival of the fortunes of the house of David.[51] In his view the references in Psalm 122:5 ("the thrones of the house of David") and Psalm 132:10 ("do not turn away the face of your anointed") imply that a David is still reigning, and thus point to a pre-exilic date.

This view in turn, however, goes beyond the evidence: the references in Psalms 122:5 and 132:10 are not clearly pre-exilic (122:5 may be a reference to the past, and 132:10 is not specific about the present situation of YHWH's anointed) and in any case are not decisive for the date of the collection as whole. In general, though the Songs of Ascents make it clear what *kind* of situation Zion and those who worship on Zion find themselves in, they are ambiguous as to the precise historical background. Although a post-exilic dating for the collection is favored, nothing can conclusively demonstrate this.[52] Whether or not the collection originally

49. See R. Borger, "Zu שׁוּב שׁבוּ/ית," *Zeitschrift für die alttestamentliche Wissenschaft* 66 (1954): 315-16; M. Ben-Yashar, M. Zipor, "שְׁבוּת/שְׁבִית," *Theologische Wörterbuch zum Alten Testament* VII, 958-65; I. Willi-Plein, "*ŠWB ŠBWT* — eine Wiedererwägung," *Zeitschrift für die Althebräistik* 4 (1991): 55-71. The phrase שׁוּב שׁבית/שׁבות is frequently attested, and seems to involve a play on two linked ideas in many of the passages where it is used in reference to Israel or Judah (e.g., Jer. 32:44; 33:26; Ezek. 16:53; 39:25; Joel 4[3]:1): (a) YHWH's "turning back" to his people, or (what amounts to the same thing) YHWH's "restoring the fortunes" of his people; (b) YHWH's "bringing back the captives" of his people. But we should not assume that this double connotation was originally intended at every passage where this phrase occurs.

50. *Le Psautier*, p. 247.

51. *Le Psautier*, pp. 251-52. He compares the oracles concerning the restoration of Israel in Jer. 30–31 and notes that the ideas of the Songs of Ascents fit with the aims of the deuteronomic reform.

52. This includes the unusual linguistic features of the collection. On this, cf. Beaucamp, *Le Psautier*, p. 242: "Des particularités stylistiques, aussi fortement marquées, constituent un argument sérieux en faveur de l'unité de l'oeuvre. Elles ne portent pourtant pas la marque d'une époque déterminée, et n'aident guère à la dater. Les quelques traits d'aramaïsme qu'on y relève, l'emploi du lamed par exemple, ne sont pas décisifs."

came into being in the post-exilic period, it would have been highly appropriate for use during that period.

IV. Perspectives on Zion in the Songs of Ascents

In what follows the Songs of Ascents are dealt with in groups of three. Each triad is also presented under a heading which seems to encapsulate a leading theme of that triad. These are both to some extent rationalizations for ease of presentation. The schema adopted finds some justification in the fact that the opening and closing three psalms do seem to form distinct groups.[53] It also has the advantage that it gives due weight to the major progression in the Songs of Ascents (from enemy lands to temple, from alienation to blessing and worship in the temple), but also takes account of continuities and, at points, striking contrasts of mood between the individual Songs (one of the advantages of a literary arrangement such as the Songs of Ascents, in which separate psalms are united into a larger whole, is that it allows such continuities and contrasts to be clearly articulated). There are links between individual Songs, however, which do not fit neatly into this suggested structure, particularly those between Psalms 124 and 129, and perhaps also those between Psalms 120, 123, and 130.[54] Other views of the structure of the Songs of Ascents are also possible, as for example, Seybold's division into three groups (Pss. 120–122, 123–132, 122–134) under the headings "arrival," "back to Zion," and "departure"[55] or Beaucamp's division of the Songs of Ascents into three groups (Pss. 120–122, 123–128, 129–134), on the grounds that each group displays a similar movement from lament to blessing.[56]

53. Note further the following points: Ps. 123 (plea for mercy), Ps. 124 (review of past deliverance), and Ps. 125 (describing the security of God's people) in some ways recapitulate the movement of Pss. 120–122 (from alienation to security/fellowship enjoyed in Zion); compare also Pss. 121:2 and 124:8; the next triad (Pss. 126–128) ends with the same words as Pss. 123–125: שלום על־ישראל; Pss. 129–131 are linked by the fact that they all begin in the first singular, but address the concerns of Israel as a whole.

54. See the comments on Ps. 130 below.

55. *Die Wallfahrtspsalmen*, pp. 71-72.

56. *Le Psautier*, p. 252. P. Auffret has suggested a division into three blocks of five, Pss. 120–124, 125–129, 130–134 (*La sagesse a bâti sa maison. Etudes de structures littéraires dans l'Ancien Testament et spécialement dans les Psaumes*, Orbis biblicus et orientalis 49 [Göttingen: Vandenhoeck & Ruprecht, 1982], pp. 439-

A. Psalms 120–122: Journey to Zion

From a number of viewpoints, Psalm 122 represents the climax to Psalms 120–122. This is true as regards geography: in Psalm 120 the speaker describes himself as dwelling in foreign lands ("Woe to me that I sojourn in Meshech, that I dwell alongside the tents of Kedar," v. 5);[57] in Psalm 121 the speaker's eyes are on the hills around Jerusalem;[58] in Psalm 122 the focus is on Jerusalem and worship in the temple. There is also a progression in the sentiments and mood expressed, from grim determination verging on despair (Ps. 120) to joy at the prospect of worshipping in Jerusalem (Ps. 122).[59] This is linked to another move in these psalms, from alienation and insecurity, from the hostile slander of those who "hate peace" (Ps. 120:6), to fellowship, peace, and security (Ps. 122).[60] Accordingly, the first singular perspective of Psalms 120 and 121 opens out to include the first plural voice in Psalm 122. The play between first singular and first plural perspectives in

531). Auffret argues that the Songs of Ascents are chiastically arranged, on the basis of an exhaustive treatment of verbal links between the individual Songs of Ascents. Although a number of the verbal links he suggests are plausible, his criteria for establishing verbal links seem to me in general too loose (see also Crow, *Songs of Ascents,* pp. 134-35). In addition, Auffret pays no attention to one aspect which seems to me important for coherence and thematic development in the Songs of Ascents, namely, changes of person between and within Songs.

57. Suggestions concerning this notorious crux include: the place names are simply metaphorical for "barbaric" hostility (Allen, *Psalms 101–150,* ad loc.); the speaker in the psalm is the king, representing the nation Israel surrounded by hostile nations (J. H. Eaton, *Kingship and the Psalms,* 2nd ed. [Sheffield: JSOT Press, 1986], pp. 82-83). I am inclined to think that the phrase is an inclusive reference designed to include any pilgrim coming to Jerusalem, no matter from how far afield or from which quarter.

58. In the context of Psalm 122 following, scarcely any other identification is possible: it would not be an unlikely identification even if Psalm 121 were taken by itself.

59. In this respect, too, Psalm 121 acts as a transition. Taken by itself, Psalm 120 seems incomplete: v. 7 is a rather weak and unemphatic ending, which seems to invite a further development or response. This is duly supplied by Psalm 121. Verses 1-2 of Psalm 121, coming after Psalm 120, suggest a turning away from hostile and threatening neighbors towards YHWH; and the person addressed by the promises of YHWH's protection in vv. 3-8 (second singular verbs and suffixes) is, in effect, the one who lamented his circumstances in Psalm 120, now encouraged by his friends. Psalm 120 is a good example of a Song of Ascents which only makes complete sense when read as part of the entire collection.

60. A cluster of ideas linked by the word-plays on שׁאל ("ask"), שׁלום ("peace"), שׁלי ("be secure"), and ירושׁלם ("Jerusalem") in vv. 6-7.

Psalm 122, and the sense of "belonging" that this conveys, are among the strongest impressions left on the reader. Not that Psalm 122 ignores the historical and theological factors which make Jerusalem a worthy object of Israelite loyalty. Several such are referred to: the temple is there; that is where "the tribes of Yahweh went up . . . to praise YHWH's name" (v. 4); it was the royal city of the "house of David" (v. 5). Even the imagery of Jerusalem as a "city that is bound firmly together" (v. 3, NRSV) portrays it as a focus of Israelite unity. These factors, however, are strongly reinforced by the speaker's expressions of delight in fellow-Israelites and in Jerusalem itself, which, as noted, stand out by contrast with the situation depicted in Psalm 120. As we come to the end of this first triad, Jerusalem's historical and theological associations are brought to life by the speaker's intense personal devotion to Jerusalem and what Jerusalem stands for. Verses 8-9 of Psalm 122, in which, uniquely in the Songs of Ascents, Jerusalem is addressed in the second person singular, deliberately bring together the personal and historical/theological aspects:

> For the sake of my brothers and companions,
>   let me say "Peace upon you";
> for the sake of the house of YHWH our God,
>   let me seek your welfare.

B. Psalms 123–125: Hostility to Zion

Zion in the Songs of Ascents is the focus of both love ("let those who love you be at ease," Ps. 122:6) and hatred ("all those who hate Zion," Ps. 129:5). In the Songs of Ascents there are many references to hostility towards Zion, Israel as a whole, and individual Israelites.

I have suggested that Psalm 120 designedly begins the collection by sounding a note of alienation, of hostility which has to be endured. This is initially answered by the progression to Psalm 122, with its evocation of peace and fellowship in Jerusalem. But Psalm 123 returns to the mood and setting of Psalm 120 (note the similar opening verses, and the verbal parallel between Pss. 120:6 and 123:4, which both use רבת and נפש), and speaks of a hostility endured by the worshipping community as a whole.[61]

61. As in Psalm 122, the verbs and pronominal suffixes are partly first singular and partly first plural: that is, the sentiments expressed are those of a singular speaker

Whereas Psalm 122:9 has expressed the psalmist's loyalty to "the house of YHWH our God," in Psalm 123 the whole community pleads passionately to "YHWH our God" for mercy (v. 2). Belonging to the community committed to YHWH may involve joyful fellowship, but it also involves the mockery of those opposed to what Zion stands for.

In Psalm 124 the contemporary hostility of Psalm 123 is set in the context of a perennial hostility endured by Israel.[62] The first verse indicates this by encouraging the (first plural) speakers to see their experience as something characteristic of Israel throughout its history: "If it had not been that YHWH was with us — let Israel say. . . ." Throughout, the language is vivid but non-specific: the enemy is described by the most general term possible (v. 2: "when men rose against us"); the terms of vv. 3-5 (devouring monsters and raging waters) are stock Old Testament language for the forces opposed to God and God's people.[63] The aim is seemingly to evoke the whole sweep of embattled Israel's history. Towards the end a different image is used, of a bird escaping from a trap (v. 7).[64] The idea of escape only becomes explicit at the end (marked by two occurrences of the root מלט in v. 7). The worshippers can reflect that they have indeed survived up to this point,[65] and the effect is to suggest that YHWH will deliver them — will deliver Israel — in future. The formula with which the psalm ends is thus appropriate: "our help is in YHWH's name, he who made heaven and earth" (v. 8).

The confident opening of Psalm 125 follows on from this: "Those who trust in YHWH are like Mt. Zion, which will not be moved, which is established for ever." But Mt. Zion, it emerges as the psalm proceeds, is at present an enclave in enemy territory. The surrounding land is occupied: "the scepter of wickedness [Assyrian? Persian?] will not remain over the allotted territory of the righteous" (Ps. 125:3). The latter verses make a

___

who feels himself to be part of a larger group. The effect of reading Psalm 123 after Psalm 122 is that in Psalm 123 the speakers are identified as those whom Psalm 122 has portrayed as committed to "YHWH our God" and to Jerusalem's welfare. Even if Psalm 123 were considered apart from its context, the contrast between the intensity with which the speakers appeal to YHWH and "the mockery of those who are at ease" (v. 4) would suggest some such identification.

62. Again, a conceptual link is reinforced by a verbal link, נפשׁנו ("us"/"our soul") in Psalm 123:4 being picked up three times in Psalm 124 (vv. 4, 5, 7).

63. See, for example, Psalms 46:1-3; 74:12-15; 89:8-10; 93:3-4.

64. This might depict the experience of those who survived the Assyrian invasion or of those who returned from the Babylonian exile.

65. Note the emphasis of ואנחנו נמלטנו ("*we* have escaped") in v. 7a.

sharp distinction between righteous and wicked, and, apparently, a group in the middle, described as "making their ways twisted" (perhaps an Israelite group who have sided, or are tempted to side, with the "wicked").[66] The community, in fact, appears to be under considerable pressure. Psalm 125 as a whole leaves a mixed impression on the reader. On the one hand there are clear expressions of confidence in YHWH, reinforced by the language, which contrasts the immovability of Zion (a symbol for the security of God's people) with the wicked, who are described as impermanent (v. 3) and movable (v. 5); on the other there is an urgent note of appeal ("Do good, YHWH, to those who are good," v. 4). The psalmist even hints at the possibility that the righteous might cease to be loyal to YHWH (". . . in order that the righteous should not set their hands to evil," v. 3). The psalm well conveys a faith under severe strain. The final words ("Peace be upon Israel!" v. 5) are anything but an empty formula, in the light of the tensions exposed in the previous lines.[67]

In general, it seems consistent with the portrayal of Zion in the Songs of Ascents that the theme of YHWH's rule over the nations, which plays an important role in other Zion psalms (Pss. 2, 46, 48, 96, 97, 99), is not developed here.[68] The Songs of Ascents seem to be focused on the more modest aims of survival and rebuilding in the land. Though Zion is invoked as a symbol of YHWH's power at Psalm 125:1-2, it is YHWH's power as protector of his people, not as ruler of the nations, which is in view ("As for Jerusalem, it has mountains around it; and YHWH is around his people," v. 2; contrast Ps. 99:2, "Great is YHWH in Zion; he is exalted over all the nations").

A further such comparison may be made. Some of the psalms deal-

66. Perhaps the writer deliberately uses such general terms to suggest that the particular situation he has in mind (which the original hearers could presumably also identify) is part of the constant struggle against opposition which has marked Israel's history from the beginning.

67. Still less are they "quite out of place at the end" (Crow, *Songs of Ascents,* p. 58). More generally, I question Crow's view that Psalm 125 is one of the Songs of Ascents in which redactional seams are particularly apparent (op. cit., p. 57). There *is* a tension between vv. 1-2, 5b and vv. 3-5a, but this is not, in my view, due to the fact that the psalm is made up of two different types of material reflecting respectively, "the local, family-oriented wisdom tradition of personal retribution" and "the Jerusalemite tradition of the immovability of Zion" (op. cit., p. 58). Rather, the tension is that between faith and experience, a tension which can, of course, be experienced by a single person or group.

68. Though note the reference to the nations' awe (past tense) at Ps. 126:2.

ing with YHWH's rule over the nations do so by depicting the nations gathering together to attack Zion and being instantly repulsed (particularly Pss. 46, 48).[69] This is a way of expressing Zion's invulnerability. Psalm 125 takes as its starting-point the security of Mt. Zion (vv. 1-2); but the veiled allusion to the future removal from the land of the wicked and the compromisers in vv. 3-5 is at best a strikingly muted version of the theme of the "repulse of the nations."

C. Psalms 126–128: Restoration of Zion

The next three Songs, Psalms 126–128, are linked by their shared insistence (implicit in Ps. 126, explicit in Pss. 127 and 128) that it is YHWH, and he alone, who can bless, and by the fact that they tie together Zion's welfare and individual/familial prosperity. As argued above, the speakers in Psalm 126 look back to one occasion on which the fortunes of Zion were strikingly restored, and ask that they may experience something similar in their own day (Ps. 126:1-4). The metaphor of an individual reaping and sowing, it was suggested, has concerted endeavor on the part of the whole Israelite community in view. Because it focuses on an individual sowing and then harvesting his sheaves, however, the metaphor also suggests a connection between national restoration and individual prosperity. This same connection is also made in Psalms 127 and 128, which are a complementary pair:[70] in Psalm 127, by means of puns on בנה, בית and בנים and by the insistence that YHWH, whose involvement is essential for the welfare of the temple and Jerusalem, is also the one who blesses an individual with sons; in the case of Psalm 128, by linking the blessings of the "man who fears YHWH" (vv. 1-4) with YHWH's blessing from Zion (v. 5).[71] The last two lines of

---

69. Compare also Psalm 2 and Isaiah 29.

70. These two psalms complement each other conceptually: if Psalm 127 stresses that blessing comes from YHWH, and him alone, Psalm 128 makes a complementary point, that these blessings are for those who fear YHWH, and for them alone. That these points are different sides of the same coin is suggested by the similar wording of Psalm 127:5 (אשרי הגבר) and Psalm 128:1 (אשרי כל־ירא יהוה), which also creates a clear link between the two psalms.

71. I regard the half-line יברכך יהוה מציון (v. 5aα) as a hinge, picking up terms from v. 4 (יברך, יהוה) but locating YHWH's blessing in Zion. It also introduces the second singular voice which continues to the end of the psalm. Allen (*Psalms 101– 150*, p. 184) may well be correct in his view that the intended speakers of the blessing in vv. 5-6 were one or more priests.

Psalm 128 form a chiasm which intertwines the individual Israelite's hopes for longevity and descendants with wider concerns for Jerusalem's and Israel's welfare:

> . . . and may you gaze upon Jerusalem's prosperity
> all the days of your life,
> and may you live to see your grandchildren —
> Peace upon Israel! (Ps. 128:5ab-6).

The effect is to make those reciting these Songs reflect that everything they desire for themselves comes about as a result of Zion's prosperity.[72]

D. Psalms 129–131: Waiting on YHWH

Psalm 129 has a number of links with Psalm 124. The opening verses of both psalms are similarly structured and both use the phrase "let Israel say." Like Psalm 124, Psalm 129 is a historical review of perennial hostility to Israel ("they have oppressed me from my youth"),[73] using a different metaphor, that of ploughing.[74] Where Psalm 124 describes YHWH's past deliverance of Israel, however, Psalm 129, having begun by describing past oppression, goes on in vv. 5-8 to express confidence in YHWH's

---

72. Crow makes precisely this point in connection with Psalm 128, but attributes this intention to the redactor, who in his view has added the last two verses (*Songs of Ascents,* pp. 74-76). His basis for this is that Jerusalem is only mentioned in vv. 5-6 and that these verses contain phrases (יברכך יהוה מציון and שלום על־ישראל) which occur elsewhere. I do not find it necessary to split the psalm in this way: Jerusalem may not be referred to in Psalm 128:1-4, but it has been referred to at the beginning of Psalm 127, of which Psalm 128 is in many ways only a continuation. Even if we leave Psalm 127 out of consideration, it seems quite reasonable that a single writer should begin by focusing on the blessings of the individual God-fearer, and then broaden the picture by setting this in the context of Zion's prosperity. Note also Allen's point that "the pattern of ideal third person speech (v. 4) followed by specific second person language (vv. 5-6) accords with vv. 1, 2-3" (*Psalms 101–150,* p. 184).

73. The use of the first person singular, in my view, is intended as a personification of Israel (cf. the similar uses of נעורים, "youth," in connection with Jerusalem and Israel at Isa. 47:12, 15; Jer. 2:2; 3:4; Ezek. 16:22; Hos. 2:17), with which the worshippers are invited to identify themselves (יאמר־נא ישראל). It is not necessary to suppose that Psalm 129 is a communal adaptation of an individual lament.

74. Perhaps this metaphor particularly suggests enemy occupation of the land; though, as in Psalms 124 and 125, it probably also has a broader reference.

future deliverance (a move well attested in the Psalter generally).[75] The enemies who have ploughed Israel will themselves become like grass withering on a roof-top: the simile (in a way reminiscent of one of Donne's "conceits") expands ingeniously into a depiction of an aborted harvest which YHWH does not bless, expressing the futility of opposition to Zion.[76]

Coming after Psalm 129 the opening line of Psalm 130 marks a sharp contrast ("From the depths I call to you . . ."). The effect is as though the first person speaker at the beginning of Psalm 129, whose voice, immediately identified with that of Israel (v. 1), has been lost in the confident prediction of Israel's deliverance, now again makes himself heard, at greater length, and with a more despairing tone.[77] But what is Psalm 130 about, exactly? The speaker asks YHWH to hear his cry (vv. 1-2), indirectly admits to a need of forgiveness (vv. 3-4), and expresses his trust in YHWH (vv. 5-6). No plea is directly made. The thought is then broken off by vv. 7-8, which urge Israel to trust in YHWH.

Crow treats Psalm 130 as a redacted fragment:[78] what was originally part of an individual petition has been adapted by the addition of vv. 7-8 to become an example of the kind of piety Israel as a whole should display. The reason why the psalm is broken off before any request is expressed is, he argues, that the redactor was more interested in the penitent attitude expressed than in the specific request which the earlier version of the psalm then went on to express. He mounts similar arguments in connection with Psalm 131.[79]

I argue differently. Psalms 130 and 131, more than any other of the Songs, need to be read in their context in order to be fully intelligible. The unexpressed prayer in Psalm 130 is for the full restoration of Zion[80] —

75. See, for example, Psalms 6 and 22.
76. Contrast Zion's ultimately successful harvest in Psalm 126:5-6 and the depiction in Psalm 128 of the prosperity and fruitfulness enjoyed by the one who fears YHWH.
77. It may be significant that the opening of Psalm 130:1 is reminiscent of the openings of Psalms 120 and 123; that is, it suggests a return to the mood of those psalms.
78. *Songs of Ascents*, pp. 87-91.
79. *Songs of Ascents*, pp. 94-98.
80. It is thus natural that the speaker should use the figure of watchmen waiting for the dawn to describe his longing in v. 6 (cf. Ps. 127:2). I suggest, further, that the phrase "in his word I hope" (v. 5) is neither an "incubation formula" (Crow, *Songs of Ascents*, p. 89) nor a reference to a "divine ruling from the sanctuary, to be delivered

that is the element which must be supplied from the context: but with this assumed, the speaker turns to consider his own, and then Israel's, sins, which are matched by YHWH's forgiveness and commitment (vv. 4, 7-8). The emphasis of Psalm 130 on sins, forgiveness, and redemption is unique in the Songs of Ascents.[81] The sins in question are not specified: the reverse, in fact — 'he will redeem Israel from *all* his sins' (v. 8). But it seems to me most natural to view Psalm 130 as, at least in part, a meditation on Israel's need to be liberated from the continuing consequences of invasion or exile (conceived as a punishment for sins). That is to say, vv. 7-8 are necessary to complete the thought of the psalm.

Thus, if Psalm 129 has expressed certainty that YHWH will deliver Zion (v. 5), Psalm 130 points to the considerable obstacle of Israel's past (and perhaps its continuing) sins. We can again compare the book of Nehemiah, especially the long prayer in chapter 9. In Psalm 130 redemption is far from complete, though v. 8 expresses confidence that it one day will be.

More briefly, but along the same lines, there is an unexpressed question in Psalm 131, which has given rise to the former thoughts which the speaker has now learned to see as "presumptuous" (v. 1), and is the cause of the former mental turmoil which the speaker has now managed to replace with calm (v. 2). That question is: when will YHWH deliver Israel? The answer the speaker gives is: I have learned to trust YHWH; let Israel do the same, for as long as it takes: "Let Israel put its hope in YHWH from henceforth and for ever" (v. 3).[82]

Psalms 130 and 131 have a similar shape, starting with individual concerns expressed in the first singular, but broadening out to take in Israel as a whole (a move in each case marked by "Let Israel put its hope in YHWH," Pss. 130:7; 131:3). This suggests a similarity of function: the psalms both act as responses to questions raised by the confident assertions of Psalm 129.

---

by a priest" (Allen, *Psalms 101–150,* p. 196), but has in view YHWH's promises concerning Zion and David (cf. Ps. 132:9-18).

81. In Psalm 125 the speaker, by contrast, described those faithful to YHWH as "the righteous" (v. 3) and "the upright in heart" (v. 4).

82. The thought of this psalm would, thus, be similar to that expressed at Deut. 29:28.

E. Psalms 132–134: The Founding Vision and the Future

Psalms 132–134 conclude the Songs of Ascents on a fundamentally optimistic note. Psalm 132 stands out by reason of its length, and marks a climactic point in the collection: Jerusalem and David become, so to speak, the "goal" of the collection, the note on which it ends. Psalm 132 is an appeal to the initial event which constituted Zion as YHWH's "resting-place" (vv. 8, 14), the first procession of the ark up to Zion, and a plea to remember the human agent who gave the lead in that event, David (v. 1). The first half of Psalm 132 asks that the hopes which surrounded that initial event may be fulfilled, bringing joy for those committed to YHWH (v. 9) and restoration for David's descendant (v. 10). The second half of Psalm 132 is structurally parallel to the first (very closely so) and gives the answer to this plea, YHWH's oath (in the first person) concerning David and his descendants, and his promises concerning Zion.[83] Among all the voices heard in the Songs of Ascents, here YHWH's voice is for the first time heard. The effect is that many of the petitions which have been made up to this point now find their definitive answer in a reaffirmation of YHWH's choice of Zion and of David's royal line: "this is my resting-place forever . . . here I will make a horn grow for David . . ." (vv. 14, 17).

Psalm 133, as Crow plausibly argues, seems to be an implicit appeal to northern Israelites to recognize the primacy of Zion and David.[84] It begins with generalities: "How good, and how pleasant it is when brothers dwell together" (v. 1). But the intent lying behind this opening is increasingly focused by the simile of oil running down the beard (Aaron's beard, it emerges, turning our thoughts towards priests and temples) and then by that of the dew of Hermon (in the north) descending on the mountains of Zion, which is where YHWH has "commanded" blessing. Brotherly harmony turns out to involve northern brothers coming to southern Zion to worship in the temple.

Psalm 134, in which YHWH is blessed in his temple as he sends out blessing from Zion, completes the thought of this triad and of the collection as a whole.[85] The closing words are important: if the temple and Zion are a worthy focus of Israelite loyalty, it is only because the "Maker of

83. In the final verses (16-18) the two are linked together.
84. *Songs of Ascents,* pp. 109-20.
85. It is surely significant that, of the nine occurrences of the root ברך in the Songs of Ascents (124:6; 128:4, 5; 129:8; 132:15 [twice]; 134:1, 2, 3), five are found in the last triad.

126

heaven and earth" has designated them as such: "May YHWH bless you from Zion, he who made heaven and earth" (v. 3).

V. Conclusion

Here it has been argued for the coherence of the Songs of Ascents as a collection. Virtually every element in the Songs of Ascents counts, and makes its contribution to a diverse but unified whole. The sequence of the Songs juxtaposes psalms of joy, commitment, and blessing with psalms whose mood is grimmer and more despairing, thus representing both sides of the experience of those who seek Zion's welfare. The six repeated formulae and related phrases, as Crow rightly observes, stress the security of those who commit themselves to the God of Zion. Other important aspects are the imagery (Zion as an immovable mountain; sowing, reaping and fertility as symbols of national and individual prosperity; the figure of the watchman as a symbol of longing for YHWH's intervention) and the use of different grammatical voices.

How, then, can we describe Zion in the Songs of Ascents?

First, Zion remains a focus of YHWH's purposes for the future: the last three Songs in the collection respectively reaffirm YHWH's promises concerning Zion and the Davidic line, promote Zion as a worthy object of loyalty for Israelites, whether northern or southern, and state that Zion is the place where YHWH is worshipped, and from where he distributes his blessings. Continuity with the past is emphasized in this presentation of Zion: YHWH has not abandoned his promises or his people Israel.

Second, Zion is the focus of what is an inclusive vision of Israel: Jerusalem is the place where "the tribes of Yahweh went up" previously (Ps. 122:3), and at this later period the Songs of Ascents continue to affirm that "brothers" (Israelites) should "dwell together," that is, worship together in Jerusalem (Ps. 133). It is probably significant that in the one verse where the term "Israel" is more precisely defined (Ps. 122:3) the definition tends in an inclusive direction: in that verse the phrase ". . . where it is appointed to Israel to praise . . ." is preceded by "where the tribes went up, the tribes of Yahweh. . . ."[86] The juxtaposition seems to imply an ideal of Israel in which all the twelve tribes are present. One could draw parallels here with

---

86. Cf. the point made in the comments on Psalm 122 that the imagery of v. 3 (Jerusalem as a "tightly-compacted" city) suggests unity between the tribes.

PHILIP E. SATTERTHWAITE

the books of Chronicles, where unity among the Israelite tribes is similarly desirable, and the preconditions for unity are, as here, acceptance of
Jerusalem as the place of worship and acceptance of David and his descendants as YHWH's chosen kings.[87]

Third, one should note how consistently the Songs of Ascents link
the welfare of Zion and the welfare of the individual Israelite: in Psalms
120–122 the individual speaker experiences blessing and joy as he draws
closer to Jerusalem; Psalms 126–128 each juxtapose images of personal
fruitfulness and prosperity with the theme of YHWH's blessing Zion. At a
different level this link is reinforced by the use of both singular and plural
voices. The point is the same in each instance: Zion is where the individual Israelite is to find blessing.

Yet the shadow of national catastrophe hangs over this collection.
For all that Zion and the Israelite community centered around her retain a
place in YHWH's purposes, there is a poignancy about Psalms 122 and
132, because they underscore the importance of Zion and the David monarchy by (necessarily) invoking a more glorious past. Hence the note of
longing, and occasionally, impatience, which dominates some of the
Songs (Pss. 123, 126, 130, 131).

It is a distinctive picture of Zion, then, which emerges from the
Songs of Ascents. The hope Zion represents has not been abandoned, and
there are blessings in store for Israel as a whole and for individual Israelites as they seek to serve the God who has chosen Zion. If the troubles
both past and present endured by those who maintain faith with this God
also find eloquent expression, this is matched by a portrayal of YHWH's
commitment to Zion and those who worship there.

87. Beaucamp notes in this connection that there is no mention in the collection
of Judah (*Le Psautier*, p. 250).

The Personification of Jerusalem and the Drama of Her Bereavement in Lamentations

KNUT M. HEIM

The short book of Lamentations provides a literary expression for the suffering and pain of Jerusalem when the whole community has been struck by disaster. The city itself serves as an embodiment of all its inhabitants, their sins and their subsequent misery. In a special way Lamentations provides pastoral insight into dealing with grief and suffering that demonstrates the continuing relevance of Jerusalem as a symbolic expression of the cry of God's people.

I. Introduction

How can pain be overcome when a whole community is struck by disaster? The book of Lamentations wrestles with catastrophe on a national and personal level. The thesis of this essay is that the personification of Jerusalem is the most important literary device in the book of Lamentations:

I am grateful to Prof. Alan Millard, Donald Fairbairn and Daniel Bailey for reading the manuscript of this essay and for making many helpful suggestions.

129

through its personification the Jerusalem community can deal with its own pain and anxiety on a more profound level. This transformation of the city of Jerusalem and its remaining inhabitants into a single female figure enables her to express her pain and respond to the challenges she faces in the aftermath of destruction. Personified as a woman, she can be consoled through her participation in a multifaceted dialogue that may best be described as a drama of bereavement.[1]

Pain can only be experienced by individuals, even if it is in response to communal catastrophes:[2] "Each heart knows its own bitterness, and no one else can share its joy."[3] While the basic structure of the community remains intact, the individual can always find help in the religious and social institutions of the nation. But when society as a whole breaks down, nobody is left for the individual to turn to, and the normal structures of social security have disappeared. Looking for consolation, all those whom he or she will find who might — under normal circumstances — have provided reassurance and hope are suffering from similar or even worse despair, grief, and bereavement; there is no comforter. Thus when disaster strikes a whole community, pain is elevated to a different and more complex level. It needs to find an expression that is both individual and corporate in order to help individuals express their own personal pain while at the same time addressing the agony experienced by the other members of the community. In the book of Lamentations this expression of both individual *and* corporate pain has been achieved through the personification of Jerusalem. The book of Lamentations opens with a daring simile (1:1a-b):

> How lonely sits the city that was once full of people!
> How like a widow she has become, she that was great among the
> nations!

1. Jerusalem is personified in different ways in the book, sometimes as a widow, sometimes as a wife or an unmarried young woman, and so on. Significantly, these personifications are always female, presumably to evoke the impression of vulnerability and dependency typically associated with femininity in the patriarchal context in which the book was composed.
2. A. Mintz, "The Rhetoric of Lamentations," *Prooftexts* 2 (1982): 1-17, here 2.
3. Prov. 14:10 (NIV). Unless indicated otherwise, biblical quotations are taken from the New Revised Standard Version (NRSV). Reference is also made to the new Jewish Publication Society version, *TANAKH: The Holy Scriptures* (Philadelphia; Jerusalem: Jewish Publication Society, 1985), abbr.: NJPS.

The suffering of the city's community is compared with the suffering of one particular individual, and so the inexpressible plight of unnumbered people may be grasped through the experience of one (corporate) individual. As Claus Westermann writes:

> By means of this comparison the history of a people obtains a personal character. It is perceived as the fate of one person, and it is precisely this that makes suffering possible.[4]

The importance of grieving has already been mentioned. Paul Joyce, in an important study of the bearing of the grief process on the interpretation of Lamentations, has demonstrated that two fundamental human experiences form the background to the book: grief and dying.[5] Many of Jerusalem's citizens have died during and after the disastrous events presupposed in the book.[6] Their deaths (cf. 1:19-20: "my priests and elders perished in the city . . . in the street the sword bereaves; in the house it is like death") are an ever-present reality in Lamentations. Commenting on the comparison of Jerusalem with a widow in Lamentations 1:1, Joyce points out that her losses included the temple, the king, law, and prophecy:

> Israel's entire symbol system had been torn away, and the people had experienced a complete loss of meaning. That structure of belief was centred on divine election, and, pressing the image of bereaved widow, we could even say that Israel had lost her "husband," God himself.[7]

---

4. C. Westermann, *Lamentations: Issues and Interpretation,* trans. Charles Muenchow (Edinburgh: T & T Clark, 1994), p. 110; translation modified.

5. P. Joyce, "Lamentations and the Grief Process: A Psychological Reading," *Biblical Interpretation* 1 (1993): 304-20.

6. Although it is impossible to determine with certainty what these events were, there is a near consensus that the events to which the book of Lamentations reacts are those of the Babylonian crisis between 596 and 587/6; cf. Westermann, *Lamentations,* pp. 54-55, 104-5 and the literature cited in Joyce, "Grief Process," p. 304n.1; Iain Provan's conclusion that "the book as a whole may, with a degree of certainty, be dated between the 6th and the 2nd centuries B.C.; but beyond this we may not go" (I. Provan, *Lamentations,* New Century Bible Commentary [London: Marshall Pickering; Grand Rapids: Eerdmans, 1991], pp. 7-19, here p. 19) seems overly cautious.

7. Joyce, "Grief Process," p. 310. On the concept of God as the husband of his people, see esp. Nelly Stienstra, *YHWH Is the Husband of His People: Analysis of a Biblical Metaphor with Special Reference to Translation* (Kampen: Pharos, 1993).

Lady Zion, the personification of Jerusalem and its citizens, experiences bereavement and isolation. Individual psalms of lament deal with suffering on the individual level. Similarly, the book of Job tackles the issue of personal suffering. Communal psalms of lament such as Psalms 44, 58, 74, 79, 80, 83, and 106 deal with the suffering of the Israelite community. In these traditional laments there is always a shadow of hope, expressed in a plea for divine intervention or explicit avowals of confidence.[8] The book of Lamentations, however, generally lacks both features. After the defeat of Judah and the destruction of Jerusalem, including the temple, no grounds for hope remained. The covenant was broken, this time not by the people, but apparently by God himself. Had he utterly forsaken his people?[9] Why would this terrible punishment happen so soon after the sincere reforms inaugurated under Josiah (640-609 B.C.)? How was it possible that God would forsake his covenant? Why did so many innocent people have to suffer, particularly young children and babies? The book of Lamentations does not answer these questions. The answers must be given by the voice which remains silent in the book: the voice of God himself. The divine answer will be given only on the canonical level of the later writings of the Old Testament, as Christopher Seitz has demonstrated, arguing that the situation presupposed in Lamentations forms the context for Second Isaiah's announcements of Israel's restoration, especially in Isaiah 55:1-5.[10]

One of the most persistent refrains in the book is the desolate affirmation that Lady Jerusalem has no one to comfort her. Yet there is a proliferation of utterances, by a confusing array of speakers. Their number and identity are matters of dispute. Yet the crucial issue is not how many voices there are, or even who is speaking, but how the different speakers interact with one another. For the personification of the city and its re-

8. Cf. H. Gunkel, *Einleitung in die Psalmen: Die Gattungen der religiösen Lyrik Israels* (Göttingen: Vandenhoeck & Ruprecht, [4]1985), pp. 125, 132.

9. Cf. the tauntingly ambiguous expression in 5:22, discussed briefly below.

10. Cf. Provan, *Lamentations,* 24-25; C. R. Seitz, *Word without End: The Old Testament as Abiding Theological Witness* (Grand Rapids: Eerdmans, 1998), 130-49. The same pattern of "question" and "answer" has independently been argued by Seitz and myself with regard to Ps. 89 and Isa. 55:1-5; cf. Seitz, *Word,* pp. 150-67, esp. pp. 155-58, with K. M. Heim, "The (God-)Forsaken King of Psalm 89: A Historical and Intertextual Inquiry," in John Day (ed.), *King and Messiah in Ancient Israel: Papers from the Oxford Old Testament Seminar,* JSOTSup 270 (Sheffield: Sheffield Academic Press, 1998), pp. 296-322, esp. pp. 305-14.

maining inhabitants into Fair Zion has transformed them into a persona able to enter into dialogue.

The speakers in Lamentations have received attention in William Lanahan's article on the "speaking voice" in Lamentations. According to Lanahan, the different voices in Lamentations are different personae, a persona being "the mask of characterization assumed by the poet as the medium through which he perceives and gives expression to his world."[11] Lanahan found five such personae:

1. a more objective reporter;
2. the voice of Jerusalem, i.e., "the hypostatized anguish of the fallen city" (Lam. 1:11c-16, 18-22, etc.);
3. a defeated soldier (Lam. 3);
4. a bourgeois (Lam. 4);
5. a choral voice (Lam. 5), "subsuming each individual *persona* in an act of prayer which transcends the viewpoints and the inadequacies which the poet perceived and expressed through the first four chapters."[12]

In Lanahan's analysis, then, the final chapter in the book sums up the mood of the Jerusalem community, ending in a prayer consisting of questions, "suspended without a definite answer."[13] His analysis provides important new insights which will be taken up below; it is, however, limited in scope and content. First, he has not included all voices and speakers in the book. For example, while it is true that the voice of the "passers-by" in 2:15c occurs only as a quotation by one of Lanahan's personae, their contribution is nevertheless related in direct discourse and is more significant than Lanahan allows. (See below.) Second, he has not fully explored how the different personae interact with one another. Third, his analysis of the fifth persona is open to question, as the analysis below will demonstrate.

The present study will offer an analysis of the personification of Jerusalem, discuss different utterances in Lamentations, and provide a brief analysis of the dialogue resulting from the interplay between the interloc-

11. W. F. Lanahan, "The Speaking Voice in the Book of Lamentations," *Journal of Biblical Literature* 93 (1974): 41-49, here 41.
12. Lanahan, "Voice," p. 48.
13. Lanahan, "Voice," p. 49.

utors in the book. Special attention will be given to the contribution which this dialogue makes to the grieving process of the community.

II. Personification in Lamentations

The prominence of the stylistic device of personification in Lamentations has often been observed, yet few scholars have made personification the focus of their analysis. A notable exception is Alan Mintz. His 1982 article forms the basis for the first part of this study.[14] Yet Mintz is not mentioned at all in Westermann's survey of scholarship up to 1990 (ET 1994), and he receives no more than a critical footnote in Delbert Hillers' important commentary. Although Hillers notes the frequency of personifications, he explains that personifications are potentially misleading since they refer to the the city or its citizens as a whole rather than a part of it. Hillers argues that personifications serve mainly metrical purposes, and he often omits them in translation when he is unable to find thoroughly idiomatic equivalents in English. His suggestion that the device was employed so frequently because of its special popularity in the seventh and sixth centuries B.C.E. and because of its special role in the city lament genre is not convincing, since he does not explain *why* personifications were so popular, especially in city laments.[15] The daring simile in the opening statement of Lamentations (1:1a-b) sets the tone for the remainder of the book and deserves repetition:

> How *lonely sits the city* that was once full of people!
> How *like a widow* she has become, she that was great among the
>   nations!

The apparently straightforward comparison in this *simile,* where the suffering of the city's community is compared with the suffering of one particular individual, becomes a *personification* through a set of surprisingly complex transformations.

In the first line, the "city" is a *synecdoche (abstractum pro concreto)* for its inhabitants. Thus the city as a dwelling place represents the sum of the individuals that have survived Jerusalem's destruction and

14. Mintz, "Rhetoric," pp. 1-17.
15. Cf. D. R. Hillers, *Lamentations,* Anchor Bible 7A (New York: Doubleday, ²1992), pp. 30-31, 34, 37, 39.

are still living within its walls.[16] Yet the architectural site is given human features: she "sits." The ingenious employment of the verb "to sit" in the first colon, with its ascription of human characteristics to an abstract entity, paves the way in the second line for the metamorphosis of an inanimate and complex concept into a single, bereaved and suffering person, a widow — an emotionally powerful cultural image. (See below.) Yet how does personification work as a literary device? How is it possible that personified Jerusalem can represent the entire population of the city? And from where does this personification metaphor derive its power? Some further comments on the different transformations involved in the personification of Jerusalem may provide answers to these questions.[17]

The common "Saussurian" linguistic distinction between "signifier" and "signified" also applies to personifications. A personification always consists of two parts: the first part is the actual expression used, the "personifier"; the second part is the — usually implicit — entity to which the expression refers, the "personified." For example, in Lamentations 1:1 the personifier ("a widow") stands for the personified ("the city"). In this instance both parts are explicit. The "city" of the first line becomes a human being, a "widow," in the second line. Yet this is but one of several transformations operative in the personification of Jerusalem. There are four altogether:[18]

1. *ideation,* the translation of humans into an abstract idea;
2. *topification,* the translation of humans into a geographical location;
3. *personification,* the translation of a nonhuman quantity into a human being;
4. *impersonation,* the translation of a group of people into one person who speaks for them.

---

16. Alternatively, the inhabitants could be seen as the "husband" who filled her and made her great, but this would isolate the personification from its use in the context of the book. Since Jerusalem is still inhabited, despite the actual wording of this verse, the imagery should not be taken too literally.

17. The theory underlying the following discussion is based on J. J. Paxson, *The Poetics of Personification* (Cambridge: Cambridge University Press, 1994). Paxson (*Personification,* pp. 35-62) has a fairly comprehensive taxonomy of tropes involved in personifications, most of which can also be found in Lamentations.

18. The first three are explained by Paxson (*Personification,* pp. 42-43).

Each of them will be explained with regard to the example of Lamentations 1:1 and illustrated with a diagram, identifying the signifier (the result of the transformation) above the line and the signified (the actual referent before it is transformed) below the line. These transformations comprise successive stages in the personification of Jerusalem, for in each successive transformation the signifier of the previous stage has become the signified of the present stage. The functions which the signifier and the signified perform in these transformations will be indicated in parentheses, and the result of each transformation will be identified briefly.

(1) *Ideation.* In an implicit first-level abstraction which is not actually expressed in the text, the personification of Jerusalem turns human beings into inanimate, abstract ideas. This involves a reification of human beings into ideas. On this first level, all humans living in Jerusalem (signified) are lumped together under the abstract concept of the community (signifier), as the following diagram demonstrates.

Diagram 1

Ideation. *First-level Abstraction (Reification)*

Jerusalem community *(reifier)*

Citizens of Jerusalem *(reified)*

This abstraction involves a crucial step in the metaphorical expression of Jerusalem's experience. The inhumane treatment she has received from her enemies is implicitly reflected in this transformation of the citizens of Jerusalem into a less-than-human concept. This will be seen even more clearly at the second stage.

(2) *Topification.* At this second level of abstraction, the abstract concept of the human community, which had still implied the presence of human beings, is transformed into an architectural site devoid of humans: it is a city "that *was* once full of people" (cf. 1:1a). Through the metaphorical relationship of "containment," all those who are still living within Jerusalem's geographical limits (the "contained") have now been reduced to a geographical location (the "container"). The city symbolizes its citizens, and an architectural structure has replaced its inhabitants, as the next diagram shows.

Diagram 2
Topification. *Second Level of Abstraction (Localization)*

Jerusalem City *(localizer)*

Jerusalem community *(localized)*

This second level of abstraction removes those who — in contrast to what is said in 1:1a — still survive in Jerusalem even further from the surface of the text. Humans living in Jerusalem are eclipsed from sight, what remains in view is nothing but the container, a geographical location, and concern for the social well-being of Jerusalem's remaining inhabitants may comfortably be reduced to a mere archaeological curiosity.

(3) *Personification*. At the third level of abstraction, this geographical location, "the city," is "qualified" as a person by being provided with body parts (it "sits") and human sentiment (it is "lonely"). Furthermore, the title "widow" integrates it into a system of human relationships. Although the first two transmutations are integral to the nexus of transformations that are necessary to make the metaphor work, it is only this transformation that may properly be called a "personification," for it involves the endowment of a nonhuman entity, a place in this case, with human characteristics, translating it into a "person." This can be illustrated with the following diagram.

Diagram 3
Personification. *Third Level of Abstraction*

Widow *(personifier + human attributes)*

Jerusalem City *(personified)*

The city does not remain an architectural site, but is turned back into a human being full of painful emotions. The "widow," personified Jerusalem, represents the sum of the individuals living within the walls of the city. The sequence of transformations apparently has come full circle. Taken together, however, these first three transformations have produced the fourth kind of transformation.

(4) *Impersonation*. The three transformations mentioned so far — ideation, topification, and personification — have first reified multiple human beings into an abstraction, then this abstraction has become an architectural structure, and finally the geographic location has been re-

personified into a single female figure who represents the corporate identity of the many. This is detailed in the next diagram.

Diagram 4

Impersonation. *Result of Previous Abstractions (Representation)*

Widow *(impersonator/representative)*

Citizens of Jerusalem *(impersonated/represented)*

The first three transformations together have produced a fourth kind of transformation. Tracing this complex sequence of transformations reveals that the "widow" not only personifies the city, but actually symbolizes the Jerusalem community. The community, in turn, is an abstraction for the totality of individuals living in Jerusalem. This means that the personification of Jerusalem makes "daughter Zion" (as she will be called further below) the representative of every single member of the Jerusalem community. Her experience of defeat, humiliation, exploitation, and bereavement thus represents the experiences and sentiments of all the humans living in the city. Each individual can thus see his or her sufferings and painful emotions lived out in daughter Zion's plight. This representative function explains why personified Jerusalem can be depicted in surprisingly different roles, which at times appear to be mutually exclusive. She is wife, prostitute, divorcée, widow, mother, daughter, and so on, thus impersonating the various individuals suffering distress. (See below.)

The personification of Jerusalem into a widow sitting in the dust and lamenting her bereavement in a manner characteristic of ancient Near Eastern culture conjures up a powerful cultural image.[19] The emotional impact of this personification cannot be stressed enough, and may be illustrated with a negative example from the twentieth century taken from a book on personification by J. Paxson, in which two of the transformations mentioned above — reification and personification — play a crucial role. In the following example the personification of humanity transforms society, an abstraction, into a living body; this transformation, however, automatically *dehumanizes* its concrete living members. The human individuals who constitute society are *reified* into organs, limbs, tissues, and the like.

19. Cf. Job 2:13; see also H. Gese, "Der Tod im Alten Testament," in idem, *Zur biblischen Theologie* (Munich: Kaiser, 1977), p. 39.

When asked about his involvement in the holocaust despite his hippocratic oath, Fritz Klein, a low-level Nazi doctor, replied: "Of course I am a doctor and I want to preserve life. And out of respect for human life, I would remove a gangrenous appendix from a diseased body. The Jew is a gangrenous appendix in the body of mankind."[20]

Paxson comments: "only when human beings have been rhetorically made into objects and things can they be conceptually treated like things — they can be 'removed' or excised, rather than murdered."[21] This shocking example of the personification of the concept of humanity at the expense of (the reification of) the Jewish people is in some respects comparable with sections in Lamentations, but its purpose there is a positive one, and the transformations go in the opposite direction.

For example, the intensely emotional description of Jerusalem's destruction in Lamentations 2 has surprisingly few references to the city's citizens but is full of references to architectural structures: footstool (v. 1), dwellings (v. 2), strongholds (vv. 2, 5), palaces (v. 5), booth (like a garden) and tabernacle (v. 6), the walls of Jerusalem's palaces, altar = sanctuary = the house of the Lord (v. 7), the wall of daughter Zion, rampart and wall (v. 8), gates and bars (v. 9). These inanimate objects, however, are often personified. They either display human emotions or are treated like humans (altar and sanctuary are "scorned" and "disowned," v. 7; rampart and wall "lament," v. 8). Yet human beings live in these structures (elders and young girls, possibly a merismus). Furthermore, as we have seen above, the geographical location "Jerusalem" is personified and impersonates all her inhabitants. Jerusalem (and what she represents) may have been destroyed without mercy (v. 2), "cut down," "burned," and "consumed" (v. 3), shot at with arrows (v. 4), broken down (v. 6), and laid in ruins (v. 8), but this is *not* how it should be, for she is "Fair Zion," a vulnerable and pitiful woman.

Envisaging the mourning community as a widow provides an ideal platform for the development of the concept of grief (1:1). Comforters were an essential part of the grief process. Thus Fair Zion's vulnerability is cast into sharp relief in the very next verse (1:2: — "she has no one to comfort her"), and this bitter reality turns into a shattering refrain that dominates the

20. R. J. Lifton, *The Nazi Doctors: Medical Killing and the Psychology of Genocide* (New York: Basic Books, 1986), p. 16, quoted in Paxson, *Personification,* p. 51.

21. Paxson, *Personification,* p. 51.

rhythm of the entire chapter. It is not enough that the neighboring nations have become her enemies and refuse to comfort her (v. 2) and even revel in her disgrace (vv. 7-8) — those who belong to her own population are either deported (the nation, v. 3; her children, v. 5) or cannot bring comfort as they themselves suffer the same fate (her young girls, v. 4; her princes, v. 6). So great is her isolation that only *inanimate* objects mourn for her (the personified roads and gates, v. 4). Her first appeal to the Lord is preceded by the unsettling refrain (v. 9): "there is no one to comfort her," and she receives no reply. Thus she turns elsewhere, to the "passers-by," but her suffering seems nothing to them (v. 12). In heart-breaking language she expresses her anguish (v. 16): "For these things I weep; my eyes flow with tears; . . . my children are desolate, for the enemy has prevailed," the core of her lament being the realization of her isolation, echoing the refrain: ". . . for a comforter is far from me, one to revive my courage." The narrator recapitulates the bitter truth (v. 17): "she has no comforter."

This experience of isolation and estrangement reaches into all aspects of communal and religious life. The discussion has already shown that daughter Zion is isolated from her God. This may be further developed, and again it will emerge that the personification of Jerusalem serves as a powerful device to illuminate the broken relationship between Jerusalem and her God. A lasting impression in Lamentations 1 is Jerusalem's consciousness of her sins (vv. 8, 20, 22). The personification of Jerusalem is used ingeniously to depict her sin in vv. 8-10. In daring and provocative metaphors Jerusalem's corporate sin is likened to the voluntary promiscuity of a woman:

> [S]he became filthy . . . they have seen her nakedness. . . . Her uncleanness was in her skirts; she took no thought of her future. . . . Enemies have stretched out their hands over all her precious things; she has even seen the nations invade her sanctuary (1:8-10 NRSV, slightly adapted; see n. 24).

Fair Zion is described as a prostitute. Israel's adultery is a common but nevertheless powerful Old Testament metaphor for idolatry. An extended metaphor in Hosea 1–3 describes the relationship between the Lord and his people as that of husband and wife. Thus when Israel turned to other gods, the nation's behavior could be described as adultery.[22] But

---

22. See A. Fitzgerald, "The Mythological Background for the Presentation of Jerusalem as a Queen and False Worship as Adultery in the OT," *Catholic Biblical Quarterly* 34 (1972): 403-416.

Fair Zion's voluntary promiscuity has suddenly turned into unwanted rape and abuse (the enemy has stretched out his hands over all her precious things). The force of the imagery develops from the correspondence *body = temple* and *genitals = inner sanctuary* (cf. 2:20).[23] To guilt and defilement come shame and disgrace: "all who honored her despise her, for they have seen her nakedness, yea, she herself groans and turns her face away." As the narrator comments in verse 17: "Jerusalem has become a *filthy thing* among them."[24]

This overview of Lamentations 1 highlights the importance of personhood and relationships for the individual and communal grieving process. Personification helps to conceptualize and verbalize pain. Verbal expression of pain seems to have a cathartic and healing effect, and has rightly become a pillar of modern counseling methods. Furthermore, the projection of personal and communal experience ("I" and "we"/"you" [plural]) onto a third person ("she") helps the individual and the community to structure their own experience of themselves.[25] Thomas Aquinas can speak of the impossibility of a transfer of personhood onto others *(incommunicabilitas)* from a philosophical perspective, especially with regard to suffering.[26] Yet personification as a *literary* device in Lamentations enables "representation" and sets in motion an affective and cognitive process in the thought-world of both writer and reader, speaker and listener, which makes such a transferal possible. Personification helps the grieving process by unlocking the inner thoughts of the suffering individuals, breaking the boundaries of privacy and providing an interlocutor, someone to listen and to comfort. In Lamentations 1 four types of personalities emerge: the individual sufferer, the suffering community, others, and God. The individual sufferer and the suffering community have been combined through the personification of Jerusalem, the "others" have turned from "lovers" into "enemies,"[27]

23. Mintz, "Rhetoric," pp. 3-4.
24. In Lev. 12:2; 15:19-20, 26, 33; 18:19; Ezek. 18:6; 22:10; 36:17 the noun נִדָּה (cf. לְנִידָה in v. 8), here translated as "filthy thing," refers to (the impurity of) a woman's menstrual blood; cf. J. E. Hartley, *Leviticus,* Word Biblical Commentary 4 (Dallas: Word, 1992), p. 165, textual note on v. 2.
25. "Die apriorische Relationskategorie Personalität läßt die empirisch begegnende Person als eine Instanz verstehen, die sich in ihrem symbolisierenden und organisierenden Handeln im Verhältnis zu Anderem selbst erlebt" (K. Stock, "Person II," *Theologische Realenzyklopädie* 26 [1996]: 225-31; here: p. 226).
26. Cf. Stock, "Person II," p. 227.
27. This is a typical motif in individual psalms of lament; cf., e.g., Ps. 41:9.

and God has turned from somebody to complain about into someone to talk to, even though that discourse is still restricted to complaints and almost vindictive pleas for the enemies' punishment (vv. 21-22). This latter shift, however, which has occurred toward the end of the composition, is crucial: from talking to "others" and to one another *about* God as an enemy, suffering Jerusalem as a community turns again to her God in talking about her enemies.

Although Jerusalem is still personified ("Daughter Zion," vv. 1, 2, etc.) in Lamentations 2, her corporate identity begins to break up into representative members of the community: rulers (v. 2), king and priest (v. 6), king, princes, and prophets (v. 9), elders and maidens (v. 10), infants and babes (v. 11), mothers and wounded men (v. 12). The physical makeup of the city as a dwelling place is also described in more detail: palaces and strongholds (v. 5), altar, sanctuary, and walls, the temple (v. 7), rampart and wall (v. 8), the gates and their bars (v. 9), streets (v. 11). Last but not least, many of the civic institutions are specified as well: the administration (vv. 6, 9), the temple with its feasts (vv. 6-7), the law and the prophets (v. 9). All these significant parts of the city have one thing in common: they have been violated and destroyed. While Jerusalem is *talked about* by the narrator at the beginning of the chapter (utterance 6, 2:1-12, discussed below), she is *spoken to* in utterance 8 (2:13-19, discussed below), and finally speaks herself in utterance 11 (2:20-22, discussed below). She prays to the Lord for help, for the first time in the book. There is still, however, no corporate sense of guilt, despite the individual's statements (2:14, 17 in utterance 8 = 2:13-19, discussed below) which acknowledge that her present state is the result of the Lord's punishment for her sin. Thus a sense of community and individuality is regained and a dialogue is opened.

In the first part of the chapter, God was still the enemy (esp. vv. 1-9); but now (utterance 8, 2:13-19) the narrator expresses that God purposefully ordained the destruction of Jerusalem because of her sins — including the sins of individuals (vv. 14, 17). This recognition, however, generates an impassioned and urgent summons for Fair Zion to call out to the Lord for help (vv. 18-19).

While the individual is not identical with the "I" of vv. 20-22, he is nevertheless part of the community represented by personified Jerusalem. Here again the vital role of personification for the grief process is revealed. By personifying his own city as another person, the narrator becomes able not only to *speak about* her torment, but also to represent her and *speak for her.* He becomes an interlocutor who is able to express the communal grief, exhort, encourage, and console (ch. 3). The expression of Jerusalem's immeasurable grief has a key function in the chapter and the overall makeup of the book. The poet's questions (2:13):

> What can I say for you, to what compare you, O daughter Jerusalem?
> To what can I liken you, that I may comfort you, O virgin daughter Zion?
> For vast as the sea is your ruin; who can heal you?

respond to daughter Zion's question in 1:12: "is there any sorrow like mine . . . ?" (NJPS, adapted). The problem is not the amount of pain endured, but its boundlessness and lack of analogy: "the Destruction *(sic)* is as unfathomable as the ocean's depths and as extensive as its unseen reaches."[28] By distinguishing himself from his community, the poet is enabled to enter into dialogue with Fair Zion. Not only can he *speak* to Fair Zion *from outside,* as someone who has a wider perspective on the suffering endured by everybody, but, more importantly, he is someone who can *listen* to Fair Zion. And, conversely, Fair Zion is enabled to express herself, and in doing so can listen to her own expression of pain and anguish! The function of this emotional address is threefold:

1. the individual can empathize with his community (cf. the emotional language);
2. the individual can "conceptualize" Jerusalem's grief and provide a point of reference for her. Even if it is "vast as the sea," this categorization makes the catastrophe more comprehensible;
3. Fair Zion is enabled to enter into dialogue: with herself, the poet, passers-by, enemies (defiance), and God (from enemy to helper).

Thereby the individual implicitly acknowledges the severity of Jerusalem's grief and indicates that Jerusalem ultimately needs help from beyond itself, not from the passers-by or the enemies (cf. vv. 15-16) but from God alone. The rhetorical question "Who can heal you?" does not ask for the answer "No one"; rather, the answer is "The Lord alone." This is clear from the following verses (vv. 14-19), particularly v. 19: "Arise, cry out . . . before the presence of the Lord . . . for the lives of your children." This advice, given by the speaker of v. 13, makes sense only if he himself be-

28. Mintz, "Rhetoric," p. 7.

lieves that healing can come from the Lord. This interpretation is confirmed by the fact that Fair Zion responds to this appeal by directly addressing the Lord in vv. 20-22: "Look, O Lord, and consider!", the implication being that she understood the narrator in this way. And in her plea Jerusalem explicitly picks up key motifs of vv. 11-14.

These observations have demonstrated that the personification of Jerusalem has a profound effect on the whole book of Lamentations. It is not merely a literary device which provokes an emotional response to Jerusalem's suffering, but also, and more importantly, it serves an ingenious strategic purpose. As the next section will further explore, it transforms the Jerusalem community into an interlocutor who can perform different roles in the complex dialogue which dramatizes the bereavement of the survivors in Jerusalem — both on an individual and on a corporate level.

III. The Drama of Jerusalem's Bereavement

The frequent and often abrupt change of speakers in Lamentations is one of its most characteristic — and puzzling — phenomena. The problem arises because the grammatical number of the speakers repeatedly changes (from singular to plural and back). This is exacerbated by frequent shifts in perspective or attitude toward Jerusalem's fate. Furthermore, the different speeches often shift from one addressee to another, sometimes within the same discourse. Lastly, several addresses contain embedded utterances by other speakers.

A systematic treatment of these shifts and changes is lacking so far, and there is no consensus about the number of voices in Lamentations. For example, Wiesmann identifies six, Lanahan five, and Provan three voices.[29] Since Provan appears to recognize the lowest number of speakers, a brief discussion of his contribution may prove instructive. The following table outlines his analysis of the number of speakers.

Lam. 1: Two speakers:
        (1) a narrator (vv. 1-11, interrupted in vv. 9c and 11c)
        (2) a sufferer, personified Zion (vv. 9c, 11c-22)

---

29. H. Wiesmann, *Die Klagelieder* (Frankfurt: Philosophisch-theologische Hochschule Sankt Georgen, 1954); Lanahan, "Voice," pp. 41-49; Provan, *Lamentations,* pp. 6-7.

Lam. 2: Two speakers:
        (1) the narrator (vv. 1-19), with two addresses,
           (i) to the reader (vv. 1-12),
           (ii) to Zion (vv. 13-19)
        (2) personified Zion (vv. 20-22)

Lam. 3: Two speakers:
        (1) the narrator (vv. 1-33, 37-66)
        (2) personified Zion (vv. 34-36)

Lam. 4: Two speakers:
        (1) the narrator (vv. 1-16, 21-22)
        (3) the people of Jerusalem (vv. 17-20)

Lam. 5: One speaker:
        (3) the people of Jerusalem[30]

At first glance, Provan's analysis seems convincing. Yet he wonders whether the narrator of the earlier poems might be included among the "we" of chapter 5,[31] and — if one were to follow Provan's method underlying his identification of speakers — one could go further still. First, his isolation of 3:34-36 as personified Jerusalem's objection to the individual's speech in 3:1-33 stands, as he admits, on weak ground. If the speaker in vv. 34-36 is identical to the speaker in the surrounding verses, which is the natural assumption even on Provan's own account,[32] then there is only one speaker in Lamentations 3. Second, a distinction between the "we" in 4:17-20 and 5:1-22 (Provan's third speaker) on the one hand, and personified Zion on the other (Provan's second speaker), is questionable (see the section on personification, above). Third, Provan argues that the "man" in Lamentations 3 is the narrator (Provan's first speaker). Yet the narrator identifies himself as a member of the Jerusalem community, and in Provan's analysis he speaks on behalf of his community in the "we" section(s) of vv. 40-66. In the final analysis Provan's three speakers thus collapse into one. The lack of consensus already mentioned, combined with the problems in Provan's analysis of the number of speakers, suggests that the difficulty with identifying and distinguishing voices or speakers in

30. Provan, *Lamentations,* pp. 33-34, 57-58, 80-84, 109-10, 123-24.
31. Provan, *Lamentations,* p. 124.
32. Provan, *Lamentations,* p. 97.

Lamentations may not be caused by flaws in different analyses as such; rather, the problem may lie with the text itself.

Readers of Lamentations are confronted by a profusion of utterances, speakers, and voices. These utterances are directed at different audiences within the textual world of the book. They convey different, and often competing, messages, and they struggle for the readers' attention. Questions like "Whose voice is the author's? Who is speaking in a particular section? Which voice is 'right'?" are virtually impossible to answer, and the result is bewilderment and disorientation. Analyses which reduce the number of "speakers" before the "voices" have been "heard" in their own right, as distinctive contributions to a discussion of suffering and communal catastrophe *in progress,* may have missed the point. It is possible, then, that the polyphonic nature of Lamentations may not be caused by a stitching together of different sources; nor does it necessarily reflect confusion on behalf of the final editor(s) of the book. Rather, if the present analysis is correct, it may have been designed to reflect the historical situation of a community going through turmoil and crisis. Consequently, analyses of Lamentations which start from a definite number of speakers, such as Provan and others have done, may have by-passed the actual *reading process.* Readers who, apart from such a strict scheme, take each utterance identified below on its own terms may in fact be responding to the book's invitation to take part in the anguished debates of the Jerusalem community. They may, as it were, be joining the discussions in the market square or sit down with the elders outside the city gate, as they rigorously and passionately debate the nature of the disaster that has befallen them, individually and communally.

This study proposes, then, that the book of Lamentations is not a reasoned treatise on the nature of suffering; rather, it reflects a community's desperate grasping for meaning as the world around it — and the political, social, and religious framework which gave this world meaning and purpose — has collapsed. The utterances are so interwoven that only a sequential presentation may do justice to their complex interplay.[33]

---

33. Some of the following observations are based on an interesting discussion of this phenomenon by Lanahan ("Voice," pp. 41-49).

A. *Inventory of Utterances*

Since a clear identification of speakers seems impossible, the different sections in this inventory refer to utterances rather than speakers. Each utterance will be discussed with regard to those textual features which are particularly relevant to its contribution to the dialogue, and thus the treatments of specific utterances may differ in length. The following analyses do not attempt to provide comprehensive verse-by-verse comments, and for such treatments the reader is referred to the standard commentaries. The analyses take particular account of the grammatical number of the speakers, changes of addressees within specific utterances, changes of addressees from one utterance to another, and modifications of perspective and tone.

Utterance 1   The "default voice." An unmarked narrator tells of per-
(1:1-11)   sonified Jerusalem's destruction and the plight of her
                  citizens.

Lanahan's designation of this narrator as a "more objective reporter" is not confirmed by the text itself. Phrases like "How lonely sits the city. . . . How like a widow she has become . . ." (1:1) are hardly cool, descriptive statements.[34] Nevertheless, Lanahan has put his finger on a crucial point. What makes this narrator appear objective is that the narrator simply talks *about* Jerusalem in 1:1-11, *without revealing anything about himself.* A comparison with the way the narrator communicates in other parts of Lamentations may illustrate the particular nature of this first speech.

(a) In 2:1-12 (utterance 6) the narrator exposes himself in two areas: (i) he talks about his feelings (v. 11a: "my eyes are spent . . . my stomach churns . . ."); (ii) he reveals that he is a member of the Jerusalem community at the time immediately after the disaster (v. 11b: "because of the destruction of the daughter, my people"[35]).

(b) According to many scholars, the speaker who addresses Jerusalem in 2:13-19 (utterance 8) is still the narrator of 2:1-12. Yet there are two important differences: (i) he now *speaks to* Jerusalem; (ii) hints at a connection between the speaker and Jerusalem are conspicuously absent, suggesting a lesser degree of identification.

---

34. Lanahan, "Voice," p. 41.
35. NRSV's "because of the destruction of my people" obscures the personification.

(c) The speaker in 3:1-39 (utterance 12), whom many identify with the narrator, finds himself *in opposition to* his people (3:14: "I have become the laughingstock of all my people . . .").

The conclusion to be drawn is that the narrator appears to address different groups of people in Lamentations. In this opening section he addresses his *readership,* while at other times he speaks to his community, the people of Jerusalem. In the first speech he purportedly simply tells the "brute facts" of Jerusalem's fate. Yet these facts are related in a compassionate manner, designed to raise readers' sympathies for the destroyed city. What modern readers should not forget, however, is that when the book was written or edited, the readers whom the author(s) or editor(s) had in mind were of course members of the community in Jerusalem. Thus, contrary to the initial impression, the narrator's readership includes the population of Jerusalem that is addressed in the later speeches. Modern readers are historically and geographically removed from Jerusalem and her destruction, but they are drawn into the situation and take part in the discussions presented in the book, just as the originally intended readers and the "historical" interlocutors in Lamentations itself.

Utterance 2   Two speech fragments, uttered by Lady Jerusalem, are
(1:9c + 11c)   embedded in the opening narrative.

Although these phrases are put into the mouth of Lady Jerusalem, the speech fragments in vv. 9c and 11c are *reported speech* quoted by the default speaker, for v. 11c leads into Lady Jerusalem's reproach of some passers-by (utterance 3) without transition, despite the different addressee. There is no agreement among scholars as to whether Lady Zion's actual lament begins in v. 11c or in v. 12. But v. 9c is framed by the narrator's account and should more likely be regarded as reported speech. Both vv. 9c and 11c are petitions to the Lord and are very similar in language and form, while v. 12 opens with a defiant challenge to some passers-by who do not seem to be in sympathy with Jerusalem. At this point the Lord is merely talked *about.* Although this observation is not conclusive, this may suggest that vv. 12-16 and 18-22 are in fact separate utterances. Whether Jerusalem's speech begins in v. 11c or in v. 12, however, is of secondary importance. What counts is that the addressee has changed, and together with the different tone (from humble petition to defiant challenge) this leads to a fragmentation of the utterances, reflective of the

148

emotional upheaval and disagreement within the city. Jerusalem does not speak with one voice.

Utterance 3
(1:12-16)

Lady Jerusalem, in a lengthy lament replete with first person singular pronominal suffixes, describes her plight. Her speech is interrupted by a short narrative comment (v. 17) before it continues to the end of the chapter (vv. 18-22).

In emotional language, Lady Jerusalem reproaches a group of "passers-by" for failing to take pity on her. Although the meaning of the Hebrew in v. 12 is uncertain, NRSV's rendering "Is it nothing to you . . . ?" is supported by the context. The following injunction to the passers-by uses verbs for "seeing," similar to the two appeals to the Lord (utterance 2, vv. 9c, 11c, discussed above), which were clearly designed to prompt God's compassion and intervention. Furthermore, the statements in v. 12b-c, which describe what the passers-by are to acknowledge, are also designed to raise compassion.

It appears that, after having asked for divine intervention in vain, Lady Jerusalem has now turned away from the Lord. She calls on the passers-by, who turn out to be equally indifferent. Yet the passionate description of her suffering is not a simple plea for compassion but contains an implicit accusation of cruelty on behalf of the inactive onlookers. Although Lady Jerusalem acknowledges her sin in passing (v. 14, the Hebrew of which, however, is uncertain), the detailed description of her suffering, consistently emphasizing its originator, seems to suggest that the Lord's punishment is too cruel (vv. 12b-16).

But who are these "passers-by"? Different answers have been offered, ranging from the "ordinary man" (in the sense of someone who has not gone through similar sufferings) to the cynical onlookers-turned-enemies that often occur in psalms of lament (cf. v. 7c and 2:15c, utterance 9 below). The two options are not mutually exclusive. A variation of the first option, however, should also be considered. Could it be that the passers-by refer to *anybody* who learns of Jerusalem's plight, including successive readers of Lamentations? What is it to *them* that Jerusalem has suffered cruelly at the hand of her God? Readers may suddenly find themselves transformed from mere onlookers into symphathizers reflecting — with Jerusalem — on whether the severity of the divine punishment is really warranted.

Utterance 4
(1:17)
The interpolated "default voice" provides a sensitive and contextually appropriate narrative comment, describing Lady Jerusalem as she utters v. 16 (cf. catchword connections).

This utterance is a short interlude before Lady Jerusalem completes her speech. It provides the narrator's comments on her preceding address, taking up catchwords from v. 16 and highlighting the fact that she has no comforters (cf. vv. 16, 21), only enemies spurred on by the Lord. In a subtle way this sensitive comment underlines that the narrator is listening perceptively to what Jerusalem (his community) has to say.

Utterance 5
(1:18-22)
Lady Jerusalem completes her first speech.

In the second part of her speech, Lady Jerusalem's perspective has changed. She explicitly vindicates the Lord's dealings with her and acknowledges her guilt (v. 18). She points out her deteriorated relationship to former "lovers" (v. 19) who have deceived her. This speech contains two further injunctions. The first is addressed to "all peoples" and asks them to listen and learn of her plight (vv. 18b-19), while the second is directed at the Lord and urges him to punish her enemies with the same severity that she herself has received from him (vv. 20-22).

Utterance 6
(2:1-12)
The narrator, now clearly marked, gives another account of Jerusalem's destruction and the plight of her citizens.

A first person singular narrator recounts his experience of pain at the plight of his people (third person, v. 11), with whom he identifies himself closely. It appears that the narrator's perspective has changed. He responds directly to Lady Jerusalem's speech of chapter 1, reinforcing her own description of the severity of her plight and highlighting the fact that her destruction was the Lord's doing, to the point that he identifies God himself as Jerusalem's enemy (vv. 4 and 5). In the process, he details the destruction of Jerusalem's institutions on the one hand, and the suffering of her constituent members on the other. Verse 12a contains a *reported speech fragment* uttered by "infants and babes" (utterance 7). Utterances 7 and 8 (2:13-19) probably also belong to this speech.

150

Utterance 7   Infants and babes are quoted by the narrator.
(2:12aβ)

This speech fragment, reported by the first person singular narrator of utterance 6, is put in the mouths of "infants and babes" (cf. v. 11), the antecedents of the pronominal suffix in v. 12. It highlights the sheer horror of the suffering in Jerusalem and constitutes the emotive climax of the narrative in 2:1-12. Among other things, the narrator here underlines his empathy and compassion with his people. He is aware of the suffering of the most vulnerable ones, he has heard their cries and understands the cruelty of the situation in which parents who are unable to provide food for their children find themselves.

Utterance 8   The narrative voice returns.
(2:13-19)

In vv. 13 to 19 the speaker changes from a narrator into an interlocutor who plays an integral character part in the textual world of Lamentations. This second address is explicitly directed at Jerusalem and culminates in a passionate assignment for her to implore God on behalf of her children (vv. 18-19;[36] the reference may be both to her citizens and to actual suffering infants, cf. v. 20). His advice to cry out to the Lord stresses the need for urgency and persistence (at night, without respite, everywhere). It also contains reported speeches, one by some passers-by (utterance 9, v. 15c), the other by Jerusalem's enemies (utterance 10, v. 16c).

Utterance 9   Passers-by return (in an interpolation), now overtly
(2:15c)   cynical.

This speech fragment is reported to Jerusalem by the first person singular narrator. While the designation of the passers-by is the same as in 1:12, they are now no longer impartial and detached onlookers, but express open contempt and derision. They are probably not identical with the enemies (v. 16), for the passers-by and the enemies are introduced separately, with two sets of speeches. Although they both express their contempt, the enemies' speech is significantly more aggressive than that of the passers-by.

---

36. Following the emendation suggested by most commentators and adopted in NRSV etc. in v. 18a.

More important, however, is *what* they say: "Is this the city that was called 'the perfection of beauty, the joy of all the earth'?" (NRSV; citation marks added). The embedded expression is a nonliteral, but nevertheless deliberate, quotation from Psalm 48:3 (MT 48:2; cf. also Ps. 50:2). The Psalm cited by the passers-by is a doubly embedded speech: while the direct speech of the passers-by is quoted by the narrator, they in turn cite the psalm. Psalm 48 belongs to the "hymns of Zion" and is thus particularly relevant. It not only contains elaborate reflections on God's protection of "his" city (vv. 1-3) and the respect of the nations for her miltary strength, derived from the divine support she enjoys (vv. 9-11, 4-8), but also draws attention to the city's impressive fortifications. For the original psalmist, all these circumstances were guarantees of the city's perpetual security (vv. 8 and 14). Consequently, the quote not only flings Jerusalem's proud title in her teeth (so Hillers),[37] but is a deliberately torturous sneer with a *theological* twist. It drives home to Jerusalem that the tenets of the so-called "Zion theology," which constituted such a formidable obstacle to the reception of the oracles of judgment which the pre-exilic prophets of judgment had preached (cf., e.g., Isa. 1–39, Jer. 7:1-15), has been shattered. This is confirmed by a reference to false prophets (cf., e.g., Hananiah in Jer. 28) in v. 14.[38] In addition to the citation of Psalm 48:3, however, 2:15 may also allude to Psalm 50:2, the expression כְּלִילַת יֹפִי here corresponding to מִכְלַל־יֹפִי there. Is it mere coincidence that another psalm, separated only by Psalm 49 from Psalm 48, also shares an important and rare phrase with Lamentations 2:15? Psalm 50 certainly has themes which closely link it with Lamentations. For example, the covenant (vv. 5, 16) and its mutual obligations (vv. 15-16) feature prominently, and there is a somber warning that the Lord would "tear apart" his people for her sins (v. 22).[39] The sheer number of connections makes mere coincidence improbable. More likely Lamentations 2:15 contains a conscious

---

37. Cf. Hillers, *Lamentations,* p. 107.

38. So also Westermann, *Lamentations,* p. 155.

39. There is no consensus on the psalm's genre. P. C. Craigie, *Psalms 1–50,* Word Biblical Commentary 19 (Waco: Word, 1983), identifies the psalm as a covenant renewal liturgy. H.-J. Kraus, *Die Psalmen: I. Teilband,* Biblischer Kommentar: Altes Testament 15.1 (Neukirchen-Vluyn: Neukirchener Verlag, [3]1966), p. 372, classifies it as a liturgy of prophetic judgment; similarly F.-L. Hossfeld and E. Zenger, *Die Psalmen I: Psalm 1–50,* Neue Echter Bibel (Echter Verlag, 1993), pp. 308-9. Both classifications, however, underline the importance of covenant faithfulness as a way to avoid judgment.

allusion to both psalms, a sophisticated example of intertextual play. It displays a knowledge of Israel's religious literature which — uttered apparently by "passers-by" from outside the Israelite community — is surprising, if not outright improbable. A more reasonable explanation is that the author/editor of Lamentations 2 puts his *own* words into the mouths of the passers-by. Their taunt, possibly reflecting what the Jerusalem community may have *felt* their enemies were thinking of them, may in reality constitute the author's own biting sarcasm and irony.

Utterance 10   (Omniscient) enemies taunt and torture Jerusalem.
(2:16c)

This discourse fragment is also reported to Jerusalem by the first person singular narrator. Apparently the enemies' taunt includes an allusion to the "day of the Lord's anger" (cf. 2:1, 21-22). Again, it can only be seen as bitter irony that it is by her enemies that Jerusalem is told that her destruction was the Lord's doing. The reference to the "day of the Lord's anger," however, may have a further point of reference in the late pre-exilic prophecy of Zephaniah, who predicted that, because of the people's sin, the day of the Lord would be bitter not only for Judah's enemies but also for Judah herself (Zeph. 1:15–2:3). Again, such an allusion is unlikely from the mouth of Jerusalem's enemies (but cf. 2 Kings 18:25), and it may be that here, too, the author puts his own words into the mouths of others.

Utterance 11   Lady Jerusalem responds to the injunction in vv. 18-19
(2:20-22)   by calling out to the Lord.

As in her earlier requests to the Lord and the passers-by to witness her plight with compassion (cf. 1:9c, 1:11c, 1:20, and 1:12), Jerusalem asks the Lord to take account of the severity of her plight. The very harshness of Jerusalem's sufferings, especially of her most vulnerable inhabitants, serves as a motivation for the Lord to end his judgment and bring salvation. Jerusalem's lament and petition contain barely hidden suggestions that the Lord's judgment is too severe, thus putting him under pressure to intervene. The fact that Jerusalem follows the narrator's advice of vv. 18-19 demonstrates that the communication between them is effective.[40] She

40. The direct discourse is unmarked, and it is not until v. 21 that the reader will be alerted to the fact that the speaker is not the narrator but Jerusalem herself.

also responds to the narrator's rhetorical question from v. 13 by pointing out to the Lord that she has been treated more severely than anyone else.[41] With this injunction a point in the drama is reached where God — albeit implicitly — stands trial. Has he dealt too severely with Jerusalem? The following speaker will try to respond to Jerusalem's question(s).

Utterance 12   A male individual (narrator) tells of his sufferings. (3:1-39)

This is the voice of a single male speaker (אֲנִי הַגֶּבֶר) who defines himself with reference to his people (עַמִּי, v. 14). Most likely he is identical with the narrator of Lamentations 1–2. In vv. 18 and 24 he quotes himself ("his soul" in v. 24), and in vv. 22-23 he may quote a fragment of hymnic praise (see below). The "tone" of this *persona* changes several times in the chapter. The first part is a descriptive lament recalling the individual's inflictions, characterized by despair (vv. 1-20). After a transitional section in vv. 19-20, the individual describes in the second part (vv. 21-33) how his despair has turned into hope by recalling a fragment of hymnic praise (vv. 22-23) that culminates in a bold expression of confidence (v. 24). This leads on to an instructional section in vv. 25-39.

There is no consensus as to the identity of the "I" in Lamentations 3. Is it a personification (of Jerusalem), a corporate personality (= the people of Judah or Jerusalem), a historical figure (Jeremiah, King Jehoiachin), or an idealized figure (a typical sufferer, a Jewish "everyman")?[42] The most promising way to uncover his identity seems to be paying close attention to his interaction with the other voices in the drama.

As Mintz has pointed out, the specific self-introduction as a single male serves to distinguish the voice in 3:1-39 from personified Jerusalem.[43] This identification of the speaker does not simply stress the speaker's *gender,* but also the *number* of the speakers: he is one, as opposed to his community. Thus the speaker in Lamentations 3 is not the voice of personified Jerusalem, nor is it the voice of a corporate personality. This does not, however, mean that he has no connection at all with the

41. The rhetorical question "To what can I liken you?" demands a negative answer: Jerusalem's sufferings are incomparable. While this can be no comfort to her, she uses this insight to imply to the Lord that the severity of his judgment has gone beyond the measure appropriate for her sins.

42. Cf. Hillers, *Lamentations,* pp. 109, 120-23, and Mintz, "Rhetoric," p. 9.

43. Mintz, "Rhetoric," p. 9.

Jerusalem community. On the contrary, the speaker identifies himself as one of its members ("all *my* people," v. 14), albeit as one who suffers from his people's contempt.[44] The phrase "My eyes flow with rivers of tears because of the destruction of *the daughter of* my people" (3:48) recalls 2:11 ("My eyes are spent with weeping . . . because of the destruction of *the daughter of* my people"), which brings him close to the speaker of utterance 6. Furthermore, there are deliberate similarities between Lamentations 3 and the book of Job. For example, vv. 7-8 use imagery familiar from Job (Job 13:27; 33:11; 19:7; 30:20): "He has walled me in . . . though I call and cry for help, he shuts out my prayer" (cf. also 3:14 with Job 30:9 and 3:39 with Job 1:10). Consequently, the speaker of Lamentations 3 may be modelled on Job as the paradigmatic sufferer, both in his acceptance of suffering (Job 1–2) and in his obstinate accusation of God (Job 3–31), but possibly also in his role as final arbiter (Job 42:7-9). Job's relentless accusations of God as his enemy also seem to be reflected in the voice of the narrator in Lamentations 2.[45] Thus he may indeed be intended to represent a "typical" sufferer. In sum, the male individual has suffered a disaster that is similar to the fate of Jerusalem. He is a member of the Jeru-

---

44. Most Hebrew manuscripts read "my people," but the ancient Jewish Sebir, many Hebrew manuscripts, and the Syriac translation read "peoples" (followed by RSV, NEB, and NJPS), which fits much better with the larger context in Lamentations 3 (cf. vv. 45-46, 63), especially if one assumes that the speaker in vv. 40-66 is still the individual of vv. 1-39. However, the very existence of a textual comment like the Sebirin note confirms that the version of the MT was read and perceived to be difficult, which suggests, on the basis of *lectio difficilior,* that MT is to be preferred as the more "original" text (cf. E. Tov, *Textual Criticism of the Hebrew Bible* [Minneapolis: Fortress; Assen/Maastricht: Van Gorcum, 1992], p. 64). "My people" may refer to the people of Judah as a whole, but in the context of the book of Lamentations it more likely refers to the Jerusalem community. The speaker of 3:1-39 recounts in vv. 1-18 how he suffers "under the rod of *his* wrath." It is not until v. 18 that the Lord is explicitly revealed as the individual's enemy, unless one takes יְהוָה from 2:22 as the antecedent of the pronominal suffix in 3:1 (cf. Provan, *Lamentations,* p. 81). In v. 13 the individual recounts how the Lord has shot "arrows" into his body, which is followed by the information that his people held him in derision. This implies that they saw his sufferings as divine punishments for his sins, in accordance with the deed-consequence nexus underlying the Sinaitic covenant and Deuteronomistic theology in general. This brings the individual in Lamentations 3 in close relationship with the servant of Isaiah 53; see esp. Isa. 53:3-4.

45. Concerning the date of the book of Job and its constituent parts, see D. J. A. Clines, *Job 1–20,* Word Biblical Commentary 17 (Dallas: Word, 1989), p. lvii and the literature cited by Clines on pp. cxii-cxiii.

salem community. He uses similar phrases to describe experiences reminiscent of the experience of the narrator in Lamentations 2. His sufferings have made him a laughingstock for his community. Thus the chapter provides a surprisingly large amount of information about this speaker — and yet hints which might have revealed his true identity are conspicuously absent.

The conclusion to be drawn from these details is that — apart from identifications with historical individuals like Jeremiah or King Jehoiachin — most identifications suggested in previous scholarship find some warrant in the text. The solution to the identity of the voice in Lamentations 3:1-39 thus lies in a combination of adaptations of the aforementioned suggestions. Even though the speaker is not a personification, he does *represent* the people of Jerusalem, certainly in the first part of Lamentations 3. This does not mean that he constitutes a "corporate personality" or an idealized figure. But he describes himself as somebody who can identify with his people. Since he suffers pains that are characteristic of his fellow citizens, it is in this sense that he is a "typical" sufferer, and it is in this sense that his suffering represents their suffering. In this way he portrays himself as one who can understand what his people are going through, and this will give his admonition in the later part of his address additional credibility (3:25-39, utterance 12d).

Utterance 12a *The* individual quotes himself (cf. the introductory verb
(3:18)   וָאֹמַר), thus emphatically underlining his despair.

As Provan notes, "this is perhaps the lowest point in the whole poem."[46] The individual reveals his deep despair and hopelessness, and these sentiments are highlighted because the statement is couched in direct speech. Provan and others have pointed out that the individual is in dialogue with himself; but the significance of this internal dialogue is much broader: those who hear or read his words can take part in his most private thoughts and feelings. This powerfully drives home to the whole community in Jerusalem the fact that he knows deep pain and God-forsakenness from personal experience. This adds credibility to his words and paves the way for a change in tone.

46. Provan, *Lamentations*, p. 90.

Utterance 12b   Apparently the individual quotes a fragment of hymnic
(3:22-23)   praise.

Traditionally, the basis for the hope which is expressed from 3:21 onward
has been identified as belief in the mercy of the Lord.[47] While agreeing
with this identification in general, the present anlysis suggests that vv. 22-
23 are more than simple statements of faith; rather, they constitute yet another "voice" with a distinctive contribution to the discussion. This time,
however, the voice speaks from the past. If the present analysis is correct,
these verses may be fragments of an unknown hymnic composition, and
may consequently provide a unique glimpse at one of the sources behind
the text of Lamentations — a psalm of lament, the remainder of which is
now lost. Several arguments foster this suggestion. The first four are con-
textual, the fifth is based on textual observations, and the sixth on syntac-
tic considerations. (1) Form-critical observations have shown that praise
often accompanies the avowal of confidence in psalms of lament, and just
such an avowal of confidence follows in the immediate context (3:24, utterance 12c).[48] (2) In v. 21a the speaker calls something to mind which is
referred to by the (kataphoric) demonstrative pronoun זאת. The referent
of the demonstrative is then quoted in vv. 22-23. However, if the speaker
can "call to mind" what he is about to say, it must have *existed* in his mind
prior to its utterance in the present context. It would be natural to assume
that he refers to a theological truth or spiritual experience that has previously been expressed in the religious lore of his community. In the present
crisis he draws upon this tradition of faith. (3) The second person singular
pronominal suffix in the last word of v. 23 reveals the second colon in this
verse as direct speech, an address to the Lord. Taking this colon alone as
direct address, however, as NJPS has done, would alienate it unduly from
its context. It is more likely that the whole of vv. 22-23 is addressed to the
Lord. (4) Lam. 3:57 comprises another quotation of a traditional lament
(see utterance 14d below). There the fragment quoted is part of what
Begrich has identified as the so-called "salvation oracle."[49] Thus the quotation of traditional lament forms is not unique to vv. 22-23 and 24 (on v.

---

47. Cf., e.g., Hillers, *Lamentations,* p. 128; and Provan, *Lamentations,* p. 93.
48. Cf. Westermann, *Lamentations,* p. 173.
49. See Westermann, *Lamentations,* p. 186; and J. Begrich, "Das priesterliche
Heilsorakel," *Zeitschrift für die alttestamentliche Wissenschaft* 52 (1934): 81-92, reprinted in idem, *Gesammelte Studien zum Alten Testament* (München: Kaiser, 1964),
217-31.

24, see utterance 12c below). (5) Since vv. 21 and 24, like most of Lamentations 3, are uttered by an individual (first person singular), the Masoretic text of v. 22 (לֹא־תָמְנוּ "we are not consumed," first person plural), which indicates several speakers, seems out of step with its context. This may explain why the Syriac translation, the Targum, and one Hebrew manuscript have used the third person plural of the same verb ("they do not come to an end," לֹא־תָמּוּ in Hebrew, with "steadfast love" [plural in the Hebrew] as its subject), thus avoiding a change of speaker. Rather than indicating another Hebrew *Vorlage,* then, these variants may reflect unease with the sudden change of the number of speakers in v. 22 and may constitute an attempt to bring the verse in line with the surrounding material. If vv. 22-23 are recognized as a quotation from a communal psalm, however, the change in the number of speakers is not surprising but natural. (6) The construct phrase חַסְדֵי יְהוָה seems syntactically unconnected to the two following causal clauses, each introduced with כִּי. While NEB's verdict that the Hebrew is "unintelligible" may be exaggerated, renderings like NIV's "Because of the Lord's great love we are not consumed, for his compassions never fail" seem to brush over the difficulties posed by the Masoretic text. More likely is one of the solutions mentioned by Provan: "It is because of the steadfast love of the Lord that we are not consumed, that his mercies never come to an end." In this case, however, one would have expected the preposition בְ- before חַסְדֵי to produce a causal connection. Consequently, another solution mentioned by Provan should be preferred: "But this I call to mind, and therefore I have hope: the steadfast love of the Lord! For we are not consumed because his mercies never come to an end: they are new every morning."[50]

Utterance 12c The individual reports his avowal of confidence. (3:24)

Having recalled part of a traditional psalm (utterance 12b), which belongs to his community's traditional lore, the narrator now expresses his new confidence. The formal introduction through the phrase אָמְרָה נַפְשִׁי puts additional emphasis on his new hope.

50. Cf. Provan, *Lamentations,* p. 93; for an alternative analysis not discussed here, see Hillers, *Lamentations,* p. 115.

Utterance 12d   The individual makes a number of instructional state-
(3:25-39)   ments, presumably directed at his community.

Verses 26-39 should under no circumstances be divorced from v. 25,[51] as vv. 26-27 not only begin with the same letter as v. 25, but with the same word, טוֹב, which implicitly carries an instructional force commensurate with the rest of the utterance (cf. vv. 28-30).

Verses 37-38 affirm the Lord's sovereignty and goodness in the face of suffering in a way similar to Job's affirmation of the Lord's justice in the midst of his trials (Job 2:10). This naturally leads to the rhetorical question of v. 39. While different plausible translations of this verse have been suggested (cf. esp. NJPS and NRSV), the basic point of the question is clear: a sinful man is responsible for his suffering and should consequently not complain about his circumstances.[52]

Utterance 13   A communal voice, which can be separated into three
(3:40-51)   different utterances (13a, 13b, and 13c), enters.

There is no consensus about the delimitation of this section. Westermann takes vv. 40-41 with v. 39.[53] Provan sees all of vv. 42-66 as the narrator's words: in vv. 40-47 the narrator summons his fellow sufferers to repentance and prayer, in vv. 48-51 the narrator laments, mainly about the suffering of others, and in vv. 52-66 the narrator returns to lamenting his own suffering.[54] Hillers takes vv. 42-66 as a common prayer of lamentation and supplication, vv. 42-47 being the people's voice, while vv. 48-51 express the poet's grief over his people's ruin, and vv. 52-66 constitute an individual's appeal for the Lord's intervention.[55] Proper attention to the tone of the utterances and due emphasis on the addressees of different parts in this section may provide a more secure guideline. It appears that this section divides into three different utterances, two of which are apparently uttered by an individual (the narrator). This individual, however, identifies

---

51. Contra Westermann, *Lamentations,* pp. 175-79.

52. Provan, *Lamentations,* p. 99; O. Kaiser, *Klagelieder,* in H.-P. Müller, O. Kaiser, and J. A. Loader, *Das Hohelied. Klagelieder. Das Buch Ester,* Das Alte Testament Deutsch 16.2 (Göttingen: Vandenhoeck und Ruprecht, [4]1992), p. 152 with n. 39, p. 166.

53. Westermann, *Lamentations,* pp. 149-52.

54. Provan, *Lamentations,* pp. 81 and 101.

55. Hillers, *Lamentations,* pp. 123-24, 131.

himself closely with his community, and this makes a separation between him and the community extremely difficult. This circumstance may explain the lack of consensus as to the delimitation of this section.

Utterance 13a
(3:40-41)

A first person plural (cohortative) addresses the community.

This address can be interpreted in three different ways. (1) It could be an individual addressing the community. In this case several other options arise: (a) the speaker could be the individual of 3:1-39; (b) the speaker is the first person singular narrator who spoke in 2:11-19; (c) he could be both; (d) it could be an unknown individual. (2) It could be a group of people who are part of the Jerusalem community. (3) It could be the whole of the Jerusalem community. If options (2) or (3) are correct, they could be identical with the first person plural speakers in vv. 42-47.

Verses 40-41, although continuing the didactic tone of vv. 25-39, turn from an indirect instruction at an unspecified audience to a cohortative in which the instructor closely identifies himself with those he instructs with respect to the actions recommended (self-examination and earnest prayer). Thus there is continuity as well as discontinuity with the preceding section. While vv. 25-39 constituted indirect advice based on the memory of divine mercy experienced in the past (vv. 21-24) and prompted by a common experience of suffering (vv. 1-19, 20), the individual now turns to his community and includes himself in the appeal for self-examination and earnest prayer. His suffering enables him to empathize with their suffering — in fact, his suffering probably *is* their suffering — and thus he can exhort them to join him in repentance.

Utterance 13b
(3:42-47)

The Jerusalem community (or a significant part of it) responds to the preceding call to prayer.

This section cannot stand without the preceding vv. 40-41, for the antecedent of אַתָּה in v. 42 is the Lord (= אֵל) in vv. 40-41. Provan still considers this the individual's prayer, in which he wishes his community to join,[56] but two important changes signify that these verses should be considered a new utterance: the cohortative verb form changes to an indicative form, and the addressee is not the community but the Lord. Thus vv.

---

56. Provan, *Lamentations,* p. 101.

42-47 constitute the community's prayer in response to the summons of vv. 40-41. Significantly, this prayer consists of a confession of sin and a description of how the Lord has afflicted the community. A request for relief from the disastrous situation is conspicuously absent. This may be in reaction to the individual's advice in vv. 26 and 39.

Utterance 13c   The narrator (first person singular) describes his pain at
(3:48-51)   the plight of his community.

This section is characterized as a new utterance by the change of speakers from first person plural to singular, and from prayer to narrative. Utterance 13c is an individual's lament about the suffering of others, in which, however, he expresses his own grief over his people's ruin (vv. 48, 51). In contrast to the surrounding sections (utterances 13b and 14), this "lament" does not address the Lord directly. Thus these lines may be intended for the narrator's readers and listeners. He informs them indirectly of his empathy with them. Their suffering is his suffering, and that is why his exhortation to join him in repentance is convincing (cf. vv. 40-42).

Utterance 14   A narrator, whose contribution can be separated into
(3:52-66)   four different utterances, addresses the Lord in the fashion of an individual psalm of praise.

The narrator (first person singular) describes how enemies have afflicted him (vv. 52-54). Then he tells the Lord, in descriptive praise, how he had asked for deliverance and how the Lord had answered his petition (vv. 55-62). Finally, he asks the Lord to punish his enemies (vv. 63-66). In the process, he quotes himself twice (the evaluation of his desperate situation [v. 54b] and his prayer [v. 56]), and cites the Lord's response to his petition (v. 57).[57]

Utterance 14a   The narrator (first person singular) describes his afflic-
(5:52-54)   tion at the hands of unspecified enemies.

These verses may still belong to the information given to the individual's readers and listeners (cf. utterance 13c), but several features connect it to

---

57. A distinction between utterance 14 and utterance 15 may be justified by the change from narrative to prayer, but this shift in address is no proof that we are dealing with different speakers.

the following section: (1) the catchword בּוֹר "pit" (vv. 53, 55) connects vv. 52-54 with the following verses; (2) vv. 55-62 describe the Lord's response to vv. 52-54; and (3) while vv. 48-51 were lamenting the problems of the speaker's community, he now focuses on his own problems.

This does not mean, however, that the speaker in utterance 14 is different from the individual speaker of the preceding sections, as some have claimed. Hillers, for example, denies the identity of the "I" in vv. 55-66 with the "I" of the beginning because of the speaker's changed perspective. But, as Hillers himself admits, "because of the preceding collective prayer in vv 42-51, the reader is led to think that the speaker of the closing verses is praying on behalf of, or is representing, the people."[58] Even though Hillers admits that a distinction between the "I" of the end and the "I" of the beginning of the poem may appear inconsistent, he argues that

> it seems justified when one recalls that someone *reading* the poem, or a worshipper *hearing* it in a service, experiences the poem serially, starting at the beginning, and is not likely to have the end in mind at the start.[59]

There are several objections to this line of argument: (1) There is no reason to doubt that ancient readers — just like Hillers himself — were able to reread the passage in the light of its end. (2) Even those listening to the poem in the context of worship would have been able to adjust their understanding of earlier parts of the poem in the light of its end, especially since a communal setting would provide opportunity to discuss the poem's meaning, either during or after the act of worship. (3) Hillers neglects the importance of personification; if readers were already sensitive to the concept of representation, as they may very well have been on the basis of observations presented above, then there is no reason to doubt that they were able to adjust their initial understanding of the "I" in the light of the later portrayal.

Utterance 14b   The petitioner (narrator) evaluates his desperate situa-
(3:54b)   tion.

Most significant is the emphatic realism in the individual's self-evaluation: "I am lost." A self-citation has already been put to the same

58. Hillers, *Lamentations*, p. 123.
59. Hillers, *Lamentations*, p. 131; emphases mine.

use in 3:18 (utterance 12a above), highlighting dramatically the individual's desperate situation and thus encouraging his readers and listeners to identify and empathize with *his* suffering, just as he was empathizing with theirs.

Utterance 14c The narrator reports past prayers in which he had asked
(3:56) the Lord for relief from his sufferings.

Since the community's prayer in utterance 13b had not included a prayer for relief, the individual now relates his own prayer for deliverance, offering his own experience and his own pious response as a paradigm for his community.

Utterance 14d The narrator reports the Lord's response: "Fear not!"
(3:57)

The circumstance that the Lord does not speak himself, but only appears in a quotation, has led many scholars to believe that the voice of God is not heard at all in Lamentations. For example, Mintz states that lamentations as a genre (including the book of Lamentations) can be understood as "a record of man's struggle to speak in the face of God's silence,"[60] thus ignoring v. 57. Similarly, Lanahan does not even mention v. 57, and Provan speaks of "the voice that is not itself heard in the book: the voice of God himself."[61] Yet the significance of this phrase, the only divine utterance in Lamentations, should not be underestimated. "Fear not!" is the typical opening of the so-called "salvation oracle" in psalms of lament.[62] The opening phrase ("You came near when I called on you") in v. 57 is reminiscent of Psalm 69:18 (MT 69:19), where the psalmist also asked God to draw near, describing his sufferings in terms quite similar to the situation of the sufferers in Lamentations 3 (cf. Ps. 69:1-3, 14-15, etc.). It appears, then, that the function of the quotation here is similar to the comparable one in vv. 22-24 (utterances 12b + 12c). The individual makes God "come alive" to his fellow sufferers. As God responded to his faithful in the past, so he will respond to their present pleas as well. Here we are at the heart

60. Mintz, "Rhetoric," p. 16.
61. Provan, *Lamentations,* p. 25.
62. Cf. Begrich, "Heilsorakel," p. 83.

of the book of Lamentations. The author/compiler's purpose is to encourage his fellow citizens, and he achieves his aim magnificently by relating his own experience of a divine oracle in the traditional language of his people's accepted religious lore.

Utterance 15
(4:1-16)   A first person singular speaker (a member of the Jerusalem community) narrates the siege and fall of personified Jerusalem and her citizens. He also cites statements by foreigners among whom Jerusalem's citizens now live (v. 15).

The speaker is clearly identified as a member of the community (vv. 3, 6, etc.). Particularly significant for the communal discourse are the individual's statements in vv. 6 and 11-13, which state unambiguously that it was the Lord's punishment for the people's sin which has led to the horrendous sufferings described in verses such as 9-10. Verse 6 provides a further nuance to this justification of the divine punishment: the suffering was so incomparably great because the people's guilt was beyond measure (the guilt and punishment of Sodom and Gomorrah were traditionally believed to represent humanity at its worst).

Utterance 16
(4:15)   Citizens of foreign nations are quoted in stylized language, expressing their xenophobia toward the uprooted citizens of Jerusalem now living among them.

The verse is notoriously difficult, and no consensus about its interpretation has arisen. The interpretation adopted here is similar to Provan's suggestion that v. 15 is part of an extended metaphor:

> The people of Zion are *pictured* as living in the midst of the community of nations as sojourners, and as becoming unclean in the course of their sojourning. Afraid of becoming contaminated by them as they stagger through the streets (which must on this occasion be taken metaphorically), these nations decide that they must leave.[63]

There is no reason, however, not to take the statements more literally. If some of the Jerusalem community have been dispersed among the nations (cf., e.g., Jer. 41:16–43:13, esp. 42:18: ". . . You shall become an object of

63. Provan, *Lamentations,* pp. 118-19; emphasis his.

execration and horror, of cursing and ridicule . . .") in the aftermath of its defeat, those refugees were literally living among the nations. Verse 22 seems to confirm that the exile is an important concern in this chapter. Thus it appears that Lamentations 4 introduces the concerns of Jerusalem's exiles into the textual world of Lamentations.

Utterance 17   First person plural speakers narrate their final defeat
(4:17-20)   and the king's capture.[64]

The citizens of Jerusalem as a group express their recognition that no one could save them from their doom, whether those outside the community ("a nation that could not save" = Egypt) or those inside the community (the present king, "the Lord's anointed").[65] The unexpressed corollary of these statements is that there is only one who can help: the Lord. This recognition will be expressed, finally, in v. 22.

Utterance 18   A — presumably single — speaker (the narrator?) ad-
(4:21-22)   dresses Edom and Jerusalem, who are personified as
           women. This speaker is distinct from the Jerusalem
           community, but this does not preclude him from being
           one of its members.

After opening his address with a curse against personified Edom (cf. Obad. 11),[66] the individual announces to personified Jerusalem that "with the fall of the city and the beginning of the exile the flood tide of Yahweh's wrath" has passed.[67] Even though this is not an announcement of salvation and falls short of the prophetic oracle of salvation proper, its thematic similarity with the call to spread the message of comfort to Jerusalem in Isaiah 40:2 is striking. As in Second Isaiah, then, the announce-

---

64. Hillers (*Lamentations*, 150) thinks that the plural form of the first person "we" identifies the single speaker very closely with his people. Lanahan thinks that the "bourgeois" shifts to the first person plural because "he has some sense of identity with his fellow-citizens" (idem, "Voice," p. 48). The individual and the community blend into one another.

65. Concerning the messianic overtones perceived in this phrase at a later date, see esp. W. Horbury, *Jewish Messianism and the Cult of Christ* (London: SCM Press, 1998), pp. 91-92.

66. Edom may be an impersonation of the cynical passers-by in 2:15c.

67. Hillers, *Lamentations*, p. 153.

ment in Lamentations 4:22 may be prompted by God.[68] The speaker knows more than his community, and on the basis of his insight into the divine plan, he can comfort his fellow citizens with this, the only real note of unrestrained hope in Lamentations.

Utterance 19 (5:1-22)	The Jerusalem community (first person plural), bemoans, in a more traditional communal lament, the situation in the fallen city. The lament is directly addressed to the Lord.

There is only one voice in Lamentations 5, the voice of the Jerusalem community as a whole. Although the narrator of the earlier chapters is not included explicitly, he may reasonably be included with this communal voice. The hope expressed by the narrator at the end of Lamentations 4, however, is not present — at least not to the same degree. Lamentations 5 closely follows the traditional pattern of the communal lament. Most important for appreciating the contribution of this voice to the communal discourse on Jerusalem's bereavement are vv. 1 and 19-22. Verse 1 opens the lament with an appeal for God to "remember" (= "take to heart") Jerusalem's plight, the only occasion in the book when a direct address to God opens a song. Together with the plea for restoration in v. 21, this petition frames the lament and, together with the descriptive praise in v. 19, dominates its tone. The request in v. 21 is a prayer for the restoration of the Jerusalem community to its former relationship with God, and consequently the reestablishment of its former socio-political integrity. However, the accusation of God implicit in the questions of v. 20 and the doubtful question " — or have you utterly rejected us?" in v. 22, which serve as a motivation for the Lord to grant the preceding request, remain the final word in the book.[69] Jerusalem's suffer-

---

68. The close connection between Second Isaiah and Lamentations has frequently been noted; cf. Kaiser, *Klagelieder,* pp. 186-87; Seitz, *Word* (above n. 10), pp. 130-49. Pointing out thematic and theological parallels as well as literary and verbal connections between Lamentations and Second Isaiah (ibid., pp. 133-36), Seitz has argued persuasively that the crisis with which the book of Lamentations wrestles provides the proper literary and religious setting for Second Isaiah, suggesting a rather direct literary response to Lamentations in Second Isaiah: "'where is my comforter?' Lamentations asks repeatedly, with Second Isaiah responding to that plea" (Seitz, *Word,* p. 134).

69. Alternatively, v. 22 may be a descrete reminder ("unless you have utterly rejected us"); cf. Kaiser, *Lamentations,* p. 197. For convenient summaries of interpretations of this difficult phrase, see R. Gordis, "The Conclusion of the Book of Lamenta-

ing caused by her bereavement — and her concomitant doubts about the justification of the Lord's cruel dealings with her — will not be resolved, not, at least, until the Lord restores her fortunes.

B. Summary

The preceding inventory of utterances in Lamentations has revealed three major players and at least four minor voices in the public discourse about Jerusalem's bereavement. The main contributors to the dialogue are:

1. a narrator, who assumes different attitudes toward Jerusalem and her fate (utterances 1, 2, 4, 6, 8, 12a-c, 13a+c?, 14a-d, 15, 18?) and who at times can hardly be distinguished from his community;
2. Lady Jerusalem, who represents her community but raises her voice as an individual and who is addressed as an individual (utterances 2, 3, 5, 11; personified Jerusalem recurs in later utterances, but her voice gives way to the communal voice);
3. a communal voice which at times may encompass all citizens of Jerusalem, while at other times only a number of its members, or a certain group within the community, may contribute to the discussion (utterances 13b, 13a+c?, 17, 19).

The minor voices contributing to the dialogue are:

1. infants and babes (utterance 7); although they are of course part of the Jerusalem community, their vulnerability is expressed so emphatically as to set them apart as an identifiable part of the community with its own distinctive contribution to the communal dialogue;
2. passers-by (they speak in utterance 9, but are addressed in utterance 2; cf. also personified Edom, addressed in utterance 18) who cynically deride Jerusalem;
3. enemies (utterance 10) who taunt and torture Jerusalem;
4. xenophobic citizens of foreign nations (utterance 16) who reject the dispersed Israelites living among them.[70]

tions (5:22)," *Journal of Biblical Literature* 93 (1974): 298-93; Hillers, *Lamentations,* pp. 160-61, and the overview in Westermann, *Lamentations,* pp. 217-19.

70. Unfortunately this kind of reaction still prevails today and needs to be taken just as seriously as it was taken by those who compiled the book of Lamentations.

It is difficult to decide whether or not God should be included among these minor voices. Although he should have been a major contributor, he remains conspicuously quiet. He is talked about and spoken to, but never raises his voice. The only time he is heard he does not speak himself, but appears in a quote which recalls his affirmative "Fear not!" in response to the narrator's lament in a previous crisis. Similarly, even though God may have prompted the comforting note of hope for Jerusalem in 4:22, this circumstance remains implicit. In Lamentations, then, God speaks only from the margin. It is significant, however, that the note of hope and the "Fear not" are both positive statements commensurate with the purpose of the whole book.

IV. Conclusion

The book of Lamentations responds to the religious doubts and the communal and individual grief and pain of those surviving in Jerusalem after its destruction. This response, however, does not consist in a religious monologue which pre-empts the community's pain and doubts. Rather, the author(s) and/or editor(s) of Lamentations have created an artistic literary composition which reflects the real-life drama of bereavement in Jerusalem. The most important poetic strategies to achieve this end are the personification of Jerusalem and the dramatization of a public dialogue. This dialogue is recorded by means of different utterances made by speakers who sometimes change their perspective and respond to each other, just as they would do in real life.

This complex interaction, reflected by the different viewpoints in the dramatic dialogue, has been achieved through the literary creation of different personae.[71] These personae are part of the fiction in the textual world of Lamentations, characters invented for the particular artistic purpose of presenting the community's struggles for survival, literally and metaphorically, as it wrestles with the issues of faith, doubt, and meaning in the face of the disaster.

The most important persona in this public dialogue is the personification of Jerusalem. She has become a powerful cultural icon with which

71. For a definition of the term *persona* and a description of its function, cf. M. H. Abrams, *A Glossary of Literary Terms* (New York: Holt, Rinehart and Winston, [4]1981), 131.

the community can identify. She can impersonate each individual survivor in Jerusalem, from infants and babes to old men and women. They can all see and experience their own sufferings, thoughts, and emotions as they are lived out in Lady Jerusalem's plight. As she can represent both the individual members of her community and the community as a whole, she can feel, think, respond, and speak for them. The personification has transformed the community and its members into a persona who can play the leading role in the drama of Jerusalem's bereavement. In this way, their pain has found an expression that is both individual and communal, so that each person's individual pain can be faced and expressed, while the agony experienced by the other members of the community is also included.

The expression of pain, fear, doubt, and anger, however, is an important step in the grieving process, and so the book of Lamentations does not simply record a fictional drama, but provides a paradigmatic dialogue which reflects the emotional reality of the inhabitants of the world it describes. The utterances of the different personae in Lamentations do not correspond to the author's own perspective.[72] Rather, his own perspective is captured only in the individual narrator's utterances, and it is important to note how his perspective changes in the process of the dialogue. He does not dominate the other personae, for his voice is but one interactive contribution to the communal discourse. The voices of the other personae in the book are not silenced, but contribute to the understanding of the narrator and to the overall perspective of the book. The (implied) author of the book, who has taken on the persona of the narrator, identifies himself closely with his people and has, by means of the solidarity of his suffering and by his ability to listen to the other voices in the book, earned the right to speak to his people and on behalf of his people.

It appears, then, that Lamentations is a consciously "open" text which gives *multiple* answers to the complex questions related to Jerusalem's destruction.[73] In this sense it is still relevant today,[74] and it has a strong appeal in a postmodern world, where, bewildered by their own helplessness when confronted with suffering on a global and local scale, modern readers search for meaning.

---

72. Cf. Provan, *Lamentations,* p. 18.
73. Cf. U. Eco, *The Open Work* (London: Radius, 1989).
74. Cf. Provan, *Lamentations,* p. 24.

Molek of Jerusalem?

REBECCA DOYLE

Although Jerusalem provided the model for a pure faith directed toward God, there is also evidence of the presence of other darker deities in the city. This essay traces the presence of the terrible god Molech, whom the Bible remembers as demanding human sacrifices and whom biblical authors condemn repeatedly as a hideous example of the false worship that remained in contrast with that for which Jerusalem and its temple were especially set aside.

I. Introduction

Interest in the gods of the nations surrounding ancient Israel has fuelled the fires of many a scholar's imagination for some time now. Molek[1] not the least of them. Jerusalem was claimed by the Israelites and their Hebrew scriptures as the center for the worship of the High God, YHWH (יהוה); Jerusalem the holy city; Jerusalem where the temple with the name of YHWH was set (Deut. 12:5; 2 Sam. 7:13; 1 Kings 7:13; 2 Kings 11:36; Jer. 7:9-10; etc.). This Jerusalem may also have been the source of one of the more hideous forms of Canaanite worship. Was Molek first and fore-

---

1. There are a variety of spellings for this name depending on how the Hebrew or the Greek is transliterated. The spellings include Molek, Molech, and Moloch.

most Jebusite with his cultus centered in or near Jerusalem? Or was Molek imported from outside Israelite borders?

The Hebrew scriptures mention the god Molek very few times by name (Lev. 18:21; 20:2-5; 1 Kings 11:7; 2 Kings 23:10; and Jer. 32:35). This article will explore some of the debate that has engaged the scholars and what they suggest as the origins and forms of the cult of Molek. Also in this article the evidence of a god Molek in the ancient Near East (ANE) will be included to provide some perspective on the Molek of the Hebrew scriptures and deities with similar names from the surrounding nations. Lastly, Molek as presented in the Hebrew scriptures will conclude our study. As will be seen from our discussion the Hebrew scriptures are our best source of information about the god Molek; who was he and where was he worshipped?

II. The Scholars and Molek

Much ink and paper have been used to discuss the subject of Molek[2] in the Hebrew scriptures. This is, in part, because the texts of scripture that deal with Molek are not explicit and they are few, and, also in part, because there is little or nothing in the way of archaeological evidence of a cult or the worship of Molek. It is just this lack of evidence that has allowed for so much speculation.

MLK (מלך) as a simple Semitic root can be vocalised in classical Hebrew as *melek* (מֶלֶךְ) = "king" or *mālak* (מָלַךְ) = "he ruled" (Jos. 13:10) or *molek* (מֹלֶךְ cf. Jer. 22:11) in participial form. Those that have attempted to identify who "the molek" (הַמֹּלֶךְ) of the Hebrew scriptures is, are separated into at least two groups. There are those who take the position that *molek* is a title of some sort. The most extreme members of this group claim that there was no god with a name Molek; that the Hebrew letters *MLK* should be vocalized as *melek* meaning "king." In the other group are those who will go as far as to say that Molek was not only a god

---

2. Note in this section, "The Scholars and Molek," "Molek" will be used rather than "molek," as we are not translating specific passages for which a nominal sense would be determined by the presence or lack of an article. Another factor taken into consideration here is that since the scholars themselves use "Molek" as a name as against *molk* as a type of sacrifice, it would follow form to use the same spelling. So, unless a specific passage is being translated "Molek" will be used.

of Canaan, but that he was confused with YHWH, and may even have been worshipped as part of Yahwism.

A. A Very Brief History of the Scholarship

The rabbis assumed that Molek, as vocalized by the Masoretes in the first or second century A.D.,[3] was an idol, the name of which derived from the word translated as "king."[4] Up to the turn of the present century, many different views were proposed incorporating this view of Molek as an idol. Suggestions were made that human sacrifice was normative in the days of Moses and Abraham, and was excluded from Yahwism at a later date. A modern variation of this theme is that child sacrifice was legitimate in Israelite religion.[5] Another suggestion was that Baal was the god of fortune and Molek the god of misfortune in a dualistic pattern.[6]

But, with the turn of the century, the nature of the debate on Molek underwent some distinct changes. One significant change, proposed by Eissfeldt,[7] was that *MLK* in the Phoenician script on the Punic stelae from Carthage[8] was to be understood as a *type of sacrifice* and not as a god. He then applied this argument to his interpretations of Molek in the scriptures. Another argument was that *MLK* was a title or epithet, meaning "king," rather than an actual divine name.[9] These ideas have since formed the basic watersheds of the debate. The scholars have either tried to refute or confirm *MLK* as the name of a particular god, an epithet, or as a type of sacrifice.

Notable at the periphery of the debate is Jeffrey Tigay. He has writ-

3. Cf. *Anchor Bible Dictionary,* vol. 4 (New York: Doubleday, 1992), for articles on the work of the Masoretes.

4. G. C. Heider, *The Cult of Molek: A Reassessment,* JSOT Supplement 43 (Sheffield: JSOT Press, 1985), p. 2.

5. S. Ackerman, *Under Every Green Tree: Popular Religion in 6th Century Judah,* Harvard Semitic Monographs 46 (Atlanta: Scholars Press, 1992), p. 126.

6. Heider, *The Cult of Molek,* pp. 7-9.

7. O. Eissfeldt, *Molk als Opferbegriff in Punischen und Hebräischen und das Ende des Gottes Moloch,* Beiträge zur Religionsgeschichte des Altertums 3 (Halle: Max Niemeyer, 1935).

8. See below.

9. M. Buber, *Kingship of God,* trans. R. Scheimann, 3rd ed. (New York: Harper & Row, 1967). German original, 1956.

ten a treatise on the onomastic evidence of divine names (theophoric names) in the Hebrew epigraphic material. His conclusion is that there was little or no polytheism in Israel, because there is very little evidence of personal names with theophoric elements of pagan gods. However, he has made the previous assumption (following the arguments of Martin Noth 1928, Roland de Vaux 1964, and Otto Eissfeldt 1935) that *MLK* is not a theophoric element, and so discounted from his research the names including these radicals.[10] This seems to be the assumption of his conclusion in his premise.[11] However, Tigay has included several names with the elements *MLK* in his appendices.

B. Divine Name, Title, or Epithet?

Heider, in his review of the classical studies of the understanding of the way *MLK* is used, has cited Martin Buber as one who contends that *MLK* was not a divine name. He summarizes Buber: "it was a title (melek) used by syncretists who advocated child sacrifice to Yahweh."[12] Heider indicates that the Hebrew scriptures' use of *MLK* in personal names does not make it clear as to whether these radicals are used as a title or a divine name.[13] For instance, does *'bymlk* (אבימלך) read as "Molek, my father" or as "the king, my father"? Heider sides with those that consider *MLK* to be a divine name. And since this is the major contention in Heider's thesis, and because of the inconclusive nature of the evidence, he has decided not to rely on personal names with the elements *MLK* in his research. John Day makes the suggestion that an epithet *melek* would challenge the status of Yahweh:

> Everything suggests that *mlk* was the actual name of the god to whom human sacrifice was offered, since there was every reason for the Old Testament to avoid using *mlk* as the epithet of any god but Yahweh, as the word, which means 'king,' might appear to question Yahweh's sovereignty. It is consistent with this that the Massoretes felt constrained to

10. J. H. Tigay, *You Shall Have No Other Gods: Israelite Religion in the Light of Hebrew Inscriptions* (Atlanta: Scholars Press, 1986), p. 11, n. 30; p. 13, n. 38; p. 77, n. 18.

11. Private conversation with Professor John Rogerson.

12. Heider, *The Cult of Molek*, pp. 50-51.

13. Heider, *The Cult of Molek*, pp. 231-32.

bowdlerize the name (presumably originally Melek) to Molech, with the vowels of the word *bošĕt* 'shame'.[14]

While Buber suggests *MLK* as a title, Heider maintains that *MLK* actually is a divine name but concedes that the evidence is not clear, and Day remarks that *MLK* as a title would be unlikely because of the trouble that it would create for the monotheists. This brings us to the next set of arguments regarding Molek's identity. What was his name?

C. Dyphemism (Geiger)

Abraham Geiger proposed that the Masoretes, when pointing the text, used the vowels of the word *bošĕt* (בֹּשֶׁת) meaning "shame" to vocalize *MLK* when they understood them to be used as a divine name.[15] This substitution of vowels in words (dyphemism) that were detested by the scribes seems to be apparent for words such as: Baal (Bosheth), Astarte (Ashtoreth), and Tophet. Following Geiger and Roland de Vaux,[16] A. R. W. Green suggests that

> "Moloch" [*sic*] comes from the Greek versions and appears as "Molek" in the Hebrew, which was an epithet Hebrews applied to Yahweh. . . . According to the theory which tries to account for the change, the Jews considered it inappropriate to refer to a pagan god by the same epithet used for Yahweh. Hence, instead of "Melek," the designation "Molek," an apparent derogatory distortion which took the vowels *o* and *e* from *boseth* [*sic*] (shame) was used.[17]

This theory is still assumed among most of the scholars on both sides of the argument. But *MLK* can be vocalized in several different ways, as

14. J. Day, *Molech: A God of Human Sacrifice in the Old Testament* (Cambridge: Cambridge University Press, 1989).

15. A. Geiger, *Urshcrift und Ubersetzungen der Bibel* (Breslau: n.p., 1857), as cited by Day, *Molech,* p. 56.

16. Geiger, *Urschrift;* R. de Vaux, "Review of Eissfeldt's 'Molk als Opferbegriff,'" *Biblica* (1936).

17. A. R. W. Green, *The Role of Human Sacrifice in the Ancient Near East,* American Schools of Oriental Research Dissertation Series 1 (Missoula, MT: Scholars Press, 1975), pp. 179-80. He cites Pss. 5:2; 10:16; etc. for this thought and also mentions Molek was the god to whom children were sacrificed.

mentioned above. The vowels *o* and *e* were assigned by the Masoretes late in the history of the Hebrew scriptures. Do we trust the Masoretes to give us his name? Did they even know his name?

D. Tophet

Tophet is another word subject to "bowdlerizing," as Day calls it. There is no alternative form for this word, as with *molek,* but the assumption is still generally made that it has taken the vowels of the word *bosheth,* as given by the Masoretes. As will be explored in a later section, the tophet has reference to either the location of the sacrifice or the altar of sacrifice itself, and the tophet is always mentioned in relation to Jerusalem or the Hinnom Valley. The tophet is therefore associated with the valley of Hinnom as the very locus of the cult of Molek.

The origin of the word, tophet, is in dispute, so the meaning is hard to ascertain. It is most commonly suggested that *tophet* means "oven" or "fire pit." This has nicely lent itself to the impression of cremation or sacrifice by burning.[18] Tophet (תֹּפֶת) is mentioned solely in relation to passing children through the fire, with Ben-Hinnom, or with Molek. This singularity in use has served only to compound the confusion of its meaning. The scholars have borrowed the name Tophet from the Hebrew scriptures to describe sites where evidence of child sacrifice has been uncovered by archaeologists.[19]

E. Dedication, or Holocaust?

Another issue in the debate is the nature of the sacrifice given to Molek. Is this a dedication, as Weinfeld suggests? His proposal is that "pass through" (העביר) is to be understood as to pass between a set of fires as a ritual dedication or an initiation. He resists believing in the actual slaughter of the children by fire (cremation).

18. Add to this Isaiah 30:33 as mentioned later where fire and the breath of YHWH as brimstone lend to the impression of fiery destruction. Note there that the spelling of the word in Isaiah 30 is תָּפְתֶּה.
19. Cf. L. E. Stager and S. R. Wolff, "Child Sacrifice at Carthage — Religious Rite or Population Control?" *Biblical Archaeological Review* 10/1 (1984): 32.

Indeed, the problem of the very existence of child sacrifices in ancient Israel and neighbouring peoples was not my concern. The main purpose of my study [his first article, "The Worship of Molech and the Queen of Heaven," 1972] was to show that the Molech ritual, as presented in the legal and historical literature of the Old Testament, had to do with initiation and dedication to foreign cult [*sic*] (Hadad) rather than with slaying and burning babies (square brackets mine).[20]

This is Day's response to such a suggestion:

With regard to the question whether the Molech cult involved human sacrifice or simply dedication in the fire, some scholars deny that even the Old Testament itself speaks of sacrifice. But this is to overlook the evidence of the text itself, which clearly speaks of burning (Jer. 7.31, 19.5; *cf.* 32.35).[21]

The passages which use "to pass through" could possibly be understood as Weinfeld suggests — a dedication by passing between two fires. But taken on the whole with other verses which use the same imagery (i.e. the tophet, Ben-Hinnom, YHWH's rejection of the action, children and fire) the meaning seems quite clear. Jeremiah's and Deuteronomy's use of "to burn" (שׂרף Jer. 7:31; 19:5; cf. Deut. 12:31) leaves no doubt that holocaust was intended. B. P. Irwin, in his essay on Molek imagery in Ezekiel 38 and 39, concurs with Day in the opinion that the Molek cult involved complete annihilation, not simply a dedication.[22]

F. Origins

As the section on "MLK of the ANE" will demonstrate, the search for the origins of a Molek cult have led the scholars far and wide. These next three sections are presented at this point in the discussion because they are so intimately intertwined with the Hebrew scriptures themselves. This next section will look to the Israelites' claim to Palestine, then an archaeo-

20. M. Weinfeld, "Burning Babies in Ancient Israel: A Rejoinder to Morton Smith's Article in *Journal of the American Oriental Society* 95 (1975) pp. 477-79," in *Ugarit Forschungen* 10 (Münster: Verlag Butzon & Bercker Kevelaer, 1978), p. 411.
21. Day, *Molech,* pp. 82-83.
22. B. P. Irwin, "Molek Imagery and the Slaughter of Gog in Ezekiel 38 and 39," *Journal for the Study of the Old Testament* 65 (1995): 110-11.

logical site in Phoenician, Amman, Assyrian, and Canaanite origins will be considered.

1. Palestine

The Israelites occupied Palestine and claimed it as their own by virtue of divine gift (Gen. 12:7). This land was given with the stipulation that the people of God would not practice the religions of the people of Canaan (Exod. 20; Deut. 12-13). Deuteronomy 12:31 remarks specifically about what YHWH hates: "You shall not do thus to YHWH your God, for all the abominations which YHWH hates they do for their gods, even their sons and daughters they burn in the fire to their gods." But there is no extra-biblical material from Palestine that describes the cult of Molek in this land. We do not have any definite answers to the questions of the origins of a cult of child sacrifice to Molek at the tophet in Ben-Hinnom. We have only these accusations from the Hebrew scriptures that the Canaanites practiced this "abomination." It is just this paucity of evidence that leads to great speculation.

2. Phoenician Origins

There is substantial evidence that the Phoenicians during the time of the divided monarchy of Israel and Judah practiced child sacrifice. The proximity of time and cultures has led many scholars to look to Phoenicia as a source for a cult of child sacrifice. However, Weinfeld wants to put to rest the idea that there was a Phoenician influence in Israelite religion. He states:

> The most decisive argument against the theory that it was due to Phoenician influence that Molech was introduced into Judah is the fact that no hint of this cult is to be found in the Northern Kingdom. If Molech worship originated in Phoenicia, we would expect to find it specifically in the Northern Kingdom, which maintained ties with Tyre, particularly under the dynasty of Omri.[23]

Weinfeld seems to have missed the reference to child sacrifice and the Sepharvites in 2 Kings 17:31. Would he argue that this is eighth century

23. M. Weinfeld, "The Worship of Molech and the Queen of Heaven," in *Ugarit Forschungen* 4 (Münster: Verlag Butzon & Bercker Kevelaer, 1972), p. 140.

B.C. (Assyrian) whereas Omri was ninth century (Israel)? The Hebrew scriptures alone are our only source of information that there was an institution of child sacrifice in Palestine and without material evidence, it is impossible to apportion origin for certain.

Both Heider and Kempinski[24] mention a memorial stela (ca. 500 B.C.) from the Iberian Peninsula as an instance of the Punic practice of child sacrifice. The stela was first published in Spanish by Martin Almagro-Gorbea[25] as the Pozo Moro monument. The consensus is that a frieze from the reconstructed stela depicts the god of death (Mot according to Kempinski) enjoying a feast. The scene includes a pig set on a table in front of a seated god and a "small person" offered in a bowl, to this same god, by an attendant standing behind the table. Heider cites Kennedy[26] as assuming that there is a second "small person" which, as Kennedy states in a different publication, is "on the top of a low altar located alongside the banquet table itself."[27] Kempinski comes to the independent conclusion that this "second small person" is rather "an animal head, a jar and what may be a loaf of bread." Heider is the one who suggests the connection between this stela and the god Molek[28] on the basis of its depiction of child sacrifice.[29]

24. A. Kempinski, "The Early Evidence. From Death to Resurrection," *Biblical Archaeology Review* 22/5 (1995): 57-65, 82.

25. M. J. Almagro-Gorbea, "Les reliefs orientalsants de Pozo Moro (Albacete, Espagne)," in J. Duchemin, ed., *Mythe et Personification* (Paris: Société d'Édition "Les Belles Lettres," 1980), as cited by Heider, *The Cult of Molech,* p. 190; "Pozo Moro" in *Madrider Mitteilungen* 24 (1983): 177-293, as cited by Kempinski, "The Early Evidence."

26. C. A. Kennedy, "The Mythological Reliefs from Pozo Moro, Spain," in *Society for Biblical Literature.* Seminar Papers (Atlanta: Society of Biblical Literature, 1981), pp. 209-16; "Tartessos, Tarshish and Tartarus: The Tower of Pozo Moro and the Bible." Paper presented at the First International Meeting of the Society of Biblical Literature at Salamanca, Spain, 1983, as cited by Heider, *The Cult of Molek,* p. 190.

27. These two publications by Kennedy (1981 and 1983) must be very similar, at least according to the quotations that Heider cites.

28. Cf. Heider, *The Cult of Molek,* pp. 188-94.

29. Kempinski's article offers the first photos of this stela that I have seen. The figures are stylized and difficult to interpret. The "first small person" could possibly be interpreted in non-human terms just as the "second small person" has been interpreted by Kempinski, at least from the photos. Kempinski offers a line drawing with the photo to allay any question regarding his interpretation.

3. Amman

The excavations near the airport in Amman[30] where altars of a fire cult were found containing human bones mixed with animal bones offer evidence not too far afield. Hennessy renders a description of the use of the site thus:

> There can be little doubt that a major concern of the ritual at the Amman airport temple was the burning of human bodies and the scattering of the remains within the building and possibly outside. There appear to be two possible explanations for the site. It was either a mortuary temple or a temple associated with human sacrifice.[31]

The site has been dated from the fifteenth to the thirteenth centuries B.C.[32] He makes the connection of this site with Phoenicia by association, noting the combinations of the human and animal bones that have been found "in the tophets of Phoenicia" are similar to those found at Amman. It is interesting that in the final sentence where Hennessy suggests "to which god or goddess the sacrifices were made" he does not list Molek.[33]

4. Assyria (Weinfeld)

For understanding the origins of a Molek cult in Palestine, appeal is made to information regarding Assyrian deities, because Ahaz King of Israel is the first to be noted as having passed his son through the fire (2 Kings 16:3; 2 Chronicles 28:3) during the period of Assyrian influence.[34] This

30. J. B. Hennessy, "Excavation of a Late Bronze Temple at Amman," *Palestine Exploration Quarterly* 98 (1966): 155-62.
31. J. B. Hennessy, "Thirteenth Century B.C. Temple of Human Sacrifice at Amman," in *Studia Phoenicia. Phoenicia and Its Neighbours,* vol. 3 (Leuven: Uitgeverij Peeters, 1985), p. 99.
32. Hennessy, "Excavation," p. 162.
33. Hennessy, "Thirteenth Century B.C. Temple," pp. 100, 104.
34. Following this passage in 2 Kings 16:10-14, it is mentioned that Ahaz built an altar according to the design of one in Damascus. Damascus was in the center of the Aramean population which was also under Assyrian rule at the time (cf. M. Weinfeld, "The Worship of Molech and the Queen of Heaven," in *Ugarit Forschungen* 4 [Münster: Verlag Butzon & Bercker Kevelaer, 1972], pp. 146ff.). Ahaz is also credited for introducing several other foreign gods — the Host of Heaven, the Queen of Heaven, astral deities, and star gods; possibly also astrology was revived.

seems to be the first instance in the historical texts of an Israelite perform-
ing child sacrifice.

Assyrian culture and history predate earliest Israel by several centuries, and extended to the time of the Hebrew kings. Its proximity to Israel (locally as well as chronologically) is not just at the back door. Assyria (possibly with its gods) has barged its way in.[35] 2 Kings 17:29-31
mentions an Assyrian policy of re-populating the conquered nation of
Israel with peoples from other nations after the fall of Samaria in 721
B.C. Verse 31 notes in particular the Sepharvites, who sacrificed their
children to Adrammelech and Anammelech. There is not much known
about these two gods, but the assumption is often made that they are a
product of a syncretism between Molek of Canaan/Phoenicia and Adad
of Assyria.[36]

Weinfeld suggested that it was Ahaz who imported the cult of child
sacrifice from Assyria.[37] He was not the first to make this inference. Abraham Kuenen made these statements in 1874:

> It was not until Ahaz connected himself with the worshippers of Mo-
> lech, that the sacrificing of children in honour of that deity was men-
> tioned in their annals. . . . Perhaps his contact with the Assyrians, who
> sacrificed human beings, may have incited him to follow their ex-
> ample.[38]

Although Kuenen only wants to put the case that Ahaz practiced what he
learned from the Assyrians, there are others that have suggested that the
Assyrians forced their religious system on the conquered Israelite nation
as part of their military strategy. J. W. McKay presented a dissertation
refuting Theodor Östreicher's proposal that the Assyrians imposed the
Assyrian religious system as part of their program of military occupation.[39]

---

35. Green's analogy in Green, *The Role of Human Sacrifice,* p. 183.
36. J. W. McKay, *Religion in Judah under the Assyrians, 732-609 BC* (London:
SCM, 1973), p. 106, n. 98; R. de Vaux, *Studies in Old Testament Sacrifice* (Cardiff:
University of Wales, 1964), p. 89; Weinfeld, "The Worship of Molech," p. 148.
37. Weinfeld, "The Worship of Molech," p. 140.
38. A. Kuenen, *The Religion of Israel,* trans. Alfred Heath May (London: Wil-
liams and Norgate, 1874), p. 377.
39. J. W. McKay, *Religion in Judah under the Assyrians, 732-609 BC.*

5. Canaanite Origins

Suggestion is made that we do not have to go so far afield as Assyria. The sacrifices of children and the cult of Molek are associated with no other place than the Hinnom Valley. And the tophet is always mentioned in relation to Jerusalem or the Hinnom Valley (Ben-Hinnom or the Valley of the Son of Hinnom). The tophet has reference to either the location of the sacrifice or the altar of sacrifice itself. Based on these associations, the tophet is assumed to be the very locus of the cult of Molek. It is also this singularity of reference to the Hinnom Valley which John Day uses to put forward his thesis that the Molek cult is Jebusite. Jebus was the pre-Israelite name of Jerusalem (cf. Josh. 15:8; 18:16). He suggests that a cult of Molek was, in the first instance, Canaanite in origin. In other words, the cult of Molek needed neither to be imposed on, nor imported by the Israelites. He has made the boldest statement regarding a Canaanite source for a Molek cult. He turns to several passages to establish a theme of Mt. Zion, and Jerusalem, being "equated with the mountain of Paradise (cf. Ps. 46.5 [ET 4]; Isa. 8:6; Ezek. 47.1-12). . . . Accordingly, it was only natural for the deep valley below it to be associated with the underworld." He reasoned that

> Since the association of paradisical language [language identifying Mt. Zion with paradise] with Jerusalem is probably Jebusite in origin, it therefore seems plausible to suppose that the connection of the adjacent valley of Hinnom with Sheol is also Jebusite, and consequently that the god Molech was derived by the Israelites from pre-Israelite inhabitants of Jerusalem. Quite apart from this particular argument, which has never previously been put forward, even by those who have supposed Molech to be Jebusite, the fact that Molech is never mentioned in the Old Testament in association with any place other than the valley of Hinnom, and that the cult is clearly Canaanite, indic tes that it may have been appropriated from the local Canaanite inhabitants of Jerusalem, the Jebusites (brackets mine).[40]

As yet, no trace has been located through archaeological search in Ben-Hinnom or in the Kidron Valley. Jerusalem has been heavily occupied which may account for its disappearance from the valley outside of Jerusalem.[41]

40. Day, *Molech*, p. 55.
41. On the other hand, the "Tophet" of Carthage was found in an area of Tunis that has had little occupation on the site to eradicate the evidence left of a cult of child sacrifice there. My thanks to Richard S. Hess for bringing this to my attention.

G. Summary: Molek and the Scholars

A variety of issues present themselves when Molek is considered. According to some scholars *molek* is a mistakenly pointed/vocalized form of the name of a type of sacrifice, e.g., Eissfeldt. Others, e.g., Buber, maintain that *molek* is the title, meaning "king," for YHWH used by syncretists, but this would require a change in the vowel pointing. Still others regard *molek* as the name of a Canaanite god. The worship of *molek,* according to each perspective, assumes child sacrifice to be one of its main tenets.

The radicals *MLK* could take a variety of vowel points, so explanation as to why it has the particular vowels that are thrice used in the Hebrew scriptures led to Geiger's theory of dyphemism in 1857, which has also been used by most scholars from every venue to explain the spellings of such words as Boshet, Ashtoreth, Tophet, etc. These are words which are assumed to have idolatrous connections and so Geiger's theory tries to explain the consistency in the vowel pointing of this category of words.

In addition, the meaning of the word "to pass through" (הַעֲבִיר) has come into question. Does this mean holocaust[42] or simply some sort of dedication?[43] Day cites Jeremiah 7:31 and 19:5, which use the verb "to burn" (שׂרף), and Jeremiah 32:35, which uses "to pass through" to make the point that a simple dedication is not a satisfactory explanation. Note could also be made of the comparison between Deuteronomy 12:31 which uses "to burn" and Deuteronomy 18:10 which uses "to pass through." All five of these verses mention fire, except one (Jer. 32:35); and four of the five mention sons and daughters, while the other uses only sons (Jer. 19:5). Favor would seem to stand with the argument that "to pass through" and "to burn" were being used interchangeably, unless some sort of logic could be presented to suggest that these two verbs represented two different rituals. Even so, there is enough witness just by using the verses that use only "to burn" to point toward sacrificing of children by fire. Of interest also is the source of a cult of child sacrifice. Day suggests that it was Canaanite from the beginning, even Jebusite. Others are quick to point to Carthage as a contemporary community that practiced it. Still others are sure that Ahaz brought it back from Assyria. The Sepharvites may even have had Assyrian connections and they burned their children. One thing that can be ascertained from the discussion of the scholars is that there is

42. Day, *Molech.*
43. Weinfeld, "Burning Babies."

enough room for a difference of opinion as to who Molek is and where he may have come from.

Our day and age has abounded in discoveries. Archaeological digs in the ancient Near East have unearthed amazing complexes of cities with libraries and artifacts that have helped us to understand much about ancient civilizations. Comparison is often made between one discovery and another. Comparison is also made between new discoveries and what we have known or assumed for hundreds of years. This next section focuses on some of the discoveries and conclusions made about those discoveries as regards our god Molek. Does the information from dusty clay tablets, from altars and tombs give us any clues about our mysterious god of "child sacrifice" from the Hebrew scriptures?

III. MLK of the Ancient Near East

An appeal can and has been made (notably by Heider)[44] to the archaeological evidence that points to the material cultures of the surrounding nations for evidence that would describe and/or explain the nature and character of Molek. According to the evidence Molek is a chthonic god (a god of the underworld/netherworld) receiving/requiring child sacrifice. Gods of the netherworld and child sacrifice were known in the ancient world. The nations, kingdoms, and cities that have been cited for evidence bearing on these topics are Ebla, Mari, Babylon, Ugarit, Turkey, Phoenicia, Carthage, and Punic colonies. Each of these is reviewed here individually.

A. Ebla

In the material from Ebla there is a god Malik, whose nature or character cannot be discerned from the evidence available. What is known from the epigraphical material describes his relationship to/with the people who worshipped him.[45] Giovanni Pettinato used an analysis of personal names

44. Heider, *The Cult of Molek*. Heider's main thesis in this book is to refute Paul Mosca's (1975) defense of Otto Eissfeldt's (1935) conclusions regarding the *molk* sacrifice.

45. Heider mentions in a footnote that there are several examples in *Archivi Reali di Ebla Testi* and *Materiali Epigrafici Ebla* of names and places with *MLK* as an element. But little is known of them, so "the occurrence of names with *ma-lik* at Abu

which included theophoric elements (elements that could be understood as divine names) to identify gods who were popular among the peoples of Ebla. Pettinato notes, "These names grant an insight into the intimate relationship between common man and his god."[46] He then continues to explain the characteristics of the god(s) as the names depict them: "he [the one named] is the servant of the god but in recompense the god watches over him, indeed, he is like a father who protects, provides, and listens."[47] However, as Heider points out, the analysis included four different theophoric elements, *MLK* being only one of them. He comments, "it is impossible to say that his [Pettinato's] analysis revealed anything about the popular conception of Malik *in particular*" (brackets and italics mine).[48]

What this evidence does establish is that there was a god for whom the radicals *MLK* were used as a divine name in a community neighboring the ancient Canaanites. The evidence from Ebla situates Malik as a god in this area through the second half of the second millennium B.C. Heider suggests that this is the oldest evidence available.[49] The distance of this, chronologically, from the Hebrew scriptures presents difficulties in using it for application to the Israelite milieu. Its usefulness lies only in the fact that *MLK* is used as a theophoric element in personal names.

Salabikh remains the best evidence that Malik was not a local Eblaite deity" (Heider, p. 97, n. 174). Ebla (Tell Mardikh) and Abu Salabikh are two different cities, though they were contemporary cultures.

46. G. Pettinato, *The Archives of Ebla: An Empire Inscribed in Clay* (Garden City, NJ: Doubleday, 1981), p. 261.

47. As an excursus, it is interesting that Pettinato wants to make a distinction between a popular cult and an official cult at Ebla. The only means to pinpoint the differences between official and popular religion is furnished by the lists of personal names. The first observation concerns the divine elements in the personal names: some gods are witnessed here but are absent from the cultic texts. The most glaring cases are those of Malik and Damu, the two most popular gods at Ebla, if we credit the enormous number of personal names composed with these divine elements, and of the pair Il and Ya, equally frequent among the names of Eblaites (Pettinato, *The Archives of Ebla*, p. 260).

48. Heider has mentioned that the four names that Pettinato has used — Malik, Damu, Il, and Ya – were all analyzed in lump sum. It may have been helpful to have a separate description of Malik, at least for our study (Heider, *The Cult of Molek*, p. 99).

49. Heider, *The Cult of Molek*, p. 153.

B. Mari

Mari, located on the Euphrates to the south and east of Ebla, may have shared some of the same heritage. In the archives discovered at Mari, Akkadian texts with the name Muluk were deciphered. Again theophoric names have been the source for the information we have. *ANET* records the name of Malik-Dagan in a letter from Itur-Asdu:

> Speak to my lord: Thus Itur-Asdu your servant. (5) The day I dispatched this tablet of mine to my lord, Malik-Dagan, a man from Shakka. . . .[50]

According to the notes of the translator, William Moran, this letter was one that was supposedly sent to Zimri-Lim "who must have been absent from Mari. Hence our tablet, unless it was never sent, must be a copy." The element *MLK* has been found in the vocalized form Malik (as at Ebla and above) and also as Muluk. There have been several scholars who have seen this as a variation on an Eblaite theme.[51] But since the information comes from names it is difficult, once again, to gain any specific information as to the nature of this god or his cult.

C. Babylon

Further downriver (the Euphrates), Babylon may provide us with some more specific information. Nergal of Babylon is a god of the netherworld, which Molek is also said to have been. Although Nergal is traced as far back as the third millennium B.C. at Ebla and Fara,[52] his popularity as a

---

50. J. Pritchard, ed., *The Ancient Near East: Supplementary Texts and Pictures Relating to the Old Testament* (Princeton: Princeton University Press, 1969), p. 623.

51. Both Heider, *The Cult of Molek,* pp. 45-46, and Green, *The Role of Human Sacrifice,* p. 181, cite G. Dossin (1938) and A. Bea (1939) in this category. Green also includes P. Jensen (1934) who does not appeal to the Mari text in his article. G. Young edited a book titled *Mari in Retrospect: Fifty Years of Mari and Mari Studies* (Winona Lake, IN: Eisenbrauns, 1992). Though it is a substantial volume only three personal names and no divine names with the element *malik* are listed in the index. None is discussed. Gelb translates *malkum* and *maliktum* of Mari as "king" and "queen," respectively (pp. 129, 148). Cf. Heider, pp. 102-13, for further disussion of what he calls "Amorite Evidence" of *malik* and *malki/u* in personal names and as a divine name.

52. P. Steinkeller, "The Name of Nergal," in *Zeitschrift für Assyriologie* 77 (Berlin, 1987): 164.

god in Babylon extends into the first millennium B.C. Steinkeller also mentions that Nergal is equated with *"Ra-sa-ap"* at Ebla.[53] This would place the evidence in closer chronological proximity to the time of the Hebrew scriptures.

Connections have been made with Nergal of Babylon and the divine name *MLK*. Much interest in the gods of these ancient nations comes from those who are biblical scholars, however, and Heider cites Jensen and gives a synopsis of his equation of Malik and Nergal:

> The proposed equation of Molek and Nergal was approached from the other side in 1934, when the Assyriologist Peter Jensen offered evidence that the O.T. Melek, Ammon's Milkom and Moab's Kemoš were all equivalent to one another and to Nergal.[55]

The character of Nergal and the nature of the cult of Nergal are fairly well known. Jensen suggests that Nergal is the god of hell and that N-e-r G-a-l means king in Sumerian.[56] This would further suggest that *MLK* is an equivalent of Nergal, identifying Malik (of Akkad) with a deity of East Semitic origin.

As to Nergal's character, the reference is often made to "Nergal, the god of the dead," "god of death" or "god of the underworld." A. D. H. Bivar in an article on "Mithraism and Mesopotamia" gives a description of the Babylonian Nergal:

> Nergal was god of death and the underworld. When propitiated he was able to save from death. He was god of vegetation and the palm tree; hunting, war and the plague, which populate his kingdom. In certain aspects he was regarded as a sun god, perhaps in connection with the sun's daily journey beneath the earth, or with the lethal properties of the desert sun. Nergal, like Gibil, was a god of fire. He is identified with Malik,[57] the biblical Moloch, the deity who, amongst the Ammonites,

---

53. Cf. Pettinato, *The Archives of Ebla*, p. 251.

54. Day, *Molech*, p. 84; Heider, *The Cult of Molek*, pp. 32-34, 155, 163.

55. Heider, *The Cult of Molek*, p. 33.

56. P. Jensen, "Die Götter כְּמוֹשׁ und מֶלֶךְ und die Erscheinungsformen *Kammush* und *Malik* des assyrisch-bablonischen Gottes *Nergal*," in *Zeitschrift für Assyriologie und Verwandte Gebiete* (Berlin: Walter DeGruyter, 1934), p. 237.

57. Curtis 1957:149, as cited by Bivar (see n. 58).

near Jerusalem, and in Phoenicia and elsewhere, received the sacrifice of infants by fire. His attribute is the lion.[58]

It seems that at this point Bivar has confused Molek, the god of child sacrifice, and Milchom, the patron god of the Ammonites, as others have done. McKay adds to this description that Nergal "was associated with the planet Mars."[59] Both he and Jensen[60] present the equations, from the Akkadian god-lists, of Malik = Nergal, which provide us with connections with deities in both Ebla and Mari. Again, note here that *MLK* and *"nergal"* in Sumerian (as suggested by Jensen) can be understood as "king," so the equation seems quite natural.

D. Ugarit

Ugarit was unearthed on the coast in Syria due east of Cyprus. Of great interest to many scholars are the findings in the libraries at Ras Shamra, because the material found there has opened the discussion in many different areas. Intense discussion has ensued concerning the deities Baal and Asherah who are mentioned by name in the stories describing the Ugaritic pantheon. However, the Ugaritic and Akkadian tablets, found in the archives, shed only a little light on *MLK* as a god of those cultures that used those languages. Heider explains the relevance of these texts to the study of a god named *MLK* in this way:

> The Ugaritic material is written in two ways, alphabetic cuneiform (Ugaritic) and syllabic cuneiform ("Akkadian"), with a few tablets containing parallel lists of words in both. The texts written in Ugaritic are at the same time the most interesting and the most challenging: interesting, because for the first time they provide us with literary evidence of a god *Mlk* per se (not pluralized) in a context which allows us to know something of the god's nature; challenging, because they are unvocalised and thus open to greater ambiguity at the most fundamental

58. A. D. H. Bivar, "Mithra and Mesopotamia," in *Mithraic Studies: Proceedings of the First International Congress of Mithraic Studies,* vol. 2 (Manchester: Manchester University, 1975), p. 284.

59. McKay, *Religion in Judah,* p. 69.

60. Day, *Molech,* pp. 48-49, also mentions Ashur (a city state/capital of Assyria) as another source for this equation.

level of interpretation, the establishment of the correct reading. Thus, the name of the god under study is written in the same way as the relatively common word for "king," *mlk.*[61]

The texts cited for evidence at Ugarit are snake-bite texts or "serpent charms" that identify *MLK* from a place called Ashtaroth *(mlk 'ttrth).* There is a town called Astharoth in Bashan to the east of the Sea of Galilee. Astour has understood *'ttrth* in the two occurrences *(mlk 'ttrth* RS 24.244.41 and *mlk b'ttrt* RS 24.251 obverse.17) as Ashtaroth, "the very ancient Canaanite city in Bashan."[62] But Charles Virolleaud, in a publication of this material, suggests *'ttrth* is a divine name rather than a place name.[63] Virolleaud (1968:578) presents a parallel list of the gods mentioned in the snakebite texts *(Ugaritica* V.7.41; 8.17).[64] *Mlk 'ttrth* is listed toward the end of each of the two sets of gods mentioned. Astour translates *MLK* as "Milk" for the RS 24.251 occurrence. He comments on his translation saying, "This arrangement leaves one god, Milk, without a mate, but for the sake of symmetry the poet has included in the stich the god's residence Astartu."[65] Whether *'ttrth* in this context is a goddess or a place name is as yet an unresolved question. There are several names with the element *MLK* at Ugarit, but this tells us very little about the god *MLK.*

The suggestion is also made that *MLK* of Ugarit is connected to the Rpu and Rephesh (well-known chthonic gods), possibly also of Ashtaroth.[66] If this were the case, Heider's choice of translating *'ttrt* as a place name would be strengthened. This connection is made by way of the

61. Heider, *The Cult of Molek,* p. 114.

62. M. C. Astour, "Two Ugaritic Serpent Charms," *Journal of Near Eastern Studies* 27 (1968): 21.

63. His original note on p. 70 reads:

> *Mlk 'ttrth* "(le dieu) Mlk (tourné) vers (la déesse) 'Aštart." En RS 24.251,17, on lit *Mlk (b) 'ttrth* = "M. (est assis) à côté de *(b)* FAjtart," à rapprocher de 'Aštart *il ytb b 'ttrth:* "Il est assis à côté de . . . ," en RS 24.252, 2.

64. RS 24.244.41/KTU 1.100 and RS 24.251.17/KTU 1.107, respectively.

65. This translation seems warranted in that it is the only time that *b,* a preposition, is used with the name rather than *w,* the conjunction among the list of names.

66. Heider, *The Cult of Molek,* pp. 114, 124; M. H. Pope, "The Cult of the Dead at Ugarit," in G. D. Young, ed., *Ugarit in Retrospect: Fifty Years of Ugarit and Ugaritic* (Winona Lake, IN: Eisenbrauns, 1981), pp. 172-74.

67. King Og of Bashan was called the last of the Rephaim, Deuteronomy 3:11; and note also the Rephaim of Ashteroth-karnaim, Genesis 14:5. BDB has רפאים listed

Rephaim that were to reside at Bashan, Ashtaroth,[67] and *mlk 'ṭtrth* as mentioned above. Pope also mentions a *ršp 'ṭtrt* in the snakebite texts. Another association here is *MLK* = Mot, the god of death.[68] But these conclusions may be too weak to rely on. The finds at Ugarit were especially exciting to biblical scholars because of Ugarit's supposed continuity with the culture and chronology of the Hebrew scriptures. It is disappointing that the Ugaritic literature offers us no more concrete help with the character of the god in question.

E. Turkey

"Molech" is identified as the god who receives human sacrifice in Turkey. This comes from a stela recently discovered in Turkey which supposedly mentions human sacrifices that were made before a battle. The excavation and findings have yet to be published in full. The first publication is to be in Turkish. H. Shanks in his article says, "The earliest reference to human sacrifice has been found in Turkey and is expected to illuminate several puzzling Biblical passages regarding Molech, whoever he or it was."[69] Note should be made here that it is Shanks and not the stela that mentions "Molech." Furthermore, he dates this evidence to the eighth century B.C.[70]

F. Phoenicia

The Phoenician civilization, along the northern coast of the eastern Mediterranean seaboard, also was flourishing during the time of the kings of Israel. Tyre and Sidon, of Phoenicia, are mentioned as trading cities in the Hebrew scriptures (1 Kings 5:1ff.; Ezek. 27:1ff.).

In the evidence from Phoenicia proper, precious little is known of

---

twice, once translated as "shades, ghosts" and the second time "n.pr.gent. old race of giants" (952 s.v.).

68. Heider credits this to Pope, but does not give a citation for which of Pope's works from which the idea comes. The connection of *MLK* = Mot is not overtly mentioned in Pope, "The Cult of the Dead at Ugarit."

69. H. Shanks, "Who — or What — was Molech? New Phoenician Inscription May Hold Answer," *Biblical Archaeology Review* 22/4 (1996): 13.

70. Forthcoming publication of this should come from E. Carter, S. Kaufman, and/or possibly B. Zuckerman.

a god with the elements *MLK* but a great deal has been uncovered regarding burnt sacrifices of children. It is generally assumed that Phoenician influence in Israel was greatest during the eighth to the seventh centuries B.C. This was also the height of Phoenician religious practices involving child sacrifice. Phoenician trade extended throughout the Mediterranean, as far west as Spain;[71] ports were established in North Africa; and Phoenician religious centers have been uncovered in Sicily, Sardinia, and Tunis.[72]

Carthage, modern-day Tunis, founded in the ninth century B.C. by the Phoenicians, had a reputation for practicing child sacrifice even among the Roman and Greek writers of the first century A.D.[73] Carthage is further discussed in this next section as an often cited archaeological site regarding the debate over child sacrifice and its relevance to the Hebrew scriptures.

G. Carthage and Punic Evidence

It is when we turn to the Punic[74] evidence that we begin to see something of the nature of the cultus that has been ascribed to Molek. Many connections have been made between the Carthaginian practice of human sacrifice, child sacrifice, and the worship of Molek. Several levels of urns with the calcinated bones of infants, young children, and animals were found at the site of what is called a Tophet in Carthage. The first excavations began in the 1920s and were continued in the 1970s. Stager and Wolff describe the excavations and give some background to the site, as well as some discussion on the interest it holds for scholars of the ANE. They mention that the urns were marked with monuments, some of which were marked with names of the receivers or the givers of the offerings that were set in the

71. Kennedy, "The Mythological Reliefs from Pozo Moro, Spain," pp. 209-16; A. Kempinski, "The Early Evidence," pp. 56ff.

72. Stager and Wolff, "Child Sacrifice at Carthage," p. 32.

73. Day, *Molech,* cites these sources, with translations in his appendix, pp. 86-91.

74. In writing the article on "Languages, Phoenician," Krahmalkov, *Molech,* p. 222, gives this synopsis of "Punic":

Western Phoenician (Punic), the language of the Carthaginian state and its vast empire, rivaled in importance Greek and Latin in classical antiquity; it survived in N Africa well into the Christian period. . . .

urns beneath the monuments. Some of these monuments included the word *MLK*. It is unfortunate that Stager and Wolff do not give us a date for these particular monuments, but they do mention that the burial of urns in general dated from 750 B.C. to 146 B.C.[75] One seemingly significant comparison has been made between these and other Punic inscriptions (in Phoenician script)[76] with the name of Molek. The radicals *MLK* may have been used in the Punic inscriptions to describe different elements of sacrifice. *Mlk 'mr* has been understood to mean "sacrifice of a lamb," as a substitute. Another expression, *mlk 'dm,* has been translated as "human sacrifice" or "sacrifice of a man/blood."[77] Stager and Wolff suggest that *MLK* "refers to a live sacrifice of a child or animal." Taken together these two expressions give a gruesome picture of the cult at Carthage; if indeed, this is the way to understand *mlk 'mr* and *mlk 'dm.* Eissfeldt was one of the first to suggest that *MLK,* of the Punic evidence, was to be vocalized *molk* and to be understood to be a type of sacrifice.

On the other hand, Heider's "reassessment" of the research on Molek tries to draw a connection between the Punic evidence and the Hebrew scriptures from a different perspective:

> It remains true, as we shall see, that the Punic archaeological evidence provides the closest parallel to the cult of which the OT appears to speak. In both cases children were sacrificed by fire to a deity in a specific sacred precinct. Moreover, such elements as a strong mixture of the popular and official cults and, as we now know, periods of increased observance of the practice appear to be shared. While we shall take care not to assume that the two cults are identical in every respect (including their divine recipient!), there is no question that the Punic evidence provides rich confirmation that cultic child sacrifice by fire *was* known among the Iron Age Semites whose home land was Syria-Palestine.[78]

Stager and Wolff name several sites that are identified as places of child

75. Stager and Wolff, "Child Sacrifice at Carthage," pp. 39-45.
76. Heider mentions "*KAI* 61A and B," a sixth- or seventh-century stela from Malta, as the oldest example of *MLK* in Punic (*The Cult of Molek,* p. 199).
77. Weinfeld, "The Worship of Molech and the Queen of Heaven," pp. 135-37. Weinfeld does not agree with *mlk 'mr* as the sacrifice of a lamb as a substitute for a child, for several reasons; one of them being that he is not certain that *'mr* means lamb. He translates *mlk 'dm* as "king of mankind," an epithet for El (p. 137); cf. Day, *Molech,* pp. 5-9, who refutes these suggestions.
78. Heider, *The Cult of Molek,* p. 203.

sacrifice: "Phoenician Carthage, as well as similar precincts at other Phoenician sites in Sicily, Sardinia and Tunisia."[79] Heider adds to these cities
"Tharros, Sulcis, Monte Sirai, Bythia and Nova (Sardina)."[80] He also
gives a description of the similarities of the different sites that are credited
with child sacrifice:

> In sum, the Punic archaeological evidence provides ample physical proof
> that a cult of child sacrifice was practised [*sic*] from the earliest times of
> Phoenician colonisation in the West. The cult was practised in walled,
> roofless precincts, sometimes outside of the city walls, and entailed the
> burning of babies and young children (or young animals) in acts of indi-
> vidual devotion which were, after a time, commemorated by stelae.[81]

Philo of Byblos is an ancient source for information for Carthaginian religious practices. Philo in his *Phoenician History* is quoted by Eusebius and
said to have used Sanchuniathon as a source. There is some debate as to
whether Sanchuniathion was Philo's invention or an authentic individual
of the first millennium B.C.

H. Summary: Molek in the Ancient Near East

The stories in the Baal Cycle from Ras Shamra have greatly enlarged the
understanding of Baal and Asherah as deities in the ANE, but nothing of
the like has been discovered at Ugarit or elsewhere for Molek. We have
only two snakebite texts of Ugarit, where *mlk 'ttrth* has been understood
as either a compound divine name or as "*MLK* of Ashtaroth," a city in
Bashan in the Transjordan. At Ebla and Mari, *MLK* has been found in
names that have been used to identify gods which may have been in the

79. Stager and Wolff, "Child Sacrifice at Carthage," p. 32.
80. Heider, *The Cult of Molek,* p. 196.
81. Heider, *The Cult of Molek,* pp. 202-3. Green has made the somewhat spurious
connection between the sacrifice of Mesha's son in 2 Kings 3:27 and the cult in Carthage,
when he suggests that, "the reasons for such sacrifices are said to be national emergen-
cies which are brought about by wars, drought, and plagues, at which time children
would be sacrificed" (*The Role of Human Sacrifice in the Ancient Near East,* p. 183).
82. Heider includes three appendixes with his treatise: "Appendix A: Catalog of
Personal Names Containing *MA-LIK,*" "Appendix B: Catalog of Amorite Divine and
Personal Names Containing M-L-K Forms," and "Appendix C: Catalog of Personal
Names from Ugarit Containing M-L-K Forms" (pp. 409-19).

pantheons of those ancient nations.[82] At Ebla, "Malik" is identified as a god. This is also true of Mari with the addition of a god "Muluk." The Akkadian god-lists also equate Malik and Nergal. Nergal is known from Babylon as a chthonic deity whose name may mean "king." Nergal at Babylon brings the associations with Malik up to the first millennium B.C. The evidence from Phoenician civilizations brings *MLK* closer in time and proximity to Palestine. Punic inscriptions include *MLK* on stelae that were set as monuments. Eissfeldt suggests that *MLK (molk)* is a kind of offering. In the Punic city of Carthage, a large precinct with several layers of buried urns of cremated remains of young children, infants, and animals has been uncovered. Some of the burials were marked with stelae which include *MLK* in their inscriptions. But these inscriptions are not necessarily indicative of a cult of *MLK* associated with a deity by that name. Rather Baal-hamon and Tanit are the deities named as recipients of these offerings when identified.

Philological similarities have been used to find a god with the same name as Molek in the nations surrounding Palestine. Also activity has been sought that is similar to that which is attributed to the god Molek of the Hebrew scriptures. Taken all together, this points to *MLK* as a divine name in the ANE, and to places where child sacrifice was also practiced. However, these bits and pieces of evidence are separated from the Hebrew scriptures by time and cultural space, and their connections to the Hebrew scriptures are tenuous. No sure material evidence of a cult of Molek or a cult of *MLK* has been discovered in the ANE. The clearest evidence that we have of a cult of child sacrifice to a god Molek rests solely in the Hebrew material and that is sketchy at best. This next section looks more closely at what the Hebrew scriptures say for themselves.

IV. Molek of the Hebrew Scriptures

Based on the elements of 2 Kings 23:10 and Jeremiah 32:35 this discussion of *molek* will center on these elements: "ben-hinnom," "the tophet," "to pass through[83] the fire" (and by association "burn in the fire"), and "sons and daughters." These elements are chosen because they are present in these two verses which specifically name *molek* and because patterns or combinations of these elements seem to be consistent in other verses

83. עבר [Hi].

which seem to allude to the worship of *molek*. Of the twenty-three verses that are used for this survey, eleven of them mention that a son or sons and daughters or children[84] are caused "to pass through the fire," and four of them "burn"[85] the same. All of the other references but one[86] refer to the tophet. Allusions to Molek are dependent on these elements or combinations thereof. These allusions are found only in Jeremiah 7, 19, and 32; Leviticus 18 and 20; Deuteronomy 12 and 18 and several times in 1 and 2 Kings. Other elements will also be mentioned which show consistency in their association with those elements found in 2 Kings 23:10 and Jeremiah 32:35. First we will look at the name *molek* where it is found in the Hebrew scriptures.

A. *"The molek" of the Hebrew Scriptures*

Of the eight times (Lev. 18:21; 20:2-5; 1 Kings 11:7; 2 Kings 23:10; and Jer. 32:35) *molek* is mentioned by name in the Hebrew scriptures, 1 Kings 11:7 is the only time that *molek* is written without the article, i.e., "the molek." In 1 Kings 11:7 it reports that "Solomon built a high place for Chemosh, the abomination of Moab at the mountain which faces (i.e., east of) Jerusalem, and to Molek, the abomination of the sons of Ammon" (1 Kings 11:7). This is the only occasion in which Molek is identified with Ammon. The textual notes mention that the Lucianic recension of the Septuagint reads "Milchom." In addition Milchom is mentioned in 11:5 and 11:33 without textual notes for emendation. Milchom is identified on numerous occasions with Ammon, so this correction by the LXX is not surprising. Leviticus 18:21; 20:2-5; 2 Kings 23:10; and Jeremiah 32:35 all write *molek* with an article; 1 Kings 11:7 does not.[87] This is of significance, in that proper names do not take an article as it would cause a double or redundant determinacy. To place a definite article ("the") before *molek* then creates a title of what could be understood as a name. This use

---

84. The verses in Lev. 18 and 20 use the word translated "children" by some English translations, but more literally could be translated as "seed" (זרע).

85. שׂרף.

86. 1 Kings 11:7. See below.

87. 1 Kings 11:7 writes it anarthrously (וּלְמֹלֶךְ שִׁקֻּץ) which fits a pattern used when naming the gods of the neighboring nations; e.g., 2 Kings 23:13 where not one of the three divine names given takes an article (לְעַשְׁתֹּרֶת | שִׁקֻּץ צִידֹנִים וְלִכְמוֹשׁ שִׁ קֶץ מוֹאָב וּלְמִלְכֹּם תּוֹעֲבַת בְּנֵ־עַמּוֹן).

of the article with *molek* may have been a deliberate attempt at irony in the text. More will be mentioned of this later. Furthermore, none of the elements of 2 Kings 23:10 or Jeremiah 32:35 are mentioned in 1 Kings 11:7, so Molek in this verse seems to fall out of the general discussion as outlined above.

B. Places

Two places are discussed in this next section, Ben-Hinnom and the tophet. These are mentioned as the location of offerings made to "the molek."

1. Ben-Hinnom (בֶּן הִנֹּם)

Ben (בֶּן) is translated as "son," but the meaning of *Hinnom* (הִנֹּם) escapes us. We can only say what it has come to mean rather than give a plausible etymology. Most of the cultic references to the valley of Ben-Hinnom are in the book of Jeremiah. The valley of Ben-Hinnom is mentioned by Joshua as one the landmarks for the boundary of the tribe of Judah: "extend the boundary to the valley of Ben-Hinnom to the slope of the Jebusites off on the south (which is Jerusalem) and extend the boundary to the top of the mountain which is upon the face of the valley of Hinnom seaward (west) . . ." (Josh. 15:8). In Joshua 18:16 it is again mentioned, naming the tribe on the other side of the border as Benjamin. The Jebusites and Jerusalem were close to the border between Benjamin and Judah on the Judah side.[88] Jeremiah is sent to the valley of Ben-Hinnom near the Potsherd Gate in Jerusalem (Jer. 19:2) and in the next paragraph (19:14) he returns from the tophet. This equation, Ben-Hinnom with the tophet, is echoed in the phrases, "it will no longer be called the tophet and/ or the valley of Ben-Hinnom but" will be renamed the valley of slaughter (Jer. 7:32 and 19:6). Not only is the high place of the tophet built in the valley of Ben-Hinnom (Jer. 7:31), but the high places of the baal have been built there (Jer. 19:5 and 32:35). The parallel text to 2 Kings 16:3, in which Ahaz is accused of "causing his son to pass through the fire like the abomination of the nations," adds a few details. It reads, Ahaz "burned in-

88. Nehemiah mentions that the sons of Judah "settled (encamped) from Beersheba as far as the valley of Hinnom" (Neh. 11:30).
89. בער [Hi].

cense in the valley of Ben-Hinnom and he burned[89] his sons in the fire like the abomination of the nations" (2 Chron. 28:3).[90] Note that reference to Ben-Hinnom is missing from 2 Kings 16:3. Sons *and* daughters are caused to pass through the fire in this valley in Jeremiah 7:31; 32:35; and 2 Kings 23:10. Only in one case in the deuteronomistic texts is Ben-Hinnom associated with *molek:* 2 Kings 23:10.

2. "The tophet" (תֹּפֶת)

Tophet is written six times with an article and twice without.[91] Most of the occurrences are in Jeremiah. It is a place in the valley of Ben-Hinnom; Jeremiah 7:31; 7:32; 19:6; 2 Kings 23:10. Jeremiah returns from "the tophet" where he prophesied (Jer. 19:14). The city of Jerusalem will be made *like* Tophet,[92] and the houses of the city will be *"like* the place of the defiled tophet."[93] These two similes come in the midst of an illustration from the beginning of chapter 19 where Jeremiah is to purchase a vessel made of earthenware. In verse 10, the jar is to be broken and the next verse says, "thus I will shatter this people and this city as he will shatter the potter's vessel" (Jer. 19:11). As previously mentioned, twice it is written that this place "will no longer be called *tophet*[94] and Ben-Hinnom but the valley of slaughter." Another phrase is used twice: "they will bury in *tophet,* there is no room *elsewhere*" (Jer. 7:32 and 19:11). A high place of *tophet* is built in the valley of Ben-Hinnom to burn their sons and daughters in the fire.[95] In another verse, *tophet* is defiled to circumvent sons and daughters being passed through the fire to the molek.[96] Only in 2 Kings 23:10 is the *molek* directly associated with *tophet.*

One other verse is of some interest here. It may give an additional description of the tophet. Isaiah 30:33 reads:

For already from yesterday, Tophteh (תָּפְתֶּה) has been arranged,

90. Both בער and *sons* are corrected in the textual apparatus of 2 Chron. 28:3 to read עבר and *son* (ms), respectively.

91. Sometimes this word is written in the Hebrew with an article and could be translated as "the tophet." The issue of the presence or lack of an article with *tophet* is not as crucial as for those names for which the problem of divinity is in question.

92. וְלָתֵת אֶת־הָעִיר הַזֹּאת כְּתֹפֶת, Jer. 19:12; cf. BDB 681 s.v. נתן 3.b.

93. כִּמְקוֹם הַתֹּפֶת הַטְּמֵאִים, Jer. 19:13.

94. וְלֹא־יָאָמֵר עוֹד הַתֹּפֶת, Jer. 7:32; and וְלֹא־יִקָּרֵא לַמָּקוֹם הַזֶּה עוֹד הַתֹּפֶת, Jer. 19:6.

95. הַתֹּפֶת אֲשֶׁר בְּגֵיא בֶן־חִנֹּם לִשְׂרֹף אֶת־בְּנֵיהֶם וְאֶת־בְּנֹתֵיהֶם בָּאֵשׁ, Jer. 7:31.

96. לְבִלְתִּי לְהַעֲבִיר אִישׁ אֶת־בְּנוֹ וְאֶת־בִּתּוֹ בָּאֵשׁ לַמֹּלֶךְ, 2 Kings 23:10.

also for the king it (fs) is prepared,
he has made it deep, he has it made wide.
Its (fs) heap is a fire[97] and wood excessive;
the breath of YHWH as a torrent of brimstone kindling it.[98]

(Isa. 30:33)

The spelling for *tophet,* with the final *h,* is unusual here; BDB records it as a hapax legomenon and suggests it is "a place of burning, in fig. of י's judgement on Assyria" (BDB 1075 s.v. תפתה). Though there are many allusions to fire in other verses that are associated with the *tophet,* this verse alone places fire in the *tophet.* Only in Jeremiah 7:31 and 2 Kings 23:10 are fire and the *tophet* mentioned in the same verse. The majority of other verses mention either fire or the *tophet.* It would be tempting to read this verse as *"Tophteh (Tophet) has been arranged for the molek."* This would only require an adjustment of vowels for the word translated "king." In any case, this verse offers us a powerful image of YHWH using the *tophet* as an illustration for the punishment due Assyria (cf. Isa. 30:31).

Some other observations concerning the *tophet* seem warranted here. First, in none of the texts surveyed is the "passing" of children or the "burning" of children actually said to happen in the *tophet.* Jeremiah 7:31 hints in that direction, saying, "the high place of the *tophet* is built . . . for the burning. . . ." Secondly, the *tophet* must have been a place of some size as it was going to be the location of a burial (Jer. 7:32 and 19:11). Also burying in the *tophet* must have been unusual for this threat to have had any import. From the several verses which mention the *tophet,* it must have been a specific place, e.g., Jeremiah returned from prophesying there (Jer. 19:14). Add to this Isaiah 30:33, if we accept its spelling of the word as a variant, which mentions that it is to be made wide and deep, full of wood and fire. All of this added together gives one the sense that this *tophet* is different from an altar built of stone and placed somewhere, but rather that a place in Ben-Hinnom was made into a *tophet.*

97. מְדֻרָתָשׁ אֵשׁ is translated by NASB as a pyre, which is confirmed by BDB.
98. Isaiah 30:33

כִּי־עָרוּךְ מֵאֶתְמוּל תָּפְתֶּה גַּם־הוּא [הִיא] לַמֶּלֶךְ הוּכָן הֶעֱמִיק הִרְחִב
מְדֻרָתָשׁ אֵשׁ וְעֵצִים הַרְבֵּה
נִשְׁמַת יְהוָה כְּנַחַל גָּפְרִית בֹּעֲרָה בָּהּ׃

198

C. Verbs

The actions that are attributed to imagery of *molek* may be of some assistance here. Two verbs are treated in this section. They are used in each case as action that is done with children as the object. "To pass through" is used in each of these cases in the Hiphil [Hi] form and "to burn" in a simple Qal form. Leviticus 20:2-5 mentions "giving seed" to *molek*. This verb "to give" is not as descriptive as "to pass through" or "to burn" and could be understood simply as a dedication to *molek*. This discussion will focus on the two more descriptive verbs, "to cause to pass" and "to burn."

1. To Cause to Pass (עבר [Hi]) through the Fire

The phrase "to pass . . . through the fire" (עבר . . . בָּאֵשׁ [Hi]) is used five times in these texts; once in Deuteronomy and the rest in 2 Kings. In each case, children are "passed" through[99] the fire. Leviticus 18:21 uses the verb "to cause to pass," however without allusion to fire. The passage in Deuteronomy 18:10 uses a participial form of "to pass."[100] This verse comes as an injunction against allowing those who practice passing children through the fire, or any who practice divination, fortune telling, or the like, to be a part of the community (cf. 18:9-13). The pairing of illegal practices, such as "divination," "soothsaying," and "necromancy," and "causing children to pass through the fire" also occurs in 2 Kings 17:17 and 21:6. 2 Kings 16:3 likens causing children to pass through the fire to the abominable practices of the nations. Only in 2 Kings 23:10 is this practice linked specifically to the molek. Also, 2 Kings 23:10 is the only verse which mentions both the *tophet* and "to cause to pass through" together. Jeremiah 32:35, alone, uses "to cause to pass" without following it up with "through the fire." It translates as, "to cause the sons and daughters to pass to the *molek*" (Jer. 32:35). "To the *molek*" seems to stand as a substitute for "in the fire," which is missing in this phrase. What this fire is in these passages or what it means "to cause someone to pass through the fire" is not certain. The previous discussion of Isaiah 30:33 gives us some clues, but that passage does not use "to cause to pass," but only "fire" with the *tophet*.

---

99. בּ of instrumentality with עבר; cf. BDB 89 s.v. 2.a.

100. מַעֲבִיר בְּנוֹ־וּבִתּוֹ בָּאֵשׁ, Deut. 18:10.

2. "To Burn" (שׂרף) in the Fire

The phrases using "to burn" are very similar to those which use "to cause to pass." It is not unusual that these phrases use "fire" because "to burn" is obviously connected with fire. There are four verses, in the current passages under discussion, which speak of "burning" in the fire (Jer. 7:31; 19:5; Deut. 12:31; and 2 Kings 17:31). There are many other verses which speak of burning and fire together; however, these four verses are of concern here because they are in a cultic context that includes the elements mentioned above. Jeremiah 7:31 mentions that the sons of Judah built a high place of the tophet "to burn their sons and daughters in the fire." Jeremiah 19:5 says essentially the same thing, only that daughters are not mentioned, and the high places are built for *baal.* Deuteronomy 12:31 gives the injunction against not doing as the nations have done for their gods, "for even their sons and their daughters they burned in the fire to their gods."[101] Nations are mentioned by name in 2 Kings 17:31. This verse comes in the midst of the explanation of the way Assyria dealt with the Northern Kingdom of Israel after its conquest. YHWH is given credit for sending wild animals among those peoples displaced to Israel. Priests of the land, i.e., Hebrew priests, are sent to teach the ways of the god of the land, but after some time the people who are displaced there took up their own gods and worshipped them. The Sepharvites are accused of "burning their children/sons in the fire to Adrammelech and Anammelech the gods of Sepharvaim" (2 Kings 17:31).[102] Often, discussion about these verses draws attention to the *molek* element of these divine names. The tophet is mentioned in the context of the Jeremiah and the Deuteronomy passages, but not for 2 Kings 17:31.

V. The Victims

The victims of this burning or passing through the fire are consistently "sons," "children," or "sons and daughters." Leviticus also mentions "your seed" meaning offspring or children. There seems to be a clear dis-

---

101. כִּי גַם אֶת־בְּנֵיהֶם וְאֶת־בְּנֹתֵיהֶם יִשְׂרְפוּ בָאֵשׁ לֵאלֹהֵיהֶם, Deut. 12:31.

102. There is some speculation about the location of this place; cf. Hector Avalos, "Sepharvaim," *Anchor Bible Dictionary,* vol. 5 (New York: Doubleday, 1992), p. 1090. There is, it seems, a bit of play in the sound between *srph* (שׂרף) and the first three consonants of *Sepharvites* (ספרוים).

tinction between the use of the previously mentioned verbs and the imagery that goes with them and the rite of the "first-born." Both "to cause to pass" and "to burn" of children are presented as an abomination by the texts under study. Each of these issues is covered in this next section.

A. *Sons and Daughters*

These "sons and daughters" are identified as the children of the nation Israel, of the Northern Kingdom (Israel) and of the Southern Kingdom (Judah). Various combinations of בֵן and בַת with pronominal suffixes are used: "their sons and their daughters" (2 Kings 17:17), "his son and his daughter" (2 Kings 23:10), "their sons" (Jer. 19:5), or "his son" (2 Kings 16:3). These seem to follow a general pattern: when the noun *ben,* "son," or *bath,* "daughter" (בֵּן or בַּת), is singular the pronominal suffix is also singular; or both noun and suffix are plural. This may indicate some formulaic pattern in their presentation. All the occurrences of son(s) and daughter(s) in these verses are written with pronominal suffixes, none without. "Sons/children" or "son" is presented without "daughter(s)," but not vice versa. Six times, "son(s) and daughter(s)" are (or are presented as being) burned or caused to pass through fire (Jer. 7:31; 32:35; Deut. 12:31; 18:10; 2 Kings 17:17; and 23:10); Deuteronomy 18:10 is the only case of "son *and* daughter" in the singular. The presentation of "son(s)," without "daughter(s)," happens four times, twice plural (Jer. 19:5 and 2 Kings 17:31) and twice singular (2 Kings 16:3 and 21:6). The singular "son" is used to describe the activity of Ahaz and Manasseh respectively. "Sons *and* daughters" is more often found with the verb הֶעֱבִיר; four times (Jer. 32:35; Deut. 18:10; 2 Kings 17:17; and 32:10), as against twice with "to burn" (Jer. 7:31 and Deut. 12:31). The presentation is equally split between these two verbs for "son(s)" (without "daughter[s]"): "to burn," Jer. 19:5 and 2 Kings 17:31; "to cause to pass," 2 Kings 16:3 and 21:6. Again these last two references speak of Ahaz and Manasseh respectively.

1. First-born (בְּכוֹר)

Nowhere in these passages is the word for "first-born" (בְּכוֹר) used to describe the children of the cultic rite of "burning" or "passing" children through the fire. The issues of the firstborn revolve around two different foci in the Pentateuch and the deuteronomistic texts; firstly, inheritance[103] and secondly, dedication to YHWH. Inheritance is outside the present discussion, but the rites of dedication are of interest. The book of Exodus sets the stage for the dedication of the first-born with the release of the people of Israel from slavery under the Pharaoh (Exod. 4–12). Exodus 13 explains the reasoning behind the "dedication" (קָדֵשׁ, Exod. 13:2) of the "first-born" as YHWH's right of redemption for sparing all the "first-born" of Israel. All the "first-born" of man and beast were slain among all of Pharaoh's country except for those of the sons of Israel. Exodus 13:14-15 gives a synopsis of the story:

> And it shall be when your son asks you in the future, saying, "What is this?," then you will say to him, "By the strength of his hand YHWH led us from Egypt from the house of slavery. And it was that Pharaoh made it hard to send us out and YHWH slew all the first-born in the land of Egypt, from the first-born of man and even the first-born of beast; thus I sacrifice to YHWH all the males who open the womb but all the *first-born* of my sons I redeem."

The word "first-born" can be used for either humans that are first-born or for animals (e.g., Exod. 12:12; 13:2, 15; 34:20). And "open the womb" (פֶּטֶר רֶחֶם) is used only in the context of "first-born," and often in a parallel construction (cf. Exod. 13:2, 15; 34:19; Num. 3:12; 18:15). From the Pentateuch and the deuteronomistic texts, the suggestion of "sacrifice" (זבח) of the first-born is mentioned only in Exod. 13:15. "Dedication" (קדשׁ) is often used (Exod. 13:2; Lev. 27:20; Num. 3:13; 8:17; Deut. 15:19). "Give" (נתן) is used once as a description of offering the first-born.[104] This phrase follows the injunction that they shall give the wine from their presses without delay and then following this is the instruction that they are to do the same (give) with their oxen and sheep. These oxen and sheep are to be "given" on the eighth day. Exodus 13:12 reads, "you shall pass each one which opens the womb to YHWH."[105] This is the only case of the use of the verb "to cause to pass" with "first-born." It is as obscure in its meaning here as elsewhere. It lacks the mention of fire which is common with the "Molek verses."

The theme of "redemption" (פדה) is repeated in the context of the

---

103. Cf. Gen. 25–27; 48:8-22; and Deut. 21:15-17.
104. בְּכוֹר בָּנֶיךָ תִּתֶּן־לִי, Exod. 22:28 in Hebrew verse order.
105. וְהַעֲבַרְתָּ כָל־פֶּטֶר־רֶחֶם לַיחוֹה, Exod. 13:12.

firstborn several times (Exod. 13:13, 15; 34:20; Num. 3:46; 18:15, 17). Twice in Numbers (3:40, 43) and once in Deuteronomy (15:19) are "males" (זָכָר) specified as those to be set aside to YHWH. Nowhere in the texts that mention "dedication" (or "sacrifice" or "giving") of the first-born is a method of "dedication" or "sacrifice" mentioned. "Redemption" is a common theme with first-born but never used with *molek* imagery. Nor is a particular place mentioned. And of these texts, YHWH is the only recipient of the "first-born" by "sacrifice," "giving," or "dedication."

One passage is often brought into the discussion of the molek which does use "first-born." 2 Kings 3:27 reads, "and he took his son, the first-born who was to reign instead of him, and raised him up, a whole burnt of-fering upon the wall."[106] Neither "to burn" nor "to cause to pass" is used in this pericope. It is not situated in or near the Ben-Hinnom. Although the word translated as "whole" or "burnt offering" (עֹלָה) is assumed as part of the rite, the imagery here is different from the passages which allude to the *molek*. Instead of the *tophet* or Ben-Hinnom as the place of sacrifice it is the "wall" of the city. Jeremiah 19:5 mentions the burning of their sons as whole/burnt offerings.[107] This seems to be the only link in the imagery be-tween 2 Kings 3:27 and the elements of the texts mentioned above.

2. "The Passing" and "the Burning" of Children as an Abomination

Both the "passing" and "burning" of children are identified as "abomina-tions" (תועבה). Jeremiah 32:35 links the practice to causing Judah to sin.[108] Deuteronomy 12:31 and 2 Kings 16:3 both identify the practice with the "abomination of the nations." Deuteronomy 12:31 reads, "for ev-ery abomination of YHWH which he hates, they do for their gods; for even their sons and their daughters they burn in the fire to their gods." On the other hand, 2 Kings 16:3 and the parallel, 2 Chronicles 28:2-3, tell the same basic story of Ahaz with slightly different vocabulary[109] and some embellishment from the Chronicler, but the phrase "abominations of the

---

106. BDB 749 עלה s.v. Hi 8. "*cause to ascend* (in flame; These all to go up on altar), *offer* sacrifice." This has been translated as Hi impf 3ms + 3ms suffix, rather than 3mp, which does not fit the context. וַיִּקַּח אֶת־בְּנוֹ הַבְּכֹר אֲשֶׁר־יִמְלֹךְ תַּחְתָּיו וַיַּעֲלֵהוּ עֹלָה עַל־הַחֹמָה, 2 Kings 3:27.

107. לִשְׂרֹף אֶת־בְּנֵיהֶם בָּאֵשׁ עֹלוֹת לַבַּעַל, Jer. 19:5.

108. לַעֲשׂוֹת הַתּוֹעֵבָה הַזֹּאת לְמַעַן הַחֲטִי אֶת־יְהוּדָה, Qere הַחֲטִיא, Jer. 32:35.

109. E.g., וַיַּבְעֵר instead of הֶעֱבִיר.

nations" (תּוֹעֲבֹת הַגּוֹיִם) is identical between them. The only particular nation mentioned as burning children in the fire is the Sepharvites (2 Kings 17:31). The tophet, Jerusalem, and Ben-Hinnom are not mentioned here; thus, the connection that the rite of the Sepharvites has to a *molek* cult in Jerusalem is not certain. The Sepharvites were displaced to Samaria of the Northern Kingdom by the Assyrians in the eighth century, so any earlier practice of "burning" or "passing" of children cannot be attributed to their arrival in the land, e.g., 2 Kings 17:17.

VI. Conclusion

It appears that Jeremiah wants to put to rest the idea that receiving child sacrifice was part of the worship of YHWH; this, Jeremiah says, is the apostate worship of another god. Three times Jeremiah speaks for YHWH, saying, "this burning of children, I did not command it nor did it come upon my mind" (Jer. 7:31; 19:5; 32:35). Jeremiah 7:31 reads, "And they built high places in the tophet which is in the valley of Ben-Hinnom to burn their sons and their daughters in the fire which I did not command nor did it come upon my mind." Jeremiah 19:5 writes, they "built the high places of the baal to burn their sons in the fire. . . ." It is debated whether Jeremiah 19:5 is a scribal mistake or a deliberate choice to name *baal* as the receiver of the sacrifice of children. This is the only time that *baal* is directly associated with the tophet or Ben-Hinnom (cf. Jer. 19:6). Twice the sacrifice of children is mentioned outside of Ben-Hinnom (2 Kings 3:27 and 2 Kings 17:31 — neither of these references includes the imagery common to other allusions of the molek). In the Punic evidence, Baal-hamon is named as the recipient of child sacrifices at the Tophet in Carthage. And this may well have been a current event in Carthage at the time of Jeremiah. Lawrence Stager and Samuel Wolff[110] date the first level of the archaeological site at the Tophet in Carthage, Tanit I, as 750/ 725 to 600 B.C. Was Jeremiah using the name current in Carthage? Would he have known anything about Carthage? Or did he (or some scribe) get confused with the names? Only one other time in the Jeremiah-deuteronomistic texts are any gods, other than *molek*, named in relation to child sacrifice: Adrammelech and Anammelech, the gods of Sepharvites, who were displaced to Samaria of the Northern Kingdom by the Assyrians

110. Stager and Wolff, "Child Sacrifice at Carthage," p. 35.

in the eighth century B.C. (2 Kings 17:31). Focus has been given to the "melek" elements of these two names as evidence for a possible *molek* syncretism. Jeremiah 32:35 names *molek* as the deity connected with sacrificing of children, but *baal* with the high places. This is one of the few places where *molek* is mentioned in relation to another god; there is not enough evidence, here, to make any clear suggestions regarding *baal*'s relation to child sacrifice or *molek*'s relation to *baal*. There is a distinction between the cultic rites of the *molek* and the rites that concern the "first-born." The passages that present instruction about the "first-born" (Pentateuchal and deuteronomistic) give neither place nor mode of dedication. In addition, 1 Kings 11:7 does not mention "to cause to pass," "to burn," son(s) or daughter(s). However, this verse does write *molek* without the article and so it can be read as a divine name only in this one case.

We find that the rites and imagery associated with *molek* are like Jeremiah's shattered earthenware vessel (Jer. 19). There are gaps, because of the fragmentary evidence and the antiquity of the material, that can only be filled with guesses. They may be fitted together like this. *Molek* is associated only with Ben-Hinnom or the tophet, and the tophet only with Ben-Hinnom and Jerusalem — nowhere else. Ben-Hinnom is near the Jebusites and Jerusalem. The Jebusite tradition is pre-Davidic and so gives the impression of being an old tradition. "To cause to pass" and "to burn" seem to mean the same thing and may well be understood as interchangeable. Both are found in verses with the tophet, Ben-Hinnom, son(s) and daughter(s), and son(s) (without daughters). Both are used with "through the fire," quite naturally for "to burn" but not so with "to cause to pass." Both activities are called an abomination; YHWH commanded neither. Of the eight times *molek* is mentioned, it is used only with "to pass" and "to give." "To cause to pass" and any form of divination are regarded as enough to provoke YHWH to anger. "To pass," not "to burn," is associated with divination in several verses. The verb form (Hiphil) used in the Hebrew for the verb "to pass through" has a causal nuance which gives an odd sense of responsibility to the parents or the leaders of the communities engaged in this rite. The children are given no voice; they are victims of something sinister, as presented by these texts.

There is a considerable lack of material evidence within Palestine and without as to who *molek* is and what actually constituted the worship of this god. The evidence from the ANE is only circumstantial; there were gods who had names similar to *molek;* there were gods who received child sacrifice. However, we know very little of the connections of these gods of the ancient Near East and *molek* of the Hebrew scriptures. The most complete source of information that we have is the Hebrew scriptures themselves which point to a cult that may have been pre-Davidic in the valley of Ben-Hinnom just outside Jerusalem's walls. The worship of Molek of Jerusalem with the sacrifice of children by fire was an old tradition that survived in Ben-Hinnom to be condemned and its *tophet* destroyed by one of the last reforming kings of Judah, King Josiah (2 Kings 23).